Cambridge IGCSE®
Economics
Workbook
Susan Grant

University Printing House, Cambridge CB2 8BS, United Kingdom

One Liberty Plaza, 20th Floor, New York, NY 10006, USA

477 Williamstown Road, Port Melbourne, VIC 3207, Australia

314–321, 3rd Floor, Plot 3, Splendor Forum, Jasola District Centre, New Delhi – 110025, India

79 Anson Road, #06–04/06, Singapore 079906

Cambridge University Press is part of the University of Cambridge.

It furthers the University's mission by disseminating knowledge in the pursuit of education, learning and research at the highest international levels of excellence.

Information on this title: education.cambridge.org

© Cambridge University Press 2014

This publication is in copyright. Subject to statutory exception and to the provisions of relevant collective licensing agreements, no reproduction of any part may take place without the written permission of Cambridge University Press.

First published 2014
20 19 18 17 16 15 14 13 12 11 10 9

Printed in Italy by Rotolito Lombarda S.p.A.

A catalogue record for this publication is available from the British Library

ISBN 978-1-107-61231-0 Paperback

Cambridge University Press has no responsibility for the persistence or accuracy of URLs for external or third-party internet websites referred to in this publication, and does not guarantee that any content on such websites is, or will remain, accurate or appropriate. Information regarding prices, travel timetables, and other factual information given in this work is correct at the time of first printing but Cambridge University Press does not guarantee the accuracy of such information thereafter.

....

NOTICE TO TEACHERS IN THE UK

It is illegal to reproduce any part of this work in material form (including photocopying and electronic storage) except under the following circumstances:
(i) where you are abiding by a licence granted to your school or institution by the Copyright Licensing Agency;
(ii) where no such licence exists, or where you wish to exceed the terms of a licence, and you have gained the written permission of Cambridge University Press;
(iii) where you are allowed to reproduce without permission under the provisions of Chapter 3 of the Copyright, Designs and Patents Act 1988, which covers, for example, the reproduction of short passages within certain types of educational anthology and reproduction for the purposes of setting examination questions.

....

NOTICE TO TEACHERS

The photocopy masters in this publication may be photocopied or distributed [electronically] free of charge for classroom use within the school or institution that purchased the publication. Worksheets and copies of them remain in the copyright of Cambridge University Press, and such copies may not be distributed or used in any way outside the purchasing institution.

....

Every effort has been made to trace the owners of copyright material included in this book. The publishers would be grateful for any omissions brought to their notice for acknowledgement in future editions of the book.

® IGCSE is the registered trademark of Cambridge International Examinations.

Contents

Introduction		v
Section 1	Basic Economic Problem	1
Section 2	The Allocation of Resources	8
Section 3	The Individual as Producer, Consumer and Borrower	22
Section 4	The Private Firm as Producer and Employer	35
Section 5	Role of Government in an Economy	47
Section 6	Economic Indicators	60
Section 7	Developed and Developing Countries	74
Section 8	International Aspects	87
Answer Key		101
Useful Resources		248

Introduction

This workbook is designed to help you develop your understanding of economics, to build up your skills and to enable you to assess your progress.

The book can be used in conjunction with the Cambridge IGCSE Economics textbook I have written but may also be used independently. It is divided into eight sections which correspond to the sections of the syllabus and the textbook. Each section, in turn, is divided into ten parts.

The first part asks you to match terms with the appropriate definitions. Some of the terms and definitions are quite similar so you need to take care. Undertaking this exercise should reinforce your knowledge of the terms and emphasise to you the need for precision.

In the second part you have to fill in missing words. This requires you to process what you have learned to find words that ensure the sentences make economic sense.

One of the skills an economist needs is the ability to undertake calculations. The third part provides you with the opportunity to build up your numerical skills.

Parts 4 and 5 focus on two other skills of an economist. These are the ability to interpret and draw diagrams. The diagrams selected are the key ones associated with the different sections of the syllabus.

Part 6 will help you to both test your understanding and to develop your multiple choice technique. There is a total of 150 multiple choice questions in the book.

In Part 7 you can practice your ability to process and interpret economic terms by seeking to identify similarities in and differences between terms.

Part 8 involves you in producing longer answers and gives you the opportunity to interpret economic information and apply your knowledge to current, real world issues.

Part 9 provides structured questions which require longer written answers. These seek to develop the key skill of writing in a logical and lucid manner.

The final part, Part 10, is called homework assignments. These are in a similar format to the data questions in Part 8 but some require rather more depth and a number draw on a number of aspects of the syllabus. Of course, you can use any of the parts for homework assignments.

You can tackle a section of the book when you have completed that section of the syllabus or you can choose to work through all the sections towards the end of your course.

As with the accompanying textbook, this book seeks to cover all the topics in the syllabus and to provide you with additional concepts to strengthen your understanding and the quality of the answers you can provide. These additional concepts are:

Allocative and productive efficiency (pages 8, 15, 16 and 41)

Cost benefit analysis (pages 8, 15 and 17)

Average propensity to consume and average propensity to save (pages 24 and 28)

Aggregate demand and aggregate supply analysis (includes pages 49 and 51)

Velocity of circulation (page 67)

Lorenz curve (pages 74, 77 and 79)

Positive and preventive checks (page 81)

Absolute and comparative advantage (pages 87, 89, 91 and 92)

Terms of trade (pages 87, 90, 92 and 93)

Capital and financial accounts of the balance of payments (pages 91 and 94)

Expenditure reducing and expenditure switching policies (page 94).

I hope you find the tasks in this book both interesting and useful. Studying economics can be fascinating and can provide benefits both to you and to society. Alfred Marshall, a famous British economist, wrote in 1885 that his objective was to send economists "out into the world with cool heads but warm hearts, willing to give some at least of their best to grappling with the suffering around them; resolved not to rest content till they have done what in them lies to discover how far it is possible to open up to all the material means of a refined and noble life." Much has happened since Marshall wrote but this still remains a worthy objective.

Section 1: Basic Economic Problem

 Definitions

This exercise is based on some of the key terms used in economics. Match the following terms with their appropriate definitions. For instance, if you think an 'inability of workers to change jobs and location' defines 'scarcity', match 1 with c. Each term has an appropriate definition. If you find that you are left with a term and a definition which does not appear to match, you should review your other matches.

1. Scarcity
2. The economic problem
3. Wants
4. Land
5. Capital
6. Labour immobility
7. Factors of production
8. Opportunity cost
9. Economic goods
10. Free goods

a. Natural resources
b. Economic resources
c. Inability of workers to change jobs and location
d. Inability to produce everything that people want
e. Products that have an opportunity cost
f. Products that do not have an opportunity cost
g. Products people desire to have
h. Human made resources
i. An insufficient quantity to satisfy everyone's wants
j. Best alternative forgone

 Missing words

One way to become familiar with key economic words and terms is to use them. This exercise is designed to test your understanding of some economic words and terms in context. So complete the following sentences by filling in the missing word or words:

1. It is not possible to eliminate _____ as _____ grow faster than economic resources.
2. The economic problem means that people have to make _____.
3. Most land is _____ mobile but geographically _____.

4. If gross investment exceeds depreciation there is _____ investment.
5. _____ is the payment labour receives whilst _____ is the payment entrepreneurs receive.
6. A country's labour force can be increased by _____ the retirement age and _____ the school leaving age.
7. _____ is output whereas _____ is output per worker hour.
8. A key role of entrepreneurs is to bear _____ risks.
9. Another name for a production possibility curve is an _____ cost curve.
10. A production possibility curve shows the maximum output of _____ products with existing resources and _____ .

Calculations

Good economists can write clearly, interpret data and can undertake numerical calculations. At IGSCE/O level the calculations involve additions, subtractions, multiplications and working out averages and percentage changes.

1. A firm employs twenty six workers, paying each one US $ 75 a week. What is the firm's total wage cost?
2. A country produces US $ 900m capital goods in a year. There is depreciation of US $ 620m. What is net investment?

Interpreting diagrams

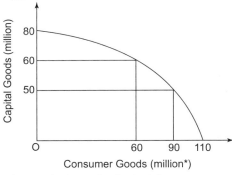

Fig. 1   * Henceforth, 'm' denotes 'millions'.

Economists make widespread use of diagrams. A diagram can be used to illustrate economic concepts, to analyse changes in economic conditions and to assess the effects of economic policies. Indeed a diagram can be worth a hundred words!

Production possibility curves can be used to show a number of economic concepts including opportunity cost.

Using Figure 1 state:

a. The opportunity cost of increasing the output of consumer goods from 60m to 90m consumer goods.
b. The opportunity cost of producing 80m capital goods.

Basic Economic Problem 3

 Drawing diagrams

It is important that you gain experience in drawing diagrams. Each diagram you draw should be clear and well labelled. You must have appropriate words on both the vertical and horizontal axes of a diagram. It is probably best to draw diagrams in pencil so that if you make a mistake, you can rub it out and start again.

Draw a production possibility curve showing the effect of an increase in the quantity of resources.

 Multiple-choice questions

Before answering a set of multiple-choice questions, check over your work on the topics covered. This preparation will build up both your understanding and confidence.

It is important to consider multiple-choice questions calmly and logically. First read the question. You may want to highlight key words. In some cases you may be able to think through an answer before you look at the options. For instance, in the case of question 2, you should consider what you understand by 'human capital'. Having decided on this, you should then look at the four options and select the one that comes closest to your understanding. This approach can also be applied in the case of questions 7 to 10.

The other questions in this section are examples of those which you have to, right from the start, consider along with the options. For example, question 3 is in effect, an integrated question. You cannot provide an answer independently of the options.

In the case of both types of questions, you need to consider the options carefully. With some questions an option may stand out as correct. With other questions, you may have to arrive at the answer by eliminating the incorrect options.

Trust your judgements. Once you have selected an answer, move on. If you are finding a question particularly difficult, leave it and then return to it at the end. Never leave a question unanswered. If you have no idea of the answer, still attempt the question. You have a 25% chance of getting the answer correct and you are not penalised for incorrect answers.

When you have completed the multiple-choice questions in a section, check over the answers and the explanations. It is particularly important to review the answers to any questions you have got wrong or are unsure about.

1. What would cause an increase in the problem of scarcity?
   - ☐ A A reduction in resources
   - ☐ B A reduction in wants
   - ☐ C A rise in productivity
   - ☐ D A rise in the mobility of resources

2. What is meant by investment in human capital?
   - [ ] A Encouraging immigration of people of working age
   - [ ] B Paying bonuses to workers to encourage them to increase their output
   - [ ] C Spending money and time on educating and training workers
   - [ ] D Upgrading the machines labour works with
3. Which item is a factor of production?
   - [ ] A The food a farmer produces
   - [ ] B The satisfaction a farmer gains from his work
   - [ ] C The tractor a farmer drives
   - [ ] D The wages a farmer pays his workers
4. Which form of air is an economic good?
   - [ ] A Air at ground level
   - [ ] B Air from an air conditioning system
   - [ ] C Air above an ocean
   - [ ] D Air in a tropical rainforest
5. Which item used in the production of textiles by a firm would an economist classify as land?
   - [ ] A Sewing machines
   - [ ] B The factory
   - [ ] C Untrained workers
   - [ ] D Water taken from a river
6. What might be the opportunity cost of using a bus to transport children to school?
   - [ ] A Increasing the earnings of the bus company
   - [ ] B Paying the wages to the driver
   - [ ] C Paying for the cost of petrol used
   - [ ] D Transporting a group of retired people on a day out
7. What is meant by 'labour' in economics?
   - [ ] A Hard physical work used to produce manufactured goods
   - [ ] B Human mental and physical effort used in producing goods and services
   - [ ] C Natural resources used in the productive process
   - [ ] D Risk taking and organising the factors of production
8. What does a production possibility curve show?
   - [ ] A The maximum combination of two types of products that can be produced with given resources

- [ ] B The prices of two types of products being produced
- [ ] C The quantity of capital and consumer goods that people would like to be produced
- [ ] D The relative profitability of capital and consumer goods

9. Which combination of economic concepts is illustrated by a production possibility curve?
- [ ] A Cost and price
- [ ] B Demand and price
- [ ] C Economic goods and free goods
- [ ] D Opportunity cost and scarcity

10. What does a point outside a production possibility curve represent?
- [ ] A A currently unattainable position
- [ ] B An inefficient position
- [ ] C The maximum use of resources
- [ ] D Unused resources

Similarities

This is another exercise to help you build up your understanding of aspects of the topics covered in this first section.

Identify one way in which each of the following pairs is similar:
1. Builders and teachers.
2. The entrepreneur and labour.
3. Forests and streams.
4. Wind and sunlight.
5. Production possibility curves and production possibility frontiers.

Differences

Identify **one** way in which each of the following pairs is different:
1. Capital goods and consumer goods
2. Economic goods and free goods
3. Capital and land
4. Geographical immobility and occupational immobility
5. Opportunity cost and financial cost

 **Data exercise**

In an economics examination your ability to interpret and analyse economic data will be tested.

The use of data puts economics in a real world context. In answering data-based questions, you should first read through the questions so that you know what you are looking for. Then read through the data. You may wish to highlight key words. Having read through the data, return to the questions. Again you may find it useful to highlight key words in the questions. For instance, in the case of question *b*, you may wish to highlight the words 'opportunity cost'. In deciding how much time to devote to each answer, take into account the marks awarded. You would obviously be expected to spend twice as long on a question with 8 marks than one with 4 marks.

A new Indian car

On 11 January 2008, Tata, an Indian producer, launched a new model, the *Nano*. On this day it became the cheapest car available, selling for half the price of the next cheapest car. For the price of 100,000 rupees, a brand new Nano could be bought or, for instance, a second hand 1993 Land Rover.

The car is intended initially for the home market. It is thought that millions could be sold in India. The firm also plans to export the car to Latin America, South-east Asia and Africa.

Although selling the car at such a low price will make car ownership more affordable for more people, there are still many millions of people who would like a car but do not have the income to buy one.

a. Using examples, identify **three** factors of production used in making cars. [6]
b. Give an example of opportunity cost from the passage. [2]
c. What evidence is there of the economic problem from the passage? [2]
d. Tata produces a range of cars. Use a production possibility curve to illustrate the effect of Tata devoting more of its resources to producing *Nano* cars. [4]

 **Structured questions**

Structured questions are divided into a number of different parts. In selecting a structured question to answer in an examination, it is important to ensure that you can answer all the question parts. It is best to answer the question parts in order as they may build on each other. As with data exercise questions, take into account the number of marks awarded to each question part.

Basic Economic Problem

1. a. What is the basic economic problem? [2]
   b. Explain **three** causes of an increase in the supply of labour in a country. [6]
   c. Discuss the relevance of opportunity cost in the following cases:
      (i) a worker deciding whether to accept a new job [3]
      (ii) a family deciding where to go for holiday [3]
      (iii) an entrepreneur selecting which new product to launch [3]
      (iv) the production of economic goods. [3]

2. Pakistan is a major producer of cotton garments, knitwear and rice. To increase its output of a range of products, the Pakistani government is seeking to improve the quality and mobility of its economic resources.
   a. What is an economic resource? [2]
   b. Explain what is meant by the mobility of economic resources. [8]
   c. Analyse **three** causes of an increase in the quality of economic resources. [6]
   d. Discuss a possible opportunity cost of Pakistan devoting more of its resources to producing cotton garments. [4]

Homework assignment

Review the work in this section and then answer the following question:

A German travel company considers its future

A German travel company decides to stop selling holidays in Italy and instead to offer holidays in a new destination. This is the Maldives, a group of islands in the Indian Ocean, famous for their long hours of sunshine and sandy beaches.

Tourism is a fast growing industry. Not all families, however, are able to go on holiday whether at home or abroad. Most of those who take holidays would like to have more holiday breaks.

a. What evidence is there in the passage of scarcity? [3]
b. Using examples, identify three factors of production involved in providing holidays in the Maldives. [6]
c. (i) Explain the difference between an economic good and a free good. [4]
   (ii) Identify a free good from the passage. [1]
d. Explain the relevance of opportunity cost for a travel firm in deciding how to use its resources. [6]

Section 2: The Allocation of Resources

 Definitions

In this section you have more terms to match with their definitions than you had in the first section. This may seem more challenging but the practice you gained in matching terms and definitions in Section 1 should help. Some of the definitions may be expressed in slightly different words to those you are familiar with. If you understand the terms, however, you should not have a problem.

1. A market economy
2. Extension in demand
3. Increase in demand
4. Supply
5. A contraction in supply
6. Market supply
7. Equilibrium price
8. A subsidy
9. A shortage
10. Price elasticity of demand
11. Elastic demand
12. Productive efficiency
13. Market failure
14. External costs

a. A measure of the sensitivity of demand for a product to a change in its price
b. This is where the quantity demanded of a product is equal to the quantity supplied
c. A situation where market forces do not result in an efficient outcome
d. Products that are more harmful for consumers than they realise and which have external costs
e. Products which are both non-rival and non-excludable
f. The willingness and ability to sell a product
g. The total benefits arising from producing or consuming a product
h. Spending by central and local government
i. Producing at the lowest possible cost
j. A situation where demand exceeds supply
k. A shift in the demand curve to the right
l. A movement along a demand curve as a result of a fall in the price of the product
m. A movement along a supply curve as a result of a fall in the price of the product
n. The total supply of a product

15. Social benefits
16. Demerit goods
17. Public goods
18. Government failure
19. Public expenditure
20. Cost benefit analysis

o. A method of comparing the total benefits and costs of a project
p. A payment to encourage the production or consumption of a product
q. An economic system which relies on the price mechanism to allocate resources
r. Harmful effects on third parties
s. When a change in price causes a greater percentage change in quantity demanded
t. When government intervention increases inefficiency

Missing words

This exercise includes twice as many sentences than in Section 1. Think carefully about the most appropriate word or words to complete the sentences.

1. Any type of economic system has to answer _____ key economic questions. One of these is how the products that are made are _____.
2. A mixed economy is one in which the allocation of _____ is determined by both the _____ mechanism and _____ intervention.
3. One of the advantages of a market economy is _____ sovereignty.
4. Economists define demand as the willingness and _____ to buy a product.
5. A _____ in the price of a product will cause a contraction in demand.
6. Rival products are known as _____ whilst products that are bought to be used together are known as _____.
7. A rise in the price of a product with inelastic demand results in a _____ in total revenue.
8. The more _____ defined a market is, the more _____ there are, so the more elastic demand is.
9. Price elasticity of supply is a measure of the responsiveness of _____ of a product to a change in its _____.
10. A market is said to be in _____ when demand is not equal to _____.
11. A market system can promote both _____ efficiency and productive efficiency by putting _____ pressure on firms.

12. A decrease in demand for a product will cause a _____ in price and a _____ in supply.
13. There will be downward pressure on the price of a product if _____ exceeds _____ .
14. A merit good has both higher _____ benefits than consumers realise and _____ effects on _____ parties.
15. Market forces will not encourage private sector firms to produce _____ goods as those wanting the products can act as _____ riders.
16. Social costs minus private costs equals _____ costs.
17. To encourage the consumption of a merit good, a government may provide a _____ to producers. In contrast, to discourage the consumption of a demerit good it may place a _____ on the product.
18. Information _____ can result in consumers paying _____ that are too high.
19. If a government overestimates the extent of external costs, it will set a tax that is too _____ .
20. Taxation is one way of financing _____ expenditure.

Calculations

Academic economists and economists working for businesses and the government frequently calculate price elasticity of demand and price elasticity of supply figures. Their findings can, for instance, help firms to decide whether to alter their prices, whether they are responding fast enough to changes in market conditions and can indicate to a government which products to tax to raise revenue.

Answer the following questions, each of which starts with a calculation:

1. It is estimated that if the price of a bar of chocolate is changed by 4%, demand will alter by 6%.
    a. Calculate the price elasticity of demand of this bar of chocolate.
    b. Is the demand elastic or inelastic?
    c. Explain one reason for the degree of elasticity you have found.
    d. If the chocolate manufacturer wishes to raise revenue, should it lower or raise price?
2. A rise in the price of cigarettes from US $ 6 to US $ 9 is found to cause demand to contract from 200,000 to 140,000 a day in an island country.
    a. Calculate the price elasticity of demand of cigarettes on the island.
    b. Is the demand elastic or inelastic?

c. Explain one reason for the degree of elasticity you have found.
d. Would taxing cigarettes be more effective in reducing smoking or raising tax revenue? Explain your answer.

3. A rise in the price from US $ 4 to US $ 4.80 causes the supply of a bunch of freshly cut roses to extend from 500 to 525 a day and the supply of a bunch of plastic roses to extend from 200 to 280.
    a. Calculate the price elasticity of supply of:
        (i) a bunch of freshly cut roses
        (ii) a bunch of plastic roses.
    b. State, in each case, whether supply is elastic or inelastic.
    c. What explains the difference in the degree of elasticity of the two products?

Interpreting diagrams

A demand and supply diagram is the best known and probably the most frequently used diagram in economics. The economist credited with introducing this diagram is Alfred Marshall (1842–1924) who included examples in his famous textbook 'Principles of Economics' published in 1890.

In this exercise, study the demand and supply diagram and then answer the questions which follow.

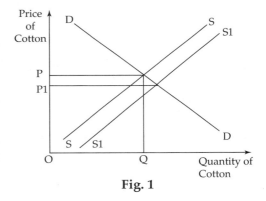

Fig. 1

a. Complete the diagram.
b. What is the change in the position of the supply curve known as?
c. Explain **one** possible cause of the change in the position of the supply curve.

Drawing diagrams

In each case, use a demand and supply diagram to illustrate the effect on the market for a newspaper of:
a. A rise in the price of a rival newspaper
b. A rise in the cost of print
c. A subsidy given to newspaper producers
d. More people finding news information from the internet
e. A major news story breaking

Multiple-choice questions

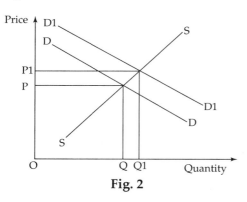

Fig. 2

In answering multiple-choice questions on demand and supply, it is often useful to draw a diagram. For example, if a question asks what effect an increase in demand would have on price and supply, a diagram such as Fig. 2 would help you to see that price would rise and supply would extend.

You are allowed to take a calculator into a multiple-choice examination. It is important that you do as a few of the questions are likely to require you to carry out a calculation. Question 12 is an example of such a question. Become familiar with using the calculator that you are planning to use in the examination.

1. Which feature is a characteristic of a market economy?
   - ☐ A Government planning plays a key role in the economy
   - ☐ B Producers respond automatically to changes in consumer demand
   - ☐ C Resources are allocated according to need
   - ☐ D There is always full employment

2. What is a mixed economy?
   - ☐ A One in which both capital and consumer goods are produced
   - ☐ B One in which both necessities and luxuries are produced
   - ☐ C One in which there is both an agricultural and a manufacturing sector
   - ☐ D One in which there is both a private and a public sector

3. A country changes from a planned to a market economy. What effect will this have?
   - ☐ A A decrease in government officials
   - ☐ B A decrease in the role of the price mechanism
   - ☐ C An increase in state ownership of resources
   - ☐ D An increase in the output of public goods

4. Which event would cause an increase in demand for petrol?
   - ☐ A An increase in concern for the environment
   - ☐ B An increase in the tax on diesel
   - ☐ C A decrease in disposable income
   - ☐ D A decrease in population size

5. What is meant by a contraction in demand?
   - A A reduction in demand due to a rise in the price of the product
   - B A reduction in demand due to a fall in the income of the population
   - C A rise in demand due to a rise in the price of a substitute product
   - D A rise in demand due to a fall in the price of a complement
6. Which event would cause the demand curve for air travel to shift to the left?
   - A A fall in the safety of sea travel
   - B A fall in the cost of air fuel
   - C A rise in the price of foreign holidays
   - D A rise in the size of the population
7. Which pair of products is an example of joint supply?
   - A Beef and leather
   - B Bread and butter
   - C Cars and petrol
   - D Computers and printers
8. Which change could explain the shift of the supply curve for a product from SS to S1S1 as shown in the diagram?
   - A A fall in price from P1 to P
   - B A rise in the quantity demanded from Q to Q1
   - C A reduction in the cost of producing the product
   - D The imposition of a tax on the product

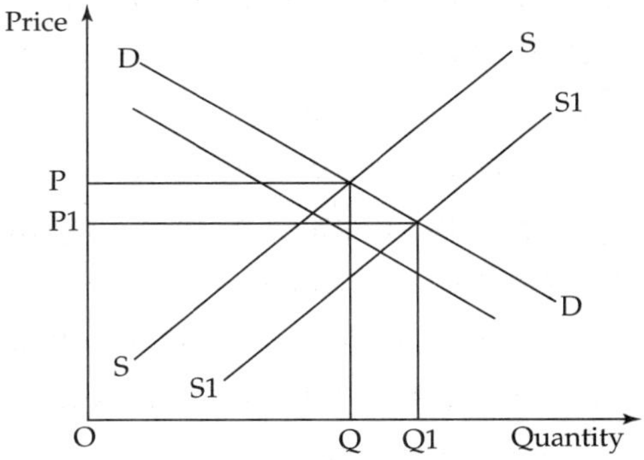

Fig. 3

9. What is meant by equilibrium price?
   - A The lowest possible price for a product
   - B The most profitable price for a product
   - C The price which equates the demand for and supply of a product
   - D The price which equates the number of buyers for and sellers of a product
10. The diagram shows the demand for and supply of gold mined in a country. Which combination of events could explain the rise in the price of gold?
    - A A decrease in the price of silver and a subsidy given to gold miners

B A decrease in the taste for gold and an improvement in the technology used in gold mining

C an increase in incomes and an increase in the cost of mining gold

D A decrease in the taste for gold and an improvement in the technology used in gold mining

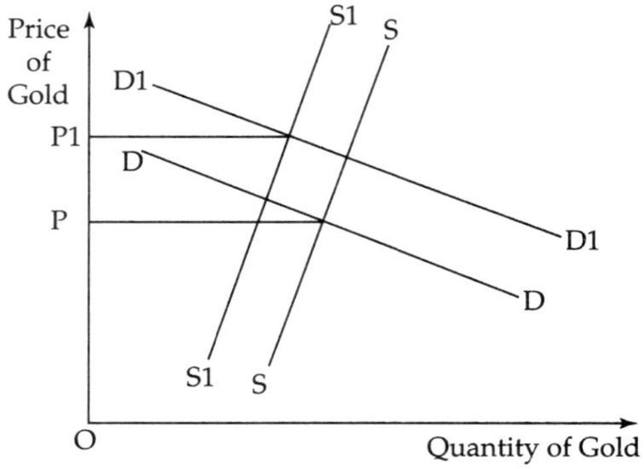

Fig. 4

11. Why does travel by private jet have elastic demand?

   A It is a luxury form of travel
   B It is a necessity
   C It has to be arranged some time in advance
   D It has no close substitutes

12. A rise in the price of a product from US $ 50 to US $ 60 causes demand to fall from 800 to 760. What is the price elasticity of demand?

   A − 0.25
   B − 0.5
   C − 2.0
   D − 4.0

13. The price elasticity of demand for a product is − 0.3. What effect will a fall in its price have?

   A A decrease in total spending on the product
   B A shift to the right of the demand curve
   C A more than proportionate change in quantity demanded
   D No change in the quantity demanded

14. What is meant by price elasticity of supply?

   A The extent to which price changes when there is a change in supply
   B The extent to which a firm can raise the price of a product whilst keeping the supply unchanged
   C The responsiveness of supply to a change in the cost of production
   D The responsiveness of supply to a change in price

15. Which advantage is a characteristic of a pure market economy?

   A An even distribution of income
   B Efficiency
   C The encouragement of the consumption of merit goods

☐ D The production of public goods

16. Which outcome is an example of market failure?
    ☐ A Consumers paying a higher price for a product whose demand is rising
    ☐ B Consumers exercising their market power by determining what is produced
    ☐ C Producers basing their output decisions on private rather than social costs and benefits
    ☐ D Producers earning a higher profit from switching from unpopular products falling in demand to producing those rising in demand

17. What would be evidence of abuse of market power?
    ☐ A A high level of competitive pressure
    ☐ B A high level of mobility of resources
    ☐ C A lack of allocative and productive efficiency
    ☐ D A lack of profit

18. What is an example of a public good?
    ☐ A Education
    ☐ B Flood defences
    ☐ C Health care
    ☐ D Postal services

19. What is a reason for public expenditure?
    ☐ A To increase external costs
    ☐ B To provide support for vulnerable groups
    ☐ C To reduce the mobility of resources
    ☐ D To subsidise demerit goods

20. What is cost benefit analysis most commonly used for?
    ☐ A Assessing public sector investment projects
    ☐ B Calculating a firm's profit position
    ☐ C Deciding whether to use labour or capital to produce a product
    ☐ D Estimating the effects of imposing a tax on demand for a product

Similarities

Identify one way in which each of the following pairs is similar.
1. What to produce and how to produce it.
2. A demand curve and a demand schedule.
3. Equilibrium price and a market clearing price.

4. Advertising and changes in disposable income.
5. Taxes and subsidies.
6. Perfectly inelastic demand and perfectly inelastic supply.
7. External costs and external benefits.
8. Information failure and abuse of market power.
9. Non-rivalry and non-excludability.
10. Market failure and government failure.

Differences

Identify one way in which each of the following pairs is different.
1. Individual demand and market demand.
2. Extension in supply and an increase in supply.
3. A market surplus and a market shortage.
4. Complements and substitutes.
5. Price elasticity of demand and price elasticity of supply.
6. Private expenditure and public expenditure.
7. Allocative efficiency and productive efficiency.
8. Merit goods and demerit goods.
9. External benefits and social benefits.
10. Conservation of resources and exploitation of resources.

Data exercises

Remember that in tackling data exercises, you need to draw on both the data and your knowledge of economics. What you are required to do is to apply the economic concepts you have learned to interpret and analyse the data.

1. The world's growing taste for tea

Between the start of 2006 and the start of 2007, the world price of tea rose from US $ 2.00 to US $ 2.40 per kilogram. A key reason for this rise was an increase in China's appetite for tea. Demand rose by 13% in 2006 and in 2007 Chinese tea consumption surpassed that of India for the first time.

A buyer for one of the major British tea selling firms said 'We are at a point now where supply and demand are so finely balanced that a drought in tea producing countries would really affect prices.' The British drink 165m cups of tea a day and 70m cups of coffee.

   a. Calculate the percentage rise in the price of tea that occurred between the start of 2006 and the start of 2008. [2]

   b. Explain what is meant by 'demand'. [2]

   c. Using a diagram in each case, explain:
      (i) why the price of tea rose between 2006 and 2008. [5]
      (ii) the effect of a drought on the price of tea. [5]

   d. (i) Is coffee a complement to or a substitute for tea? Explain your answer. [2]
      (ii) Discuss two other influences on the demand for tea. [4]

   e. Explain whether the price elasticity of supply of tea is elastic or inelastic. [4]

   f. Discuss whether a country would benefit from specialising in tea production. [6]

2. Pollution builds up in Beijing

Beijing is one of the world's most polluted cities. Its air quality is being further reduced by rising car travel. It has been estimated that there are 1,200 new cars on the roads of the capital every day. As well as creating air pollution, car travel causes noise pollution, congestion, and injuries and deaths.

To try to discourage car travel in the city, Beijing officials have tried a number of policies. These include banning cars with even-number licence plates one day and those with odd-number plates the next, raising the tax on petrol and subsidising bus travel. Some Chinese economists have suggested that the government should upgrade the city's underground rail system so that it can operate more trains.

   a. Identify **three** external costs of car travel from the passage. [3]

   b. In each case, use a demand and supply diagram to explain the effect on the market for car travel of:
      (i) a rise in the tax on petrol [5]
      (ii) a subsidy given to bus travel. [5]

   c. (i) Explain **two** ways in which a government could finance spending on an underground rail system. [2]
      (ii) Discuss how a cost benefit analysis could be used in helping Beijing officials decide whether to upgrade its underground rail system. [5]

d. Explain two reasons why demand for car travel may have increased in Beijing. [4]
e. Discuss whether a reduction in pollution will benefit a country. [6]

3. China: one country, two systems

Hong Kong returned to being a part of China in 1997. China has agreed that until 2047 Hong Kong can keep its own economic and political system and have autonomy in everything except foreign affairs, defence and national security.

Hong Kong's economic system comes closest to being a market economy. In contrast, China's economic system might be described as a planned economy moving towards a mixed economy.

Hong Kong is a high income and service-oriented economy, being particularly strong in financial services. It has low unemployment and its consumers enjoy a wide choice of good quality products.

The area does suffer from a number of aspects of market failure. For instance, it suffers from a significant amount of air pollution which it is estimated causes 2,000 premature deaths a year.

a. Distinguish between a planned and a market economy. [2]
b. Use a production possibility curve to illustrate an economy experiencing low unemployment. [3]
c. (i) Identify a benefit of a market economy mentioned in the passage. [1]
   (ii) Explain one other advantage of a market economy. [2]
d. (i) Define the term 'market failure'. [2]
   (ii) Explain why air pollution may arise in a market economy. [3]
e. Imagine you are the Prime Minister of a country. Discuss how you would decide what type of economic system to operate. [7]
f. Explain why no economy is a pure market economy. [4]
g. Discuss whether all consumers will benefit from a wide choice of good quality products. [6]

Structured questions

In answering questions on demand and supply, it is often useful to include diagrams even when the questions do not directly ask for them. This is true of questions 1b, 1c and 2a.

1. a. What is the relationship between demand and price? [3]
   b. Explain the main factors influencing demand for cinema tickets. [7]
   c. Discuss how a government could influence the market for cinema tickets. [10]
2. a. What is the difference between equilibrium and disequilibrium price? [4]
   b. Demand for mobile phones is still increasing in many countries but their price is falling. Use a demand and supply diagram, to explain this. [5]
   c. Define price elasticity of demand and explain the factors that influence price elasticity of demand. [5]
   d. Discuss why knowledge of price elasticity of demand is likely to be of use to firms selling a particular type of mobile phone. [6]
3. a. What is meant by a mixed economy? [3]
   b. Why are some countries moving from a mixed to a market economy? [4]
   c. Explain **three** causes of market failure. [6]
   d. Discuss whether the government or a private sector company should build a new airport. [7]
4. a. How are resources allocated in a market economy? [4]
   b. Why is education a merit good? [6]
   c. Explain **two** reasons why some governments provide free primary and secondary education. [6]
   d. Discuss whether health care is a public or a private good. [4]

 ## Homework assignments

These three homework assignments have been designed to test your understanding of the topics covered not only in Section 2 but also Section 1.

1. Smoking ban

A ban on smoking in enclosed public places and workplaces was introduced in England and Wales in the summer of 2007. Smoking causes a range of health problems including lung cancer, heart disease, stroke, chronic bronchitis and emphysema. It also generates a number of external costs including passive smoking and air pollution.

The UK government uses a number of measures to discourage smoking. It taxes cigarettes, requires cigarette companies to place health warnings on cigarette packets and carries out anti-smoking information campaigns.

Smoking is declining in the UK. In 1974 51% of men and 41% of women over the age of 16 smoked. By 2009, these percentages had fallen to 22% and 20%, respectively.

A higher proportion of the poor smoke than the rich. This is thought to be linked, in part, to the greater stress experienced by the poor.

    a. (i) What is the difference between private costs and external costs? [2]

         (ii) Does the information in the passage suggest that the UK government believes cigarettes are over or under-produced? [2]

    b. Using a demand and supply diagram, explain the effect of a ban on smoking in public places and workplaces on the market for cigarettes. [5]

    c. (i) What is meant by an inferior good? [2]

         (ii) What evidence is there in the passage that cigarettes are an inferior good? [2]

    d. Discuss what information you would need to assess what will happen to the market for cigarettes in a country in the future. [7]

2. Japan faces world criticism

In 2007 a number of countries, including Japan, were seeking to end the ban on whaling for commercial purposes. Since 1982 the International Whaling Commission (IWC) has banned whaling for meat. It has, however, allowed whaling for purposes of scientific research.

The Japanese have continued to capture and kill whales despite strong criticism from environmentalists, some economists and some governments. The Japanese government argues that whaling is important in order to find out the size of whale populations, their breeding and feeding habits. Others suspect that the Japanese whalers are mainly motivated by the profit that can be earned from selling whale meat to restaurants and supermarkets.

The IWC's scientists have calculated what they regard to be a sustainable catch of the most common whale species. But critics point out that there is considerable uncertainty as to how many whales there are. They also argue that it will difficult to ensure that whalers keep to any limits set. Some governments with whales living off their coasts are also concerned about how whaling may affect their tourist trade.

    a. Explain what type of resource whales are. [2]

b. Explain what is meant by a 'sustainable catch of whales'. [3]
c. (i) Explain **two** factors that could lead to a decrease in demand for whale meat. [4]
   (ii) Using a demand and supply diagram, analyse the likely impact on the market for whale meat of the removal of the ban on hunting. [5]
d. Discuss what information would help you to assess the economic arguments for and against conserving whales. [6]

3. The price of basmati rice soars

In the year 2007, the price of basmati rice doubled. There had been a poor harvest that year whilst demand increased.

The aromatic, long-grain rice is grown in northern India and Pakistan and is eaten throughout the world. It is becoming a luxury product. It now costs between two and three times the price of American long-grain rice.

Despite the rise in the popularity for basmati rice, farmers are not growing more of it. The cultivation of basmati rice is very labour-intensive and yields between one and two tonnes per hectare, compared with six tonnes for rival grains. Wheat has increased in price by more than basmati rice and farmers are switching to higher-yielding and more profitable crops.

Attempts have been made to grow the Himalayan rice strain in Italy and some other rice growing countries. These have, however, failed to produce an acceptable product. Some basmati growers in India and Pakistan are trying to make the supply of the prized rice more elastic but this may not prove to be easy.

a. (i) Draw a demand and supply diagram to illustrate why the price of basmati rice changed in 2007. [3]
   (ii) Using information from the passage, explain three reasons for this change in price. [3]
b. (i) What is meant by the cultivation of basmati rice being 'labour-intensive'. [2]
   (ii) Apart from labour, identify and give an example of another factor of production used in growing rice. [2]
c. From the passage, identify:
   (i) an opportunity cost to farmers of growing basmati rice. [1]
   (ii) a superior good. [1]
d. (i) Explain what is meant by elastic supply. [2]
   (ii) Discuss why products have different degrees of price elasticity of supply. [6]

Section 3: The Individual as Producer, Consumer and Borrower

Definitions

As in the previous sections match the terms with their correct definitions. In some cases, such as a and b, g and h, and j and k, the definitions may appear on first glance to be similar. Closer examination, however, should reveal that they are not.

1. Specialisation
2. Division of labour
3. Money
4. Legal tender
5. Retail banks
6. Merchant banks
7. Stock exchanges
8. Dividend
9. Piece rate system
10. Trade unions
11. Elasticity of supply of labour
12. Earnings
13. Wage differentials
14. Job security
15. National minimum wage
16. Collective bargaining
17. Savings

a. Organisations that enable public limited to raise companies finance
b. Organisations of workers that act in the interests of their members
c. Disposable income that is not spent
d. Organisations of workers negotiating with representatives of employers
e. A lower limit set by the government on the pay of workers
f. Wages plus other payments to workers
g. A payment based on the productivity of workers
h. A payment to shareholders.
i. A form of money that has to be accepted in settlement of a debt
j. High street banks that lend to individuals and firms
k. Banks that lend mainly to large firms
l. Workers undertaking particular tasks
m. An item used to buy products
n. Differences in wages earned by different groups of workers
o. A situation where share prices are rising
p. Protection from being made redundant
q. The extent to which the supply of labour alters when the wage rate changes

The Individual as Producer, Consumer and Borrower   23

18. Savings ratio
19. A bullish market
20. Investment income

r. The concentration on particular tasks or products
s. The proportion of disposable income that is not spent
t. Profit, interest and dividends

Missing words

Some of the sentences here require you to fill in three missing words, some two and two sentences have one missing word. Think carefully about the most appropriate words. You may find it useful to read out the sentence aloud once you have put in the words to make sure it makes sense.

1. Workers _____ can be referred to as _____ of labour.
2. Two of the functions of money are to act as a _____ of exchange and a _____ for _____ payments.
3. The key characteristic that an item has to possess to act as _____ is that it is _____ _____ .
4. A _____ bank acts as the bank to the government and issues _____ and _____ .
5. _____ is the price of _____ money and the reward for _____ .
6. A stock exchange is a market for second hand _____ and government _____ .
7. A group of workers is likely to be highly paid if demand for their labour is _____ and the supply of their labour is _____ .
8. Earnings minus overtime pay equals the _____ paid to a worker.
9. A worker may be prepared to stay in a relatively low paid job if it has good fringe _____ _____ working hours and long _____ .
10. _____ workers are usually better paid than unskilled workers because they are _____ productive.
11. A national minimum wage will raise the pay of _____ paid workers if it is set _____ the market _____ wage rate.
12. An increase in demand for pilots will be likely to _____ the wage rate of pilots and cause the supply of labour services of pilots to _____ .
13. The supply of labour to a particular occupation refers to the number of _____ of work offered by the labour _____ .

14. Elasticity of _____ of labour measures the responsiveness of the supply of labour to a change in the _____ rate.
15. A trade union is likely to have more bargaining _____ if unemployment is _____ and its workers are _____ skilled.
16. As people become richer, they usually spend more in total but a _____ proportion of their disposable _____.
17. People tend to save more if the rate of interest _____ and income tax is _____.
18. Dissaving occurs when people spend more than their _____.
19. The poor tend to have a higher average propensity to _____ and a lower average propensity to _____ than the rich.
20. Real disposable income is income that has been adjusted for _____ and after the deduction of _____ taxes.

Calculations

The **three** calculations here are relatively straightforward. It is important, however, that you do not rush them. Take your time and double check your answer.

1. A person borrows US $ 250 for a year at a rate of interest of 8%. How much will she repay at the end of the year?
2. The current market price of a share in a company is US $ 40 and the dividend paid per share is US $ 2. What is the yield?
3. A small firm employs nine workers. The wages it pays to these workers are US $ 200, US $ 220, US $ 280, US $ 300, US $ 310, US $ 320, US $ 330, US $ 350 and US $ 390 a week. What is the average wage paid?

Interpreting diagrams

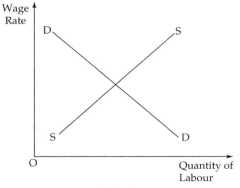

Fig. 1

This question is based on applying demand and supply analysis to a labour market.

a. Identify the equilibrium wage rate.
b. Explain why the demand curve is downward sloping whilst the supply curve is upward sloping.

Drawing diagrams

Using a demand and supply diagram in each case, show the effect on the wage rate of university professors due to:
a. An increase in the number of students studying law
b. A decrease in the wage rate of lawyers
c. An increase in the qualifications needed to become a university professor of law.

In each case, start with the labour market being in equilibrium. Then consider which curve or curves would shift and draw it/them in. Finally show the impact that the change would be expected to have on the wage rate and the quantity of labour.

Multiple-choice questions

All questions in a multiple-choice examination receive the same number of marks. Some questions, however, require more careful consideration than others. So do not worry if you find yourself spending more time on some questions than others. For example, you may find that you can arrive at a correct answer for question 20 more quickly than you can for question 12.

1. What does the extent to which workers can specialise depend on?
   - [ ] A Division of labour
   - [ ] B Opportunity cost
   - [ ] C Taxation
   - [ ] D The size of the market
2. Which function of money is most closely linked to saving?
   - [ ] A Medium of exchange
   - [ ] B Standard for deferred payment
   - [ ] C Store of value
   - [ ] D Unit of account
3. Which financial institution acts as a lender of last resort?
   - [ ] A A central bank
   - [ ] B A commercial bank
   - [ ] C An investment bank
   - [ ] D A savings bank
4. Why might division of labour increase unit costs?
   - [ ] A Days lost due to sickness may be reduced
   - [ ] B Labour turnover may be higher
   - [ ] C Training time may be reduced
   - [ ] D Workers may concentrate on what they are best at

5. What is the main form of money used in Europe?
   - [ ] A Bank accounts
   - [ ] B Coins
   - [ ] C Gold
   - [ ] D Notes
6. Which feature is a characteristic of money?
   - [ ] A Durability
   - [ ] B Indivisibility
   - [ ] C Intrinsic value
   - [ ] D Unlimited supply
7. What impact would an increase in the rate of interest be likely to have on borrowing and saving?

	Borrowing	saving
[ ] A	decrease	decrease
[ ] B	decrease	increase
[ ] C	increase	increase
[ ] D	increase	decrease

8. Which change would lead to a rise in consumer expenditure?
   - [ ] A A fall in optimism
   - [ ] B A fall in saving
   - [ ] C A rise in interest rates
   - [ ] D A rise in income tax
9. What is a main function of a commercial bank?
   - [ ] A To hold the country's reserves of foreign currency
   - [ ] B To issue the shares of companies
   - [ ] C To lend to its customers
   - [ ] D To regulate the banking system
10. In which situation would the demand for labour be inelastic?
    - [ ] A Demand for the product produced is elastic
    - [ ] B It is difficult to replace workers with machines
    - [ ] C It takes a short time to train new members
    - [ ] D There is high unemployment in the economy
11. Which one of the following types of trade union represents engineers?
    - [ ] A Craft union
    - [ ] B General Union
    - [ ] C Industrial union
    - [ ] D White collar union

12. A trade union persuades an employer to raise the wage he pays his workers above the equilibrium level. What is the most likely outcome?
   - A More workers will be employed as it will be easier to recruit them
   - B Some workers who retire or leave for other jobs will not be replaced
   - C The firm will increase its output to raise the revenue needed to pay the higher wages
   - D The firm will raise the wage rate higher to ensure demand equals supply

13. Which characteristic would strengthen the power of a trade union?
   - A Demand for the product produced by the workers is elastic
   - B It is difficult to substitute the workers by machines
   - C Its members are unwilling to take industrial action
   - D The wages form a high proportion of the industry's total cost

14. When is a labour market in equilibrium?
   - A When the degree of elasticity of demand for labour equals the degree of elasticity of supply of labour
   - B When the number of hours of work demanded is equal to the number of hours supplied
   - C When the number of workers employed equals the number of machines in use
   - D When the number of workers is equal to the number of employers

15. The diagram shows the market for bus drivers. What change could have caused the change in the wage rate paid to bus drivers?
   - A A decrease in the qualifications needed to be a bus driver
   - B A decrease in the wage paid to train drivers
   - C An improvement in the bus drivers' working conditions
   - D An increase in bus travel

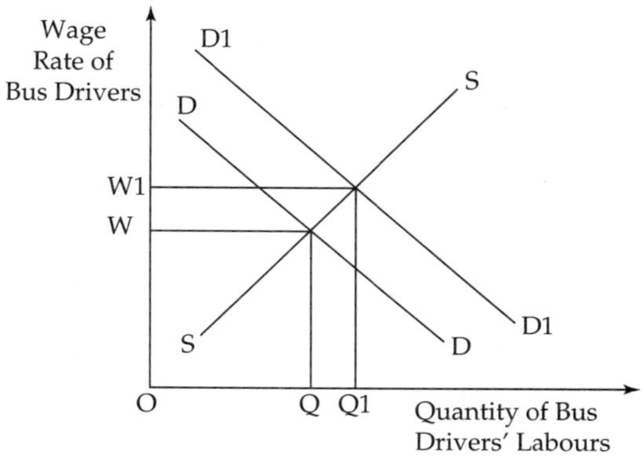

   Fig. 2

16. What could cause an extension in the supply of farm workers' labour?
   - A A decrease in the number of hours farm workers have to work
   - B A decrease in the dangers included in farm work
   - C An increase in the wage rate paid to farm workers
   - D An increase in the non-wage benefits received by farm workers

17. Which change in the nature of a job would be most likely to increase the number of people willing to do it?
    - [ ] A A decrease in job satisfaction
    - [ ] B A decrease in holiday entitlement
    - [ ] C An increase in job insecurity
    - [ ] D An increase in on the job training

18. Which group of workers is likely to spend and save the most?
    - [ ] A Cleaners
    - [ ] B Doctors
    - [ ] C Factory workers
    - [ ] D Railway porters

19. A woman's disposable income is US $ 300 and she spends US $ 270. What is her average propensity to save?
    - [ ] A 0.1
    - [ ] B 0.3
    - [ ] C 0.7
    - [ ] D 0.9

20. Which group spends the highest proportion of their total expenditure on leisure goods and services?
    - [ ] A The poor
    - [ ] B The middle income group
    - [ ] C The rich
    - [ ] D The very rich

Similarities

Two benefits of this exercise are that it should help to clarify your understanding and help you remember the examples of various economic topics.

Identify **one** way in which each of the following pairs is similar:
1. Specialisation and division of labour.
2. Unit of account and standard for deferred payments.
3. Bonus and overtime payment.
4. Working conditions and working hours.
5. Trade unions and professional organisations.
6. The Federal Reserve Bank of the US and the Bank of England.
7. Shares and bank loans.
8. Time rates and piece rates.

9. Location and career prospects.
10. Work to rule and overtime ban.

 **Differences**

This exercise should help you to avoid confusing some key terms and appreciate to a greater extent some key differences.

Identify **one** way in which each of the following pairs is different.
1. Specialisation and diversification.
2. Commercial banks and investment banks.
3. Bullish market and bearish market.
4. External finance and internal finance.
5. Wages and earnings.
6. Equilibrium wage rate and disequilibrium wage rate.
7. A craft union and an industrial union.
8. Wealth and income.
9. Earned income and investment income.
10. Saving and dissaving.

 **Data exercises**

Questions which ask you to state or identify, you can answer relatively briefly. It is important, however, that you do not answer higher marked questions which require you to explain, analyse or discuss, in note form. Writing brief notes on such questions will only get you a maximum of half marks.

1. Vast bonuses at Goldman Sachs

In 2006 the US investment bank, Goldman Sachs, paid their senior executives and star traders based in London £10 million or more each in bonuses. The London branch of Goldman Sachs had enjoyed record profits because of favourable financial market conditions. It had advised on some important mergers.

Traders at Goldman Sachs, whilst enjoying high wages and spectacular bonuses, work long hours. However, everyone was not highly rewarded for their work. Its office cleaners in the same month that the large bonuses were paid out were protesting outside the bank complaining about their wages and working conditions.

   a. Identify **two** functions of an investment bank. [2]
   b. Why might a firm pay a bonus to its staff? [4]
   c. Explain two reasons why senior executives are paid more than cleaners. [6]

d. Discuss whether cleaners would be likely to raise their wages by taking industrial action. [8]
e. Explain how 'favourable financial market conditions' may result in an investment bank enjoying record profits. [4]
f. Discuss whether high bonuses will prevent senior executives moving from Goldman Sachs to another bank. [6]

2. Should the government force people to save more?

Some economists and politicians argue that people should be compelled to save an amount that will give them an adequate income in retirement.

It is thought that some people are too short-sighted to save enough while others are confident that the government will look after them when they are old.

There are, however, problems with compulsory saving. It is difficult to decide what would be an adequate retirement income. Some people are also too poor to save.

Forcing people to save may discourage some people from saving voluntarily. It may also mean that some people who are being made to save more than they want, may borrow to maintain their level of consumption. In both cases, national saving may not increase much.

a. What is the opportunity cost of saving? [3]
b. What evidence is there of market failure in the passage? [4]
c. Explain one influence on saving referred to in the passage. [3]
d. Why might the level of saving vary between countries? [5]
e. Discuss what factors may lead to an increase in borrowing. [5]
f. Explain two ways a government could encourage people to save more. [4]
g. Discuss what effect the introduction of a generous state pension may have on saving. [6]

3. A boom in the Indian TV industry

In 2008 110 million Indian households had a TV. Of these, forty per cent had a one channel, black and white set. The situation, however, is changing. In 2008 more colour sets were sold and there was a growth in the number of households with two sets and in the number of households with cable and satellite TV. India is also forecast to become Asia's most lucrative pay-TV market by 2015 with the number of households with TVs expected to double within a few years.

In 2008, in anticipation of rising demand, more new channels became available. One problem found in launching the new channels was a lack of qualified production staff. A number of Indian cinema owners expressed concern that the increased popularity of TV viewing would affect their revenue.

   a. How many million Indian households had a colour TV set in 2008? [2]
   b. Explain what factors influence demand for TVs. [5]
   c. Using a demand and supply diagram, analyse what was likely to have happened to the pay of Indian TV production staff in 2008. [5]
   d. (i) Explain the likely relationship between TV viewing and cinema attendance. [2]
      (ii) You are the owner of a cinema. Discuss how you would try to increase the sale of cinema tickets. [6]
   e. Explain two reasons why cinema attendance might increase. [4]
   f. Discuss whether a person would benefit from specialising as a producer of TV sports programmes. [6]

Structured questions

1.   a. Explain what is meant by specialisation. [3]
    b. How does money promote specialisation? [4]
    c. What are the key functions of commercial banks? [6]
    d. Discuss whether a commercial bank should specialise or diversify in terms of the services it provides. [7]
2.   a. Explain **three** influences on the supply of labour to a particular occupation. [6]
    b. Why might the occupational mobility of labour increase? [6]
    c. Discuss why dentists are paid more than waiters and waitresses. [8]
3.   a. What is meant by a trade union? [3]
    b. Explain **three** ways a trade union could use to try and raise its members' wage rates. [6]
    c. Why despite a rise in wages, may people spend less? [5]
    d. Discuss how a more even distribution of income may affect the pattern of expenditure in an economy. [6]
4. In Bangladesh 66% of the labour force is employed in agriculture.
    a. What factors influence demand for farm workers? [6]

b. Explain the reasons why some people may continue to be farm workers despite being offered better paid jobs as factory workers. [7]
c. Discuss the benefits farm workers may gain from joining a union. [7]

It is useful to answer structured questions in order. Such a strategy helps you to avoid overlap and assists you in framing your answers. For instance, in the case of question 1, writing about specialisation and then the functions of commercial banks, should clarify your thoughts on these topics and give you ideas on how to approach the last question part.

 Homework assignments

The last question in each of these assignments carry the highest number of marks. These require you to answer in some depth. Carefully think through your answer before you start writing it. Think about which economic concepts you can bring into your answer.

1. Growth in bank lending declines in India

In 2007 and 2008 a number of banks in the USA and UK got into difficulties as a result of lending to high risk customers. The problems they faced led banks throughout the world to review their lending policies.

The growth in loans in India, for instance, fell from 40% the year before to 20% in 2008. Inflationary pressure forced the Reserve Bank of India, the country's central bank, to keep interest rates high. This made bank loans expensive. A number of India based banks became more reluctant to lend to low income earners. Citigroup, for instance, decided to concentrate more of its efforts on lending to India's emerging middle classes.

ICICI, India's largest private sector bank, decided to stop giving small loans to personal customers and to concentrate on large loans to personal customers and to firms.
  a. Why did Indian banks become more cautious in their lending in 2008? [3]
  b. Did bank lending in India increase or decrease in 2008? Explain your answer. [2]
  c. Identify **two** functions of a central bank. [2]
  d. Explain **two** factors that influence demand for bank loans. [4]
  e. You are a manager of an Indian firm. You want to open new branches. Discuss what factors you would take into account in deciding how to finance the expansion. [9]

2. German airports hit by workers' strike

In March 2008 thousands of German public sector workers went on strike in support of their 8% wage rise claim. The action taken by baggage handlers, check in staff, ground crew and firefighters caused hundreds of flights to be cancelled. The German airline, Lufthansa, was particularly badly affected.

Germany's 1.3 million public sector workers had been offered a 5% pay rise over two years tied to increased hours. Frank Bsirske, chairman of Verdi, the largest public sector union, said that an 8% rise in one year was justified as inflation was running at 2% and workers in other industries had recently received similar pay rises.

Further negotiations between government officials and union leaders were expected. Not many people anticipated that these would be successful and union leaders were considering a range of further industrial action. The government was getting prepared to refer the case to independent arbitration.

Industrial unrest was also occurring in other sectors of the German economy. Chemical workers, for example, were demanding higher wages and better working conditions on the basis that it was becoming increasingly difficult to recruit workers to the industry.

a. What is meant by 'public sector workers'? [2]
b. Using information from the passage, explain **three** arguments a union might make for a wage rise. [6]
c. Apart from strikes, identify two other forms of industrial action a union could take. [2]
d. What is meant by arbitration? [2]
e. Discuss how an employer could attract more workers. [8]

3. Rising Polish spending

In 2007 spending was rising rapidly in Poland. Wage rates were increasing, including those of construction workers and travel agents, and unemployment was falling. Household borrowing was also increasing and was 33% up on the previous year. It was forecasted that spending would increase at an even faster rate in the future with unemployment falling, wage rises accelerating and the country hosting the 2012 European football championship.

Poles had been spending a higher proportion of their total expenditure on energy, largely due to higher energy prices, and on leisure products as a result or rising affluence. More Poles were driving cars and fewer Poles were using bus transport. Indeed between 1991 and 2007 the number of cars on Polish roads had doubled.

One disadvantage of the rising spending was a rise in the country's consumer prices index. In response to the higher inflation rate, the Polish central bank raised its interest rate from 4% to 5% in 2007.

a. What is meant by 'borrowing'? [2]
b. Explain **two** reasons why a fall in unemployment may cause spending to rise. [4]
c. What evidence is there in the passage that car travel is a normal good whilst bus travel is an inferior good. [4]
d. Explain **two** reasons why the wage rate of construction workers may rise. [4]
e. Discuss the impact that a rise in the rate of interest may have on spending. [6]

Section 4: The Private Firm as Producer and Employer

 Definitions

Remember here you are seeking the best definition for each term and that you have to find an appropriate match for each term.

1. Tertiary sector
2. Public limited companies
3. Multinationals
4. Limited liability
5. Average cost
6. Average variable cost
7. Profit maximisation
8. Sales revenue maximisation
9. Profit
10. Perfect competition
11. Monopoly
12. Barriers to entry
13. Conglomerate integration
14. Horizontal integration
15. Internal economies of scale

a. An excess of revenue over costs
b. The aim of making as much profit as possible
c. A market situation with only one seller
d. Circumstances that make it difficult or impossible for new firms to enter a market
e. Companies that sell their shares to the general public
f. The stage of production involved with the production of services
g. Companies that produce in more than one country
h. Two firms that operate in different industries combining
i. Reorganisation of production to reduce costs
j. A restriction placed on the amount shareholders can lose
k. Benefits that firms in an industry gain when that industry grows in size
l. Lower cost and greater ease of raising finance when a firm grows in size
m. Higher long run average costs resulting from an industry growing too large
n. A rise in long run average costs occurring as a result of the growth of a firm
o. Earning as much revenue as possible

16. Financial economies of scale   p. Total cost divided by output
17. External economies of scale   q. A market situation with a high number of buyers and sellers
18. Rationalisation   r. Lower long run average costs resulting from the growth of a firm
19. Internal diseconomies of scale   s. The merger of two firms at the same stage of production
20. External diseconomies of scale   t. Total variable cost divided by output

Missing words

You should now be familiar with filling in the missing words. You may find some of these sentences, for example 4, more straightforward than others, for instance 20.

1. Fishing is an example of a _____ sector industry whilst the production of toys is an example of a _____ sector industry.
2. _____ limited companies have limited _____ and can only sell their _____ to known individuals.
3. If it is thought that a _____ corporation will work more efficiently in the _____ sector, a government may decide on _____.
4. As an economy develops, resources tend to move first from the _____ sector to the _____ sector and then to the _____ sector.
5. _____ costs are costs which do not alter in the _____ run even when the amount produced changes.
6. Average _____ cost minus average variable cost equals average _____ cost.
7. Total revenue divided by the quantity sold equals _____ revenue which is the same as _____.
8. A firm's _____ would increase if the gap between its _____ and costs increased.
9. A market in which there is a low degree of _____ concentration and free _____ and exit is described as perfectly _____.
10. A monopoly has _____ to entry and exit which can enable it to enjoy _____ profit.
11. A firm may remain _____ because of the _____ of its _____ or because the owner is experiencing difficulty raising _____ to expand.

12. A decrease in a long run _____ cost curve may be caused by _____ of scale.
13. As a firm grows in size, it may diversify. This would enable it to take advantage of _____ _____ economies.
14. If a firm reduces its output, its _____ cost may rise as it may no longer receive a _____ when it buys its raw materials.
15. Those running a firm may be more concerned with _____ rather than profit maximisation as their salaries and status may be more linked to the size of a firm.
16. A rise in output must reduce average _____ cost.
17. A _____ _____ is a business owned by one person.
18. In the short run it is not possible to alter all the factors of _____ employed. The one which is usually in fixed _____ is capital.
19. Oil production is _____ intensive whilst catering is _____ intensive.
20. A monopolist is a price _____ and so as its output and sales rise its _____ revenue rase falls.

Calculations

You will need a calculator to carry out these calculations. You may also need to go back to the definitions of costs before attempting them.

1. A firm employs 85 workers and its total output is 2,210 units. What is the average product of labour?
2. A firm's total cost increases from US $ 400 to US $ 700 when it produces its first unit of output. The output of a second unit raises total cost by a further US $ 200. What is the average variable cost of the second unit?
3. A firm's average fixed cost is US $ 10 and its average variable cost is US $ 80. Its total cost is US $ 3,960. What is its output?

Interpreting diagrams

The diagram shows a firm's cost curves. Label them appropriately.

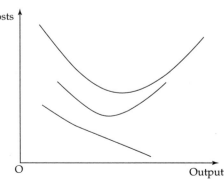

Fig. 1

Drawing diagrams

In each case, draw a cost curve diagram to show:
a. Internal economies of scale
b. External economies of scale
c. Internal diseconomies of scale
d. External diseconomies of scale

Multiple-choice questions

1. Which stage of production covers house-building?
   - A Primary
   - B Secondary
   - C Tertiary
   - D Quaternary
2. Which business organisation operates in the public sector?
   - A A nationalised industry
   - B A private limited company
   - C A public limited company
   - D A sole trader
3. Which type of business organisation is most likely to suffer from diseconomies of scale?
   - A A sole trader
   - B A partnership
   - C A private limited company
   - D A nationalised industry
4. Which type of business organisation does not usually have shareholders?
   - A A multinational company
   - B A partnership
   - C A private limited company
   - D A public limited company
5. A firm's fixed cost is US $ 4,000 a week. The average total cost of producing its output is US $ 5 and its average variable cost is US $ 3 a week. What is its weekly output?
   - A 500
   - B 800
   - C 1,000
   - D 2,000

6. The table below shows the total cost of a firm at different levels of output.

Output	Total cost (US $)
0	20
1	30
2	38
3	42
4	50
5	60

    What is the average fixed cost of producing five units of output?
    - A US $ 4
    - B US $ 12
    - C US $ 20
    - D US $ 60

7. Which cost is a variable cost?
    - A Interest payments on a bank loan
    - B Pensions paid to former employees
    - C Rent paid to a landlord
    - D Wages of workers paid on a piece rate basis

8. What is meant by fixed costs?
    - A Costs that do not alter a firm's profits
    - B Costs that only change in the long run
    - C Total cost of raw materials
    - D Total cost plus variable cost

9. What is a motive for privatising an industry?
    - A To ensure production decisions are based on social benefits and costs
    - B To increase state control
    - C To reduce competition
    - D To reduce productive inefficiency

10. A firm sells 30 units of output which cost US $ 600 to produce and it makes a total profit of US $ 150.

    What is the firm's average revenue?
    - A US $ 5
    - B US $ 15
    - C US $ 20
    - D US $ 25

11. What is a characteristic of a monopoly?
    - A A low market concentration ratio

- [ ] B High barriers to entry and exit
- [ ] C Many buyers and sellers
- [ ] D Perfect knowledge about market conditions

12. Why may a monopoly benefit consumers?
- [ ] A It may restrict output to drive up prices
- [ ] B It may restrict the entry of new firms into the industry
- [ ] C It may spend some of its supernormal profits on research and development
- [ ] D It may use some of its high revenue to pay large bonuses to directors

13. The directors of a firm decide to buy out another firm in the same industry. This is despite the fact that a report indicates that the new combined firm will experience diseconomies of scale. What is likely to be the short term objective of the directors?
- [ ] A Diversification
- [ ] B Growth
- [ ] C Profit maximisation
- [ ] D Reduced market share

14. Which combination of circumstances is most likely to encourage a firm to invest?

	Rate of interest	Retained profits
A	high	high
B	high	low
C	low	low
D	low	high

15. What could explain a rise in a firm's production but a fall in the productivity of the labour it employs?
- [ ] A Higher wages paid to workers
- [ ] B Improved training
- [ ] C Less skilled workers being recruited
- [ ] D More efficient machines being used

16. Which type of merger aims to ensure control of retail outlets?
- [ ] A Conglomerate
- [ ] B Horizontal
- [ ] C Vertical backwards
- [ ] D Vertical forwards

17. A sweet manufacturer buys a local newspaper. What type of merger is this?
- [ ] A Conglomerate integration
- [ ] B Horizontal integration

- [ ] C Vertical integration backwards
- [ ] D Vertical integration forwards

18. Which economy of scale is an external economy?
- [ ] A Ability to buy raw materials in bulk
- [ ] B Ancillary industries providing goods and services for the industry
- [ ] C Costs reduction achieved by using more efficient machines
- [ ] D More efficient use of the skills of workers

19. Which feature is an advantage of small scale production?
- [ ] A Diversification
- [ ] B Division of labour
- [ ] C Economies of scale
- [ ] D Flexible production

20. What can cause internal economies of scale?
- [ ] A A firm's costs rising by more than its output
- [ ] B A reduction in a firm's productive efficiency
- [ ] C An increase in the size of a firm's factories
- [ ] D A rise in the number of firms in the industry

Similarities

Identify **one** way in which each of the following pairs is similar. There may be differences between the two items in some of the pairs, but remember you are looking for similarities.

1. Sole proprietor and partnership.
2. Public limited companies and multinational corporations.
3. Advances in technology and a cut in corporation tax.
4. Average fixed cost and average variable cost.
5. Overheads and fixed costs.
6. Sales revenue maximisation and profit maximisation.
7. A patent and brand loyalty.
8. Barriers to entry and barriers to exit.
9. Vertical integration backwards and vertical integration forwards.
10. Risk bearing economies and managerial economies.

Differences

Identify **one** way in which each of the following pairs is different.

1. A firm and an industry.

2. Public limited companies and public corporations.
3. Fixed costs and variable costs.
4. Short run and long run.
5. Revenue and profit.
6. Perfect competition and monopoly.
7. Normal profit and supernormal profit.
8. Internal growth of firms and external growth of firms.
9. Vertical integration and horizontal integration.
10. Internal economies of scale and external economies of scale.

 Data exercises

These exercises focus on real world examples and provide you with an opportunity to apply your knowledge and understanding. There are some challenging questions here, for instance 2e.

1. Ryanair's profits fall

In February 2008 Ryanair, an Irish low-cost airline, announced a fall in profits. This was the result of a rise in costs and a fall in demand.

Among the costs which had increased were fuel, staff pay and the fees charged for take off and landing slots at the airports the airline uses. Oil had risen in price by 15% over two months. The airline's charges at Stansted airport in the UK, its main base, had doubled. Crew costs had increased by 18%. The airline has to compete with a number of other airlines for its pilots and cabin crew.

The announcement of lower profits resulted in a fall in the airline's share price. To try to turn round its fortunes, Ryanair was considering cutting its fares to attract price-sensitive customers.

a. Define profit. [2]
b. Explain whether the cost of fuel is a fixed or a variable cost for an airline. [3]
c. Apart from a rise in pay, explain **two** other ways Ryanair could seek to attract workers. [4]
d. (i) What is meant by 'price sensitive consumers'. [2]
   (ii) Comment on whether a cut in its fares would increase Ryanair's revenue. [2]
e. You are a business consultant. Discuss the advice you would give to Ryanair's executives on how they could increase the company's profits. [7]
f. Explain two ways that Ryanair could influence an expansion in its operations. [4]

g. Discuss a goal, apart from profit maximisation, that a firm such as Ryanair may pursue. [6]

2. South Korea sells off KDB

South Korea already has a large private sector but its government is still selling offsome of its assets. In 2008 it privatised the Korean Development Bank (KDB). The bank had previously promoted South Korea's industrialisation by providing loans for large industrialised projects. The government, however, argued that having the bank under private sector ownership would promote economic growth. It also plans to sell off other state-owned banks, including the Industrial Bank of Korea, if market conditions are right and is intending to sell off other state concerns such as shipbuilding.

a. Identify **three** types of business organisations in the private sector. [3]
b. What effect may the sale of state-owned enterprises have on government revenue? [4]
c. Explain what is meant by 'if market conditions are right' in the context of the passage. [4]
d. In which stage of production do banks and shipbuilding operate? [2]
e. Discuss whether the interest rate charged to borrowers by private sector banks would be lower than that charged by state owned banks. [7]
f. A state-owned enterprise usually operates as a monopoly. Explain two characteristics of a monopoly. [4]
g. Discuss whether consumers benefit more from perfect competition than from monopoly. [6]

3. Rentokil running into difficulties

Rentokil is a UK public limited company which employs 79,000 people and has branches in more than forty nine countries. It is one of the biggest business services companies in the world. Its diverse businesses range from pest-control to parcels and washrooms.

The company's profits fell from £210m in 2005 to £160m in 2006 and then to £140m in 2007. This decline was largely due to losses made on the company's parcels business.

As a result of the disappointing profit performance the company's chief executive, Doug Flynn, was dismissed in 2008. He was accused of pursuing expansion of the company, at the expense of profits.

The company's announcement of its disappointing profit performance led to a 25% fall in its share price.

a. What was the percentage fall in Rentokil's profits from 2005 to 2007? [2]
b. What evidence is there in the passage that Rentokil is a multinational company? [2]

c. Explain **one** advantage and **one** disadvantage of running a company with a 'diverse business range'. [4]
d. Analyse the possible effects of a fall in its share price on a company. [5]
e. Discuss whether the expansion of a company will necessarily reduce its profits. [7]
f. Explain two reasons why a firm may make a loss. [4]
g. Discuss whether a firm will benefit from producing in more than one country. [6]

Structured questions

1. a. How may a firm become large? [4]
   b. Analyse what factors may attract a multinational company to set up in a country. [6]
   c. Explain who carries out the role of the entrepreneur in a multinational company. [3]
   d. Discuss why a multinational company may not maximise profits. [7]
2. a. Explain the difference between total cost and average cost. [3]
   b. An insurance company moves into a larger rented office and replaces some of its temporary staff by permanent staff. Explain the impact these changes are likely to have on its fixed and variable costs. [4]
   c. What factors will influence the insurance company's choice of resources to employ? [6]
   d. Discuss the possible impact that the growth of the insurance industry may have on this company's average cost. [7]
3. a. Why do so many firms exist in the car repair industry? [5]
   b. What type of internal economies of scale are available to a car manufacturer? [7]
   c. Discuss whether a car manufacturer would benefit more from merging with another car manufacturer or with a company selling cars. [8]
4. In 2008 the number of Chinese tourists visiting Indonesia fell by 48%.
   a. What impact would the reduction in the number of Chinese tourists be likely to have on the costs, revenue and profits of Indonesian hotels? [6]
   b. Explain the factors that may have caused the number of Chinese tourists to Indonesia to fall. [6]
   c. Discuss whether a decline in the Indonesian tourism industry would result in unemployment in Indonesia. [8]

 Homework assignments

These questions provide you with another opportunity to apply your knowledge and understanding.

1. Tata takes over Jaguar and Land Rover

Tata is an Indian multinational company with interests which range from car production and tea plantations to IT. In 2008 it bought out UK based car producers, Jaguar and Land Rover, from the Ford motor company. This will expand the range of vehicles that Tata produces into the luxury end of the vehicles market.

In 2000 the company took over Tetley, the famous tea brand, and seven years later it bought the Anglo-Dutch steelmaker Corus and the Ritz-Carlton hotel in Boston Massachusetts.

It is expected that Tata's UK based branches will generate more of the company's revenue than its India based branches. Its India based branches, however, are expected to be more profitable. Tata is planning to send some of its senior managers to the UK to help run its UK based operations.

a. What evidence is there in the passage that Tata has been involved in conglomerate mergers in the past? [3]
b. Explain **three** types of economy of scale Tata may gain from taking over Jaguar and Land Rover. [6]
c. What does the passage suggest is the relationship between costs and revenue in its India based branches and its UK based branches? [4]
d. Discuss what factors a multinational company should take into account when deciding whether to operate in a country. [7]

2. A price war breaks out

In early 2008 Tesco, the UK's largest supermarket company, was facing fierce competition in the home delivery market from Ocado, a firm that concentrates on the home shopping business. This was surprising as Ocado had made a loss of £30m the year before. The firm, however, claimed to have a large share of the lucrative grocery home shopping market in London. It had a large automated warehouse near London and was planning to expand its business. It said it would match Tesco's prices on more than 3,000 products and would even sell some products at a lower price. Table 1 shows a selection of products and their prices from the two retailers, a week after Ocado launched its campaign.

Table 1. A price comparison

Product	Ocado	Tesco
Wholemeal bread	£1.23	£1.20
Biscuits	£0.76	£0.75
Cleaning fluid	£2.30	£2.38
Batteries	£5.99	£4.97
Tinned beans	£0.49	£0.49

a. Explain **two** possible advantages that Ocado may have over Tesco. [6]
b. Using Table 1, comment on the outcome of Ocadao's price campaign. [3]
c. Explain **two** ways a firm could finance the expansion of a business. [4]
d. Discuss measures, other than price reductions, that Ocado could use to attract more customers. [7]

3. The co-operative movement

The co-operative movement started in the UK in 1844. The Rochdale Society of Equitable Pioneers was founded by twenty eight poor weavers. The men had just been forced back to work after an unsuccessful strike. They were experiencing difficulty affording the prices charged by local shops. Despite their savings being low, each man was able to give £1 to set up a shop selling cheap but good quality food.

The principles on which this initial shop was set up, still remain the basis of co-operative enterprises around the world. These principles include democratic control, the opportunity for everyone to become a member, limited return on the finance invested and the sale of good quality products.

Although the UK Co-operative Group still sells mainly food, it has diversified into, for instance, travel, pharmacy and funeral arrangements. It is a significant business organisation in the UK, employing more than 87,000 people and is the fifth-largest food retailer in the country.

The Co-operative Group has a good record in innovation. For instance, in 1992 the Co-operative Bank became the world's first bank to introduce a customer-led ethical policy and in 1998 fairtrade products were introduced into stores.

a. How does a co-operative differ from a public corporation? [2]
b. Explain **two** factors that would increase the chances of a strike being successful. [4]
c. What may enable a co-operative to sell food that is not only of a good quality but also cheap? [5]
d. What are the benefits of diversification? [4]
e. Discuss whether introducing an ethical policy would reduce a firm's profits. [5]

Section 5: Role of Government in an Economy

 Definitions

Match the following terms with the appropriate definitions. Note that some of the terms relate to government policies for the whole economy whilst some are connected with policies designed to influence particular markets.

1. Full employment
2. The unemployment rate
3. Economic growth
4. Aggregate supply
5. Balance of payments
6. Imports
7. Microeconomic policies
8. Competition policy
9. Regulation
10. Macroeconomic aims
11. Macroeconomic policies
12. Fiscal policy
13. Monetary policy
14. Supply-side policy measures
15. Proportional tax
16. Corporation tax

a. The percentage of income paid in tax
b. Government measures seeking to improve the performance of particular markets
c. A policy that influences the price or quantity of money
d. A policy designed to put pressure on firms to be efficient
e. Rules and laws
f. Unrecorded economic activity
g. Taxes on expenditure
h. A country's total output
i. A record of a country's economic transactions with other countries
j. A tax on companies' profits
k. A government's decisions on its spending and taxation
l. Products bought from other countries
m. A government's objectives for the whole economy
n. A tax on the profit made from the sale of assets
o. A tax that takes an equal percentage of the income from the rich and the poor
p. As low an unemployment rate as possible

17. Capital gains tax
18. Tax burden
19. Informal economy
20. Indirect taxes

q. Policies designed to increase an economy's productive capacity
r. Policies designed to influence the whole economy
s. An increase in real GDP
t. Those without work but seeking it as a percentage of the labour force

Missing words

You should now be very familiar with supplying the relevant missing words. So, as before, complete the following sentences by filling in the missing words.

1. A government may operate a natural _____ and may either produce public goods itself or pay _____ sector firms to produce them.
2. Price stability is usually taken to mean a _____ and stable rate of _____.
3. If _____ economic growth exceeds actual economic growth, an economy will be producing at a point inside its _____ curve.
4. Total spending on a country's products is known as _____ demand and consists of _____, government spending, investment and _____ minus _____.
5. A government can redistribute income from the _____ to the _____ by raising progressive _____ and increasing the benefits paid to the poor.
6. A budget _____ occurs when government spending exceeds _____ revenue.
7. A deflationary _____ policy seeks to reduce _____ demand by raising _____ or reducing _____.
8. If demand is _____, the main burden of an indirect tax will fall on the producer.
9. A maximum price will result in a _____ if it is set _____ the equilibrium price.
10. Two of the qualities of a good _____ are that it is convenient to pay and that it is flexible.
11. _____ _____ are designed to raise revenue and discourage imports.
12. A government may raise its spending by too much if it underestimates the size of the _____.

Role of Government in an Economy

13. Supply-side policies always seek to _____ aggregate supply and never to _____ it.
14. _____ taxes take not only more of the income of the rich but also a higher _____ of their income _____.
15. Forms of government spending and taxation that alter without any change in government policy are known as _____ _____.
16. A rise in the rate of interest is an example of deflationary _____ policy whilst a cut in income tax is an example of _____ _____ policy.
17. If a government introduces new taxes but cuts tax rates, the tax _____ will widen whilst the tax _____ may fall.
18. Government measures taken to increase total spending may reduce unemployment but may cause an increase in the country's _____ rate.
19. A shift to the _____ of a country's aggregate demand curve and its aggregate supply curve may raise both _____ and _____ economic growth.
20. To reduce spending on imports, a government may _____ income tax and _____ domestic producers.

Calculations

In each of these questions, the answer is a whole number. In questions where this is not the case, it is advisable to give an answer to two decimal places.

1. A country has a population of 20 million, a labour force of 12.5 million and 2 million unemployed workers. What is the unemployment rate?
2. A country with a total income of US $ 20 billion has a tax burden of 40%. How much tax revenue does its government receive?
3. A person earns US $ 30,000 a year, of which US $ 25,000 is taxable. The rate of income tax is 20% on the first US $ 5,000 of taxable income and 30% on all taxable income above that level. How much tax will be deducted from this person?

Interpreting diagrams

a. What economic problem is illustrated by point X?
b. What macroeconomic aim may be achieved by the movement from AB to CD of the production possibility curve?

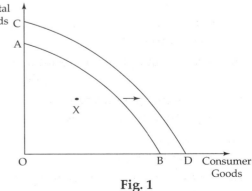

Fig. 1

Drawing diagrams

Use a demand and supply diagram to:
1. a. Illustrate the effect of the imposition of an indirect tax on a product with perfectly inelastic demand.
   b. Analyse how the burden of the tax will be shared out.
2. a. Illustrate the effect of the granting of a subsidy to producers of a product with elastic supply.
   b. Analyse how the benefit of the subsidy will be shared out.

   In these two cases, the diagrams you draw should help you with the analysis in part b. Do ensure, however, that you do not only explain who will be mainly affected by the tax and subsidy but also why.

Multiple-choice questions

A number of the questions here test your ability to distinguish between different types of macroeconomic policies. It is important to be able to differentiate between fiscal, monetary and supply-side policies. Remember fiscal and monetary policies are designed to influence aggregate demand whilst supply-side policies aim to increase aggregate supply.

There are a number of questions on taxation. Some questions on taxation are based on the microeconomic impacts of changes in taxation whilst others are placed in a macroeconomic context.

1. The production of which type of products has to be financed by taxation?
   - [ ] A Those that are unprofitable
   - [ ] B Those that are both non-rival and non-excludable
   - [ ] C Those that have higher social costs than private costs
   - [ ] D Those that are luxury items

2. What is a macroeconomic policy objective?
   - [ ] A To increase employment
   - [ ] B To increase the output of the car industry
   - [ ] C To reduce the price level
   - [ ] D To reduce economic growth

3. Which change is most likely to reduce aggregate demand?
   - [ ] A An increase in investment
   - [ ] B An increase in savings
   - [ ] C A reduction in government tax revenue
   - [ ] D A reduction in imports

4. What effect will a subsidy given to producers of a product have on the price and demand for that product?

      Price   *Demand*
- A decrease   contract
- B decrease   extend
- C increase   extend
- D increase   contract

5. How may fiscal policy increase aggregate demand?
- A By cutting the rate of interest
- B By cutting the rate of taxation
- C By increasing the budget surplus
- D By increasing the money supply

6. Which policy measure is an example of monetary policy designed to reduce aggregate demand?
- A A limit placed on bank lending
- B A reduction in interest rates
- C A rise in income tax
- D A switch in government spending from consumer to capital goods

7. What does a government's budget position show?
- A How the exchange rate influences the country's trade position
- B How the rate of interest influences the money supply
- C The relationship between export revenue and import expenditure
- D The relationship between government spending and tax revenue

8. What effect is a supply-side policy measure designed to have on a country's aggregate supply curve and production possibility curve (PPC)?

      AS curve   *PPC*
- A decrease   decrease
- B decrease   increase
- C increase   increase
- D increase   decrease

9. Which policy measure would be classified as a fiscal policy instrument?
- A A cut in the rate of interest
- B An increase in the money supply
- C The imposition of a quota
- D A rise in government spending on defence

10. Which economic problem may cause a government to cut taxation?
    - [ ] A A current account deficit
    - [ ] B Cyclical unemployment
    - [ ] C Demand-pull inflation
    - [ ] D A high, unsustainable rate of economic growth
11. Which government policy measure may be classified as either a fiscal policy measure or a supply-side policy measure?
    - [ ] A A decrease in the exchange rate
    - [ ] B A decrease in the rate of interest
    - [ ] C An increase in corporation tax
    - [ ] D An increase in government spending on education
12. In which circumstance must a government be saving?
    - [ ] A When it operates a budget surplus
    - [ ] B When it privatises public corporations
    - [ ] C When it reduces government spending and taxation by an equal amount
    - [ ] D When it switches from relying on direct taxes to relying on indirect taxes
13. A government sets a maximum price on rented accommodation above the equilibrium price. What will be the likely outcome?
    - [ ] A An unofficial market in rented accommodation will develop
    - [ ] B Rents will remain unchanged
    - [ ] C Landlords will provide more rented accommodation
    - [ ] D Some potential tenants will be unable to find accommodation
14. What is meant by the incidence of taxation?
    - [ ] A How the tax burden is shared between consumers and producers
    - [ ] B The extent to which tax is evaded
    - [ ] C What proportion of the country's products are taxed
    - [ ] D Who receives the tax revenue raised
15. What is meant by a regressive tax?
    - [ ] A One designed to create a more even distribution of income
    - [ ] B One which is impossible to evade
    - [ ] C One which is earning less tax revenue than previously
    - [ ] D One which takes a larger percentage of tax from the poor than the rich
16. A government wants to reduce income inequality. Which tax should it increase?
    - [ ] A Excise duties
    - [ ] B Import duties
    - [ ] C Income tax
    - [ ] D Sales tax

17. What is a disadvantage of a progressive system of income tax?
    - [ ] A It discourages the growth of the informal economy
    - [ ] B It may increase the mobility of labour
    - [ ] C It redistributes income form the poor to the rich
    - [ ] D It may act as a disincentive to work

18. Which feature is a quality of a good tax?
    - [ ] A Convenience
    - [ ] B Divisibility
    - [ ] C Durability
    - [ ] D Homogeneity

19. What would be an argument for removing a sales tax on food?
    - [ ] A To decrease aggregate demand
    - [ ] B To decrease income inequality
    - [ ] C To increase disposable income
    - [ ] D To increase the tax base

20. What effect would an increase in labour productivity have on an economy?
    - [ ] A A decrease in aggregate demand
    - [ ] B A decrease in the rate of economic growth
    - [ ] C An increase in aggregate supply
    - [ ] D An increase in the labour force

Similarities

Find **one** similarity between each of the following pairs. Your answer to 6 should be helped by the work you did in answer to the questions on using diagrams.

1. Essential products and public goods.
2. Economic growth and redistribution of income.
3. Fiscal policy and monetary policy.
4. Competition policy and price controls.
5. Income tax and corporation tax.
6. The impact of an indirect tax on a product with inelastic demand and the granting of a subsidy on a product with inelastic demand.
7. Convenience and economy.
8. Increase in government spending and a decrease in the rate of interest.
9. Reforming trade unions and privatisation.
10. Tariffs and taxes on demerit goods.

Differences

Find one way in which the two terms in each pair is different. You will note that 7 includes the same terms as 3 in the similarities part but this time you are seeking to identify one way in which fiscal policy differs from monetary policy.

1. Employment and unemployment.
2. Aggregate demand and aggregate supply.
3. Budget position and the balance of payments.
4. Macroeconomic policies and microeconomic policies.
5. Actual economic growth and potential economic growth.
6. Progressive taxes and regressive taxes.
7. Fiscal policy and monetary policy.
8. Subsidies and taxes.
9. Income tax and inheritance tax.
10. Direct taxes and indirect taxes.

Data exercises

1. Milan introduces a congestion charge

In January 2008 the city of Milan in Italy introduced a congestion charge on motorists wanting to enter the centre of the city. The intention is to reduce traffic and pollution.

The charges are levied on a sliding scale of engine types, with the most polluting vehicles being charged the most and the least polluting ones, such as scooters and electric cars, being exempt. The charge applies on weekdays from 7.30 am to 7.30 pm. Residents can pay a fixed annual fee or buy discounted multiple entry passes.

It is expected that the scheme will raise €24m a year, two thirds of which will be used to subsidise public transport.

In the same month, France announced green taxes on cars such as 4 x 4s land cruisers and high powered sports cars which emit high levels of CO_2. Purchases of small cars will receive a government payment of up to €1,000 – an ecological subsidy.

a. Identify an external cost caused by traffic congestion. [1]
b. Explain how a congestion charge can reduce travel time for motorists. [3]
c. Using a demand and supply diagram, analyse how a subsidy given to bus companies would affect the market for bus travel. [6]
d. Identify two other items, other than subsidising public transport, that the Italian government could spend the congestion charge revenue on. [2]
e. Discuss the effect that the congestion charge and the green tax may have on the output of car producers in Italy and France. [8]

f. Explain why a congestion charge may not apply at night. [4]
g. Discuss two measures, other than imposing a congestion charge and subsidising public transport, that could reduce traffic congestion. [6]

2. South African Unemployment

One of the main aims of the South African government is to reduce unemployment. In 2006 it introduced an Accelerated and Shared Growth Initiative. To date, this has involved spending more than 300 billion rand on public sector projects, including road building. The intention is to raise aggregate demand and increase employment. It is also using supply-side policy measures. For instance, it has reduced regulations on small and medium-sized firms.

Table 1. South African unemployment rate

Year	%
2001	28
2002	30
2003	31
2004	26
2005	27
2006	28
2007	26
2008	26

a. Identify two supply-side policy measures. [2]
b. Explain how the Accelerated and Shared Growth Initiative may reduce unemployment. [4]
c. What is meant by raising 'the economic growth rate'? [3]
d. Comment on the extent to which the Accelerated and Shared Growth Initiative has been successful. [4]
e. Discuss the effectiveness of supply-side policy measures in reducing unemployment. [7]
f. Explain two government aims, other than full employment and economic growth. [4]
g. Discuss whether a reduction in unemployment will cause economic growth. [6]

3. State intervention in the Brazilian Economy

A 2007 report which commented on the ease of doing business in 175 countries placed Brazil 121st. The average firm in the country takes 2,600 hours to process its taxes, a world record. The government imposes a considerable amount of regulation on the country's firms. The tax burden is also high with most tax revenue coming from sales tax. In 2006 Brazilian tax revenue was equivalent to 35% of GDP. This compared with 22% in Argentina and 18% in Mexico. The high level of taxation and regulation is thought to be discouraging investment.

The Brazilian government spends the tax revenue on three main items. One is generous pensions for Brazilian government workers and state pensions which are paid to everyone who has contributed to the system for 35 years regardless of their age. Another is public sector workers' pay and the third is on transfers to the regional authorities of the country's 27 states which spend the money mainly on health, education and administration.

Public sector workers, on average, earn more than twice as much as workers in the private sector and have better working conditions. Most of those receiving the country's minimum wage are private sector workers.

    a. Does Brazil receive most of its tax revenue from direct or indirect taxes? Explain your answer. [2]
    b. Describe **two** ways in which taxes place a burden on Brazilian firms. [4]
    c. Explain one advantage and **one** disadvantage of regulations. [4]
    d. Identify from the passage **three** reasons why a Brazilian would probably prefer to work for the government than a private sector firm. [3]
    e. You are a Brazilian government minister. Discuss whether you would recommend that the government should cut taxes. [7]
    f. Explain why a government may impose a national minimum wage. [4]
    g. Discuss whether an increase in government spending on education would increase a budget deficit. [6]

Structured questions

1.   a. Explain the difference between income tax and a sales tax. [4]
    b. What are the qualities of a good tax? [6]
    c. Explain the difference between a progressive and a regressive tax. [3]
    d. Discuss whether a government should shift the burden of taxation from direct taxes to indirect taxes. [7]
2.   a. What is the difference between a minimum price and a maximum price? [3]
    b. Explain why a government may impose price controls. [4]
    c. Why does the government produce some products? [5]
    d. Discuss how you would assess whether an industry should be privatised. [8]
3.   a. What does the term 'full employment' mean to governments? [3]
    b. Explain what may happen to unemployment if investment increases. [5]
    c. Apart from full employment, explain two other government macroeconomic aims. [4]

d. Discuss whether the unemployment of labour is more serious than the unemployment of other factors of production. [8]
4. In 2008, firms in the Philippines were urging the government not to raise income tax and corporation tax. They also asked the government to increase its spending on education and infrastructure.
   a. Why would firms want corporation tax to be reduced? [3]
   b. Explain how firms might benefit from an increase in government spending on education and infrastructure. [7]
   c. Discuss one way a government and one way a central bank might influence private sector firms. [10]

 ## Homework assignments

1. The problem with plastic bags

In 2008 the UK government was considering how to dissuade people from using plastic bags for their shopping. They are seen as a waste of resources and a source of pollution. On average, each bag is used for only 20 minutes before being thrown away. It has been estimated that it takes up to 1,000 years before a plastic bag degrades. This means that unless they are disposed of carefully, they form long-lasting litter.  They can also kill animals. Indeed, the United Nations Environmental Programme has estimated that more than a million seabirds and 100,000 marine mammals are killed annually by plastic in the oceans.

Some other countries have already taken action against plastic bags. China has banned all shops from providing free bags and has banned production of very thin bags. In Germany, Ireland and Sweden shoppers have to pay for plastic bags provided by shops.

As well as considering passing legislation requiring shops to charge for plastic bags or banning their use, the UK government was also investigating some alternative measures. These included promoting the use of fabric which last much longer than plastic bags. Such a measure, however, would divert some resources from food production.

   a. Does the information in the passage suggest plastic bags are under or overproduced? Explain your answer. [3]

b. Identify **two** external costs from the use of plastic bags. [2]
c. Explain **one** advantage and one disadvantage of using a ban to achieve a government aim. [4]
d. Using a demand and supply diagram, analyse the effect on food production of an increase in the production of fabric bags. [5]
e. Discuss the possible effect on shops' profits of legislation requiring them to charge for plastic bags. [6]

2. Farmers strike in Argentina

In March 2008 Argentinian farmers started a strike in protest at the Argentinian government's decision to raise a tax on the export of soya from 35% to 45% and to place new taxes on other farm exports. The rise in tax burden on farm exports was designed to raise government tax revenue. The strikes reduced food supplies in the country's shops and reduced the country's exports of food.

Farming is an important part of the Argentinian economy which has been growing in size due to the increasing demand from China and India for soya beans and other agricultural products.

Indeed, soya production increased by 72% between 2001 and 2006. Over this period, Argentina's economy grew by an average of 8.2% a year. The government, however, had problems controlling inflation which averaged 11%.

In the same month Cambodia banned all exports of rice due to fears that shortages could provoke food riots. It was anticipated that global demand for rice would outstrip the supply by 3m tonnes on the 424m tonnes required.

a. Identify two government macroeconomic aims referred to in the passage. [2]
b. What were the motives behind the Argentinian and Cambodian governments intervention in their countries' agricultural markets? [2]
c. Explain a government macroeconomic aim the Argentinian tax on the exports of soya may have harmed. [4]
d. Use a diagram to illustrate the relationship between demand and supply in the global market for rice in March 2008. [5]
e. Discuss whether a government should subsidise food production. [7]

3. Green Taxes

Green Taxes are taxes that are imposed with the main aim of improving the environment. In countries that impose green taxes, it is usual for fuel duty to account for most of the revenue from such taxes.

Imposing a tax on petrol both raises revenue and makes consuming petrol more expensive. The UK, and a number of other countries, also now charge a higher road tax on cars that use a significant amount of petrol and omit high levels of carbon dioxide. As a result, UK drivers are switching to diesel-powered cars and away from petrol-powered cars.

In 2008, however, drivers were finding that diesel was more expensive than petrol because oil companies had failed to predict the rise in demand. The growth in demand for diesel had surprised them and they had not made sufficient investment in diesel production.

As well as using taxation to improve the environment, governments use a variety of other policy measures. One such measure is an emissions trading scheme which is based on the use of tradeable permits.

    a. Comment on whether the objectives of a petrol tax conflict. [3]
    b. What is the demand relationship between diesel-powered cars and petrol-powered cars? [2]
    c. What is meant by a tradeable permit? [2]
    d. Using a demand and supply diagram, explain what might happen to the price of diesel in the future. [6]
    e. Discuss how price elasticity of demand influences the incidence of tax revenue. [7]

Section 6: Economic Indicators

 Definitions

Match the terms with the appropriate definitions. Be careful as a number of the terms here have some similarity.

1. The retail/consumer prices index
2. Monetary inflation
3. Hyperinflation
4. Menu costs
5. Stable inflation
6. Self employment
7. Unionised labour
8. Employment rate
9. The claimant count
10. Technological unemployment
11. Frictional unemployment
12. A recession
13. Labour force participation rate
14. Gross Domestic Product
15. Short run economic growth
16. Transfer payments

a. A situation where people are in between jobs
b. A measure of the change in the cost of living
c. An economy making fuller use of existing resources
d. The proportion of those of working age who are economically active
e. A very rapid rise in the general price level
f. Workers who belong to trade unions
g. People who work for themselves
h. Negative economic growth over two successive quarters
i. A rise in the general price level caused by the money supply increasing faster than output
j. The expense of changing prices as a result of inflation
k. Domestic output produced over a period of a year
l. The quality of people's lives
m. Adjusting payments to reflect changes in the cost of living
n. The movement of income and spending round an economy
o. A measure of living standards which includes components like education, health and output
p. A measure of unemployment based on those receiving unemployment benefits

17. Living standards
18. The circular flow of income
19. Index-linking
20. The Human Development Index

q. People out of work due to structural changes in the economy
r. Income payments not related to output
s. The proportion of people of working age who are in employment
t. A steady rise in the general price level

Missing words

Fill in the missing words to ensure these sentences make sense and are logically consistent.

1. Two of the stages in constructing a consumer prices index are selecting a _____ year and attaching _____ to different categories of expenditure.
2. Demand-pull _____ is likely to occur when an economy is producing close to full _____.
3. Inflation can redistribute income from lenders to _____ and from workers with _____ bargaining power to workers with _____ bargaining power.
4. A reduction in inflation will reduce _____ _____ costs as households and firms will be able to leave money in existing bank accounts.
5. _____ flexibility is the ability to change when people work whereas _____ flexibility is the ability to change where people work.
6. A _____ in the wage rate paid and a _____ in the school leaving age would increase the labour force participation rate.
7. Two ways of measuring unemployment are to count those receiving unemployment related _____ and to conduct _____ surveys.
8. An increase in aggregate demand should reduce _____ unemployment but may not reduce _____ or _____ unemployment.
9. The effects of unemployment will be more serious, the _____ the unemployment rate and the _____ the duration of the unemployment.
10. An increase in unemployment may result in a budget _____ as tax revenue is likely to _____ whilst government spending on _____ is likely to rise.

11. Real GDP is GDP at _____ prices and has been adjusted for _____.
12. The size of a country's informal economy may increase as a result of an _____ in tax rates and a _____ in the chance of being caught for tax evasion.
13. For economic growth to continue it is important that both aggregate demand and aggregate supply _____ and that the growth is _____.
14. One country may have a higher real GDP per head than another country but most of its citizens may experience lower _____ _____ if income is very _____ distributed.
15. _____ _____ inflation is more likely to encourage producers to expand than _____ _____ inflation.
16. Public sector workers are employed by the _____ and may have higher job security than those employed in the _____ sector.
17. When people have been unemployed for a _____ time, employers tend to become reluctant to employ them and some become out of date with advances in _____ and working _____.
18. In the short run, economic growth may _____ the output of consumer goods, but it is likely to _____ their output in the long run.
19. A country may have a higher HDI ranking than its real GDP per head ranking if its citizens enjoy a longer _____ _____ and a more expected years of _____.
20. Two measures of living standards are the Index of _____ Economic _____ and the Happy Life _____ Index.

Calculations

Do not rush these calculations and check over your answers.

1. The consumer price index in a country rises from 150 to 153 over a period of a year. What is the rate of inflation?
2. The table below shows the weights and the price changes of three categories of products that are used to construct a weighted price index. Use this information to calculate the change in the price level.

Item	Weight	Price Change (%)
Food	½	5
Clothing	¼	10
Leisure goods	¼	16

3. In a country three million people are unemployed and 21 million people are employed. What is the country's unemployment rate?

Interpreting diagrams

An aggregate demand and aggregate supply diagram is a useful tool to analyse changes in the macroeconomy.

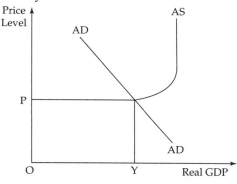

Fig. 1

a. Explain **three** of the labels in the diagram.
b. Identify **two** possible causes of shifts in the AD curve.
c. What effect would an increase in AD be likely to have on inflation and employment in this case?

Drawing diagrams

In each case use a production possibility curve to illustrate:
a. An increase in unemployment
b. Actual economic growth
c. Potential economic growth.

You should now be very familiar with production possibility curves, so this task should be straightforward.

Multiple-choice questions

With some of the questions here, the correct answer may stand out immediately. In other cases, you may have to arrive at the correct answer by eliminating the other three options.

1. What does a consumer prices index show?
   ☐ A How the price of domestically produced products has changed over time
   ☐ B How the price of a representative basket of goods and services has changed over time

- [ ] C How the wages of consumers have changed relative to the change in the price level
- [ ] D How the wages of consumers have changed relative to the costs of production

2. A country is experiencing a high rate of inflation. Which item would be the least desirable store of wealth?
- [ ] A Money
- [ ] B Property
- [ ] C Land
- [ ] D Shares

3. In which circumstance would an increase in aggregate demand be most likely to cause inflation?
- [ ] A It is caused by an increase in investment undertaken by expanding industries
- [ ] B It is the result of higher government spending on training which raises labour productivity
- [ ] C It occurs when there is a low level of spare capacity in the economy
- [ ] D It takes place when there is net immigration occurring

4. What is a cause of cost-push inflation?
- [ ] A A reduction in direct taxes
- [ ] B A reduction in the rate of interest
- [ ] C An increase in bank lending
- [ ] D An increase in the price of raw materials

5. What is a cause of demand-pull inflation?
- [ ] A A fall in labour productivity
- [ ] B A fall in investment
- [ ] C A rise in the budget deficit
- [ ] D A rise in a current account deficit

6. In which circumstance would a rise in a country's inflation rate increase the international competitiveness of the products it produces?
- [ ] A The quality of the products produced by other countries improves at a more rapid rate
- [ ] B The price level of other countries increases at a more rapid rate
- [ ] C The country's exchange rate increases
- [ ] D The productivity of the country's labour force decreases

7. Which group is economically active?
- [ ] A Full time students
- [ ] B Those who are too sick to work
- [ ] C Those who are officially classified as unemployed
- [ ] D Those who have retired early

8. What is the cause of frictional unemployment?
   - A A lack of aggregate demand
   - B The introduction of new technology
   - C A lack of information about job vacancies
   - D Domestic consumers buying more imports
9. Which factor may cause official unemployment figures to understate the actual level of unemployment?
   - A People being ashamed to admit they are unemployed
   - B People being prepared to cheat the system
   - C People who have found employment since the measure was taken
   - D People working in the informal economy
10. What type of unemployment is caused by workers changing jobs?
    - A Cyclical
    - B Frictional
    - C Regional
    - D Structural
11. An increase in which variable may cause unemployment?
    - A Bank lending
    - B Disposable income
    - C Government spending
    - D Imports
12. Why might a fall in unemployment increase the inflation rate?
    - A It will increase aggregate demand
    - B It will increase aggregate supply
    - C It will reduce workers' wages
    - D It will reduce spare capacity in the economy
13. Which government measure would be most effective in reducing structural unemployment?
    - A Increasing government spending on training
    - B Increasing the rates of unemployment benefit
    - C Reducing income tax
    - D Reducing the rate of interest
14. Which of the following payments would be included in the measurement of Gross Domestic Product?
    - A Payments to those in the informal sector
    - B Retirement pensions
    - C Salaries of government ministers
    - D Unemployment benefit

15. Which combination of changes may enable an economy to grow despite a rise in unemployment?

	Occupational mobility	Productivity
A	decrease	decrease
B	decrease	increase
C	increase	increase
D	increase	decrease

16. What is a possible disadvantage of economic growth?
    - A Environmental improvement
    - B Extra consumer goods produced
    - C Higher tax revenue
    - D Structural unemployment

17. Which method is one of the ways of measuring GDP?
    - A The consumption method
    - B The expenditure method
    - C The import method
    - D The payment method

18. Which factor may stop economic growth?
    - A Automatic stabilisers
    - B A lack of skilled labour
    - C A large multiplier effect
    - D A rise in net exports

19. Which is the most accurate measure of living standards?
    - A GDP
    - B GDP per head
    - C Real GDP
    - D Real GDP per head

20. Why may an increase in GDP be accompanied by a decrease in living standards?
    - A Illiteracy may have decreased
    - B Negative externalities may have increased
    - C The population may have decreased
    - D Working conditions may have improved

Economic Indicators

Similarities

State what the items in each of these pairs have in common.
1. Retail prices index and consumer prices index.
2. Menu costs and shoe leather costs.
3. Claimant count and labour force survey.
4. Borrowers and workers with strong bargaining power.
5. Search unemployment and seasonal unemployment.
6. Lost output and lost tax revenue.
7. Income method and expenditure method.
8. Rise in quantity of resources and rise in quality of resources.
9. Pensions and unemployment benefits.
10. Nominal GDP and GDP at current prices.

Differences

State one way in which the items in each pair differ. Take care with 7 – remember you are looking for a difference here and not a similarity.
1. Cost-push inflation and monetary inflation.
2. The organised sector and the unorganised sector of the economy.
3. Private sector employment and public sector employment.
4. The labour force participation rate and the employment rate.
5. Structural unemployment and cyclical unemployment.
6. Employed and self-employed.
7. Human Development Index and Index of Sustainable Economic Welfare.
8. Cost of living and standard of living.
9. Economic growth and recession.
10. Velocity of circulation and the circular flow of income.

Data exercises

1. The UAE's action to reduce inflation

In 2008 the United Arab Emirates (UAE) government announced plans to build up strategic stockpiles of essential foodstuffs to slow down inflation and meet the government's new inflation target of 5%.

Inflation rose in 2007 to 10%. Inflationary pressures in 2008 were coming from rising government spending, low interest rates and rising food prices.

The UAE's booming economy and fast growing population has encouraged a number of multinational supermarkets to set up in the country. French supermarket, Carrefour, had a large presence in the country in 2008 and UK supermarket, Waitrose, was expanding in the country. The UAE government was considering imposing price controls on food sold in the country's shops. Another measure, under review, was subsidising essential foodstuffs for its citizens.

  a. Explain what is meant by 'stockpiles'. [2]
  b. What is meant by a rise in inflation? [2]
  c. Explain **two** reasons why a multinational supermarket may set up in a foreign country. [4]
  d. Using a demand and supply diagram, analyse the effect of imposing a limit on food prices on the market for food. [5]
  e. Discuss whether an increase in government spending will always cause inflation. [7]
  f. Explain what is meany by a 'booming' economy. [4]
  g. Discuss whether inflation is more harmful that deflation. [6]

2. Changes in government policy in the Philippines

In 2006 the government of the Philippines was running a large budget deficit. To correct this, it broadened its value added tax (VAT) base, increased the VAT rate and sought to reduce tax evasion. It also cut back on government spending plans, including cancelling some road projects and some measures to reduce poverty. These measures did reduce the budget deficit from 3% of GDP in 2006 to 1% of GDP in 2008.

The government, however, was not successful in raising its economic growth rate from 4%. It was considering using both monetary and supply-side policy measures in a bid to increase economic growth.

Government spending in the Philippines usually forms more than a tenth of the country's aggregate demand but the government is keen to increase the proportion of investment in the country's aggregate demand. The table below shows some of the components of the Phiiippines' aggregate demand.

Table 1. Selected components of the AD of the Philippines 2008

Consumption 72%	Exports 49%
Government spending 12%	Imports 51%

a. What is meant by a reduction in the budget deficit? [3]
b. What type of tax is value added tax? [2]
c. What impact will a cut in government spending have on aggregate demand? [3]
d. (i) What percentage contribution did investment make to aggregate demand in 2008? [2]
   (ii) Did the Philippines have a trade deficit or a trade surplus in 2008? Explain your answer. [3]
e. Discuss whether monetary policy or supply-side policy measures would be more effective in increasing economic growth. [7]
f. Explain two influences on consumption. [4]
g. Discuss whether an increase in consumption will always benefit an economy. [6]

3. Spanish growth slumps

In 2008 Spain was suffering from both the effects of the international credit squeeze and a downturn in its property boom.

Due to problems that banks in the US had got into by lending to high risk customers, banks throughout many countries became more reluctant to lend. This reduced the growth in Spanish consumption and investment. House building had been contributing more than 10% of the country's GDP but in 2008 the number of building projects declined.

It was being predicted that Spain's economic growth would decline and that unemployment might rise. Economic growth rates and unemployment rates tend to be inversely related. The table below shows the economic growth rates and unemployment rates of a number of countries.

Table 2. Economic growth rate and unemployment rate of selected countries 2008

Country	Economic growth rate	Unemployment rate
China	9.8	9.5
India	7.8	7.2
Egypt	7.1	9.0
Venezuela	5.5	6.7
Czech Republic	4.7	5.9
South Korea	4.5	3.0
Spain	2.4	9.0

To try to prevent unemployment rising, the Spanish government announced that it would increase its spending on infrastructure projects such as high-speed trains and that it was considering cutting tax rates.

  a. Identify **three** components of aggregate demand referred to in the passage. [3]
  b. Explain what is meant by a decline in economic growth. [2]
  c. Describe **two** consequences of unemployment. [4]
  d. Comment on whether the information in the Table supports the view that 'economic growth rates and unemployment rates tend to be inversely related'. [4]
  e. Discuss what information you would need to assess whether cutting tax rates would increase economic growth. [7]
  f. Explain two consequences of a recession. [4]
  g. Discuss how house building and economic growth are related. [6]

Structured questions

1. a. What are the main causes of unemployment? [4]
    b. What are the disadvantages of unemployment in an economy? [6]
    c. Explain two ways a government could increase spending by households. [4]
    d. Discuss whether an increase in spending will increase employment. [6]
2. a. What is meant by a consumer prices index? [4]
    b. Explain the costs of inflation. [8]
    c. Discuss how a government might reduce inflation. [8]
3. a. How is economic growth measured? [3]
    b. Why might a more rapid rate of economic growth result in balance of payments problems? [4]
    c. Explain two ways of measuring living standards. [6]
    d. Discuss whether economic growth is always desirable. [7]
4. In 2007 Malaysia had a real GDP of US $ 130bn, an average life expectancy of 74.3 years and an inflation rate of 1.7%. In contrast, Egypt had a real GDP of US $ 89.4bn, an average life expectancy of 72.2 years and an inflation rate of 8.1%.
    a. Why may a country have a higher real GDP but a worse economic growth performance than another country? [4]
    b. Explain **three** reasons why a country's inhabitants may have a higher average life expectancy than another. [6]
    c. Discuss whether an economy experiencing 8.1% inflation would face more serious problems than one facing an inflation rate of 1.7%. [10]

Homework assignments

1. The transformation of the Georgian economy

Between 2004 and 2008 the economic performance of the Georgian economy improved radically. Its World Bank ranking for ease with which firms can set up and operate went from 112th to 18th. The government reduced corruption, simplified the tax system and carried out a privatisation programme. Corruption had been widespread in the police and civil service. The taxation system had been complex with over twenty different taxes. These were reduced to five and the different income tax rates were replaced by one rate of 25%.
Although some industries, including the operation of gas pipelines stayed under state control, many other industries were sold to the private sector.

The tax reforms and privatisation raised government tax revenue, some of which was spent on improved infrastructure. Foreign direct investment was attracted into the country. Construction, communications and the financial sector did well. The agricultural sector, however, which employed 48% of the labour force did less well. It was hit by floods, drought and Russian trade restrictions.

a. Explain **two** economic indicators you would examine to assess whether a country's economic performance has improved. [4]
b. Identify **two** supply-side policy measures used by the Georgian government in the period 2004 to 2008. [2]
c. You are a government minister. Explain **two** recommendations you would make to attract investment from abroad. [4]
d. What would be likely to happen to the size of the Georgian agricultural sector as the economy develops? [3]
e. Discuss whether a cut in tax rates will raise or lower tax revenue. [7]

2. Measuring price changes

In March 2008 the UK's Office for National Statistics (ONS) announced changes to the basket of 650 goods and services used to calculate the retail prices index and the consumer prices index. The ONS also collects 120,000 prices each month. Combined, the information is used to calculate changes in the cost of living.

The first ever basket was calculated in 1947 and included lard, unskinned rabbits, a gallon of lamp oil and Brussels sprouts.

Among the items which were added in 2008 were fruit smoothies drinks, muffins, peppers and Clementine oranges. Items which were removed included frozen vegetarian ready meals and CD singles. The weights of the items included were altered to reflect changes in consumer spending and lifestyles. For example, transport was given a weighting of 152 parts out of a thousand; food, drink and tobacco a weighting of 152; household fuel, water and related bills a weighting of 115 and audio, visual and related products a weighting of 27.

   a. Explain how the basket of goods and services is used to calculate the consumer prices index. [4]
   b. Why are items added and removed from the basket? [3]
   c. Did UK households devote a higher proportion of their spending to transport or household, fuel, water and related bills? Explain your answer. [3]
   d. Explain what you would expect to happen to the weighting of audio, visual and related products in the future. [3]
   e. Discuss whether an increase in the cost of living will reduce people's living standards. [7]

3. A Caribbean and Chilean success story?

Barbados had a higher Human Development Index (HDI) ranking than all other Latin American countries and Caribbean countries. Its unemployment in 2007 was at an all time low of 7%, down from a peak of 27% in 1993.

The country faces the possibility of significant change in the future. Demand for its sugar is likely to fall when the European Union removes its preferential treatment of exports from the Caribbean in 2015. There may, however, be oil production as experts believe there is oil off the coast of Barbados.

Another country in the region which has seen unemployment fall is Chile which in 2008 also had an unemployment rate of 7%. Despite the drop in its unemployment, almost one million workers, 15% of the labour force, were earning less than the legal minimum take home pay of just over US $ 200 a month. The Chilean government, nevertheless, claimed that the economy was performing better than other Latin American countries including Argentina, Mexico and Venezuela – see the table.

Table 3. Selected data on selected Latin American countries – 2008

Country	Economic growth rate (%)	Inflation rate (%)	Unemployment rate (%)
Argentina	6.2	11.4	8.1
Chile	4.5	5.4	7.3
Mexico	2.8	3.8	3.5
Venezuela	5.1	19.8	8.5

a. Describe **one** reason why a country may enjoy a higher HDI ranking than other countries. [2]
b. Explain **two** advantages of a fall in unemployment. [4]
c. What type of unemployment may arise from the change in the economy of Barbados described in the second paragraph? [3]
d. Analyse the likely effect of a fall in unemployment on the wage rate. [4]
e. Using the data in the table, discuss whether the Chilean economy was performing better than the other Latin American economies shown. [7]

Section 7: Developed and Developing Countries

 Definitions

Matching the definitions to the appropriate terms should help you distinguish between a number of similar terms.

1. Economic development
2. Dependency ratio
3. Birth rate
4. Death rate
5. Income inequality
6. Distribution of wealth
7. Absolute poverty
8. Relative poverty
9. Lorenz curve
10. Natural increase in population
11. Net emigration
12. Population pyramid
13. Ageing population
14. Foreign aid
15. Sex distribution

a. A diagram showing the degree of inequality
b. A diagram showing the age structure of a population
c. The average number of children born to each woman in the country
d. The international transfer of loans and grants on favourable terms
e. Loans and grants given from one country to another on favourable terms on condition that the aid money will be spent on exports of donor country only.
f. Assistance given from one country to another
g. An improvement in people's lives including a rise in self-esteem
h. The number of births in a year per thousand of the population
i. The number of deaths in a year per thousand of the population
j. A rise the average age of the population
k. A situation where people lack the income to participate in the normal activities of the country
l. A situation where people lack some of the basic necessities of life
m. Movement of people between countries and regions
n. How assets are shared out among households
o. An uneven distribution of income between households

Developed and Developing Countries   75

16. Fertility rate
17. Preventive checks
18. Migration
19. Tied aid
20. Bilateral aid

p. The increase in population resulting from an excess of births over deaths
q. More people leaving the country than entering it
r. The percentage of the population who are not of working age
s. The ratio of males to females in the population
t. Factors which reduce the birth rate

Missing words

Fill in the missing words, taking particular care with 8, 11 and 19.

1. Developing countries tend to have low rates of _____ due to low income but _____ rates of population growth.
2. A vicious circle of poverty can be present in developing countries with low saving leading to low _____ which in turn leads to low _____ which results in low _____.
3. A country may achieve economic growth without experiencing economic _____ if the choices facing people are _____ and the distribution of income becomes more _____.
4. A more uneven distribution of wealth would tend to lead to a more uneven distribution of _____, as wealth generates _____.
5. Cutting progressive taxes, charging for state education and abolishing a national _____ wage would make the distribution of _____ more _____.
6. A rise in the income of the poor is likely to reduce _____ poverty but _____ poverty may increase if the income of the rich increases at a greater rate.
7. Economists measure the distribution of income by assessing how much is earned by _____ and _____ of the population.
8. The birth rate of a country is likely to be low if a _____ proportion of women go to university, a _____ of women work and it is _____ to bring up children.
9. Net immigration will tend to _____ the labour force of a country and reduce the _____ ratio as most immigrants are of working age.
10. The _____ theory of population claims that population growth outstrips the growth of _____ production.
11. A _____ in the infant mortality rate in a country may reduce the birth rate as it may encourage families to have _____ children.

12. An ageing population will _____ the dependency ratio and create a _____ demand for health care.
13. Net emigration would be disadvantageous if a country's population is _____ the optimum level.
14. A high level of international debt will be more difficult to repay if interest rates _____ and if the country's export revenue _____ .
15. _____ substitution increases reliance on _____ production and reduces reliance on foreign production.
16. The United Nations and the _____ Bank provide _____ aid as opposed to bilateral aid.
17. The ownership of land is very unevenly distributed in Latin America. This inequality results in both _____ and _____ poverty.
18. Children of the poor tend to grow up poor as they usually have _____ years of education and _____ access to health care.
19. A triangular population pyramid shows a high birth rate and a _____ death rate and is more likely to be found in a _____ country than in a _____ country.
20. More money may flow from _____ countries to _____ countries if debt repayments are greater than foreign aid.

Calculations

Question 1 here tests your understanding of 'a natural increase in population' and question 3 requires you to know what is meant by 'cumulative percentage'. Be careful with question 2 – check what it is asking.

1. A country starts the year with a population of 120m. By the end of the year 2m children have been born, ½ m people have died and there has been net emigration of ½ m. What was the natural increase in population?
2. A country has a population of 30m, 80% of whom live above the level of absolute poverty. How many of its people are living in absolute poverty?
3. From the table below, calculate the cumulative percentage of income.

Group	% share of income
Poorest 20%	7
Next poorest 20%	11
Middle 20%	18
Next richest 20%	22
Richest 20%	42

Interpreting diagrams

Using the diagrams below, explain two reasons why Country B is likely to be a more developed economy than Country A.

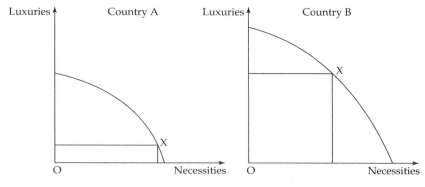

Fig. 1

Drawing diagrams

From the following information, plot the Lorenz curves for the two countries on one diagram and comment on which country has the most even distribution of wealth. It would be helpful to use graph paper if possible.

Table 1. Distribution of wealth

Cumulative % share of wealth	Country A	Country B
20	15	2
40	32	8
60	51	20
80	73	40
100	100	100

Multiple-choice questions

Read the options carefully as in a number of cases they are very similar.

1. Which change could cause a natural decrease in population?
   - A A fall in the death rate
   - B A fall in the birth rate
   - C Net emigration
   - D Net immigration

2. What is meant by 'absolute poverty'?
   - [ ] A An income level that is insufficient to meet basic needs
   - [ ] B An income level that is less than 25% of the national average
   - [ ] C A lack of any income
   - [ ] D A lack of any wealth
3. What may promote both economic growth and economic development?
   - [ ] A A more uneven distribution of income
   - [ ] B Improved education of the poor
   - [ ] C Increased output of heavy polluting firms
   - [ ] D Increased tax on company profits
4. What is meant by the 'optimum population'?
   - [ ] A A population which produces the highest output per head
   - [ ] B A population with an equal number of males and females
   - [ ] C A population which is static
   - [ ] D A population with a low average age
5. What is meant by the term 'overpopulation'?
   - [ ] A There is a high geographical density of population
   - [ ] B There is a high population relative to the available area of cultivatable land
   - [ ] C There is a high population relative to the economic resources available
   - [ ] D There is net immigration
6. What impact would economic development have on adult illiteracy, infant mortality and life expectancy?

	Adult illiteracy	Infant mortality	Life expectancy
A	reduce	reduce	increase
B	increase	reduce	reduce
C	increase	increase	reduce
D	reduce	increase	increase

7. Two countries have the same size of population. One country has a lower number of hospital beds per 100,000 people but is considered to have a better standard of health care. What could explain this?
   - [ ] A Life expectancy is lower in this country
   - [ ] B Patients are treated more efficiently in this country
   - [ ] C This country has fewer doctors per 100,000 people
   - [ ] D This country is more prone to infectious diseases
8. What would indicate a country is experiencing economic development?
   - [ ] A A fall in its death rate
   - [ ] B A fall in its savings rate

Developed and Developing Countries

- [ ] C A rise in its economic inactivity rate
- [ ] D A rise in its malnutrition rate

9. As an economy develops, what usually happens to the population of workers employed in the primary and tertiary sectors?

	Primary	Tertiary
A	decrease	decrease
B	decrease	increase
C	increase	increase
D	increase	decrease

10. Which of the following may be a barrier to economic growth?
- [ ] A A reluctance to lower the school leaving age
- [ ] B A resistance to change
- [ ] C A high level of investment
- [ ] D A high level of productivity

11. What does the 45 degree line on a Lorenz curve show?
- [ ] A A perfectly even distribution of income
- [ ] B A distribution of income that a government is aiming to achieve
- [ ] C The extent to which income is unevenly distributed
- [ ] D The income earned by 50% of the population

12. A country has a lower real GDP per head than another country but also a smaller percentage of people living in absolute poverty. What could explain this?
- [ ] A The country has a lower rate of inflation
- [ ] B The country has a lower population
- [ ] C The country has a more even distribution of income
- [ ] D The country has more people employed in the primary sector

13. What tends to happen to a country's birth rate and death rate as it develops?

	Birth rate	Death rate
A	decrease	decrease
B	decrease	increase
C	increase	increase
D	increase	decrease

14. Which of the following may increase the birth rate in a country?
- [ ] A Improved health care
- [ ] B A rise in the school leaving age
- [ ] C Reduced job opportunities for women
- [ ] D The introduction of a generous state pension scheme

15. Which activity by a US multinational company with a branch in the Philippines may increase the economic development of the Philippines?
    - A The payment of wages at a lower rate than in the USA but at a higher rate than in the Philippines
    - B The pressure on the government of the Philippines to cut its spending on health care
    - C The purchase of imported raw materials from the US
    - D The transfer of profits back to the US

16. Which form of foreign aid is most likely to be successful in promoting economic development?
    - A Tied, bilateral aid
    - B Tied, multilateral aid
    - C Untied, bilateral aid
    - D Untied, multilateral aid

17. What is meant by a country's population growth?
    - A The difference between a country's birth rate and death rate plus immigration
    - B The difference between a country's birth rate and death rate plus net migration
    - C The increase in a country's population in a year expressed as a percentage of the working population at the beginning of the year
    - D The increase in a country's population expressed as a percentage of world population at the beginning of the year

18. What could lead to a virtuous circle?
    - A Low savings
    - B Low tax revenue
    - C High imports
    - D High productivity

19. A country has a low real GDP per head. What must this mean?
    - A Everyone in the country is poor
    - B Government spending on welfare benefits is high
    - C On average income levels are low
    - D There are no millionaires living in the country

20. What would increase the ratio of males to females in a country?
    - A A fall in the death rate of males
    - B A reduction in the infanticide of female babies
    - C A rise in the emigration of males
    - D A rise in the immigration of females

Similarities

Identify one way in which each pair is similar. You may have to spend a little longer on some of these, for instance 4, 7 and 8, than on others.

1. Real GDP per head and the Human Development Index.
2. Birth rate and death rate.
3. A low level of savings and poor infrastructure.
4. A national minimum wage and generous state benefits.
5. Emigration and immigration.
6. Deciles and quintiles.
7. Rise in birth rate and fall in death rate.
8. Rise in the dependency ratio and increase in the cost of state pensions.
9. International debt and reliance on primary products.
10. Unemployment and old age.

Differences

Identify **one** way in which each pair differs. You may find this relatively easier than the previous task.

1. Economic growth and economic development.
2. Developed and developing countries.
3. Natural change in population and migration.
4. Emigration and immigration.
5. Positive checks and preventive checks.
6. Import substitution and export promotion.
7. Vicious circle and virtuous circle.
8. Distribution of income and distribution of wealth.
9. Over-populated and underpopulated.
10. Growing population and ageing population.

Data exercises

1. Are rich countries really helping poor countries?

The US Centre for Global Development publishes an index which ranks countries according to how much help they provide to developing countries. The criteria on which the index is based are the size and quality of overseas aid, openness to poor countries' exports, policy regimes that promote good investment in and technology

transfer to the developing world, openness to immigration, controlling greenhouse gas emissions and combating corruption.

In 2007 the Netherlands topped the rankings followed by Denmark and Sweden. The USA was only placed 14th largely because of poor environmental performance. Climate change can lead to flooding and can reduce the agricultural output of developing countries. The UK ranked well on investment but its position was lowered to 9th because of its poor record on admitting migrants from the developing world and its arms exports.

In 2007 the Centre examined, for the first time, the environmental performance, and economic impact of the emerging economies of Brazil, China, India and Russia. China in that year, for instance, was the world's top consumer of iron ore, aluminium, copper, nickel and zinc and the second largest consumer of oil.

   a. What is meant by the 'quality of overseas aid'? [2]
   b. Analyse how investment can promote development. [5]
   c. Explain **two** ways in which developed countries can hinder the development of developing economies. [6]
   d. Discuss whether the growth of the Chinese economy will promote economic growth in other economies. [7]
   e. Explain what is meant by 'openness to poor countries exports'. [4]
   f. Discuss whether allowing more immigration would increase unemployment in a developed country. [6]

2. India's future

India is making economic progress. One sign of this is India joining the space race. In October 2008, it launched an unmanned space rocket to the moon. Indian MNCs are investing throughout the world, and more and more high tech business parks are being set up in the country.

India, nevertheless, faces a number of problems. More than 450 million Indians live below the poverty line. Its population growth presents a challenge. It is predicted that it will become the world's most populous nation by 2050 at around 1.6 billion. The country's literacy rate is also a concern. For men it is 70.2% and for women it is 48.3%.

The Indian government is launching a number of campaigns to raise literacy. In March 2008 it started a campaign focused particularly on raising female literacy. It is offering cash incentives to poor families to send their daughters to school.

   a. What is meant by a 'poverty line'? [2]
   b. Why may the growth in India's population be lower than predicted? [4]

c. Explain **one** measure by which a government could increase literacy rates. [5]
d. Discuss the benefits of educating girls. [9]
e. Explain what is meant by 'economic progress'. [4]
f. Discuss whether a space programme will promote 'economic progress'. [6]

3. Income distribution in Brazil

Income is very unevenly distributed in Brazil. In 2007 the country recorded the fourth most uneven distribution in the world, coming behind Sierra Leone, Central African Republic and Swaziland. The poorest 20% of the population had 2.2% of total income whilst the richest 20% enjoyed a 64.1% share of the country's income.

It has been estimated that 35m Brazilians live in poverty, lacking the resources to meet basic human needs, including minimum nutrition needs and adequate medical treatment. In 2007 the official poverty line was set at 120 reais a month per person.

Reducing income inequality is the Brazilian government's top priority. The government is using a variety of methods including the Bolsa Familia. This is a conditional benefit of up to 95 reais a month that requires parents to keep their children in school and take them to clinics for health check-ups and have them vaccinated against common diseases. It is designed to break the cycle of poverty by ensuring that children are healthier and better educated than their parents. In addition, the government is providing agricultural training, financial incentives, water cisterns and, in some cases, houses for people living in rural areas. It is hoped that these measures may also help to reduce some of the problems caused by the rural to urban migration in the country.

The government has had some success in reducing income inequality. Between 2002 and 2006 the share of the country's income going to the poorer half of society increased from 9.5% to 11.9% and the share going to the richest tenth fell from 49.5% to 47.1%.

a. What was the share of Brazil's total income received by the richest 50% in 2006? [1]
b. What type of poverty is being discussed in the second paragraph? Explain your answer. [3]
c. What is meant by the 'cycle of poverty'? [2]
d. Explain **two** possible problems of rural to urban migration. [6]
e. Discuss whether the Brazilian government should spend more on education. [8]
f. Explain how improved health care can increase people's income. [4]

g. Discuss whether a government should try to reduce income inequality. [6]

 Structured questions

1. a. What is meant by economic development? [3]
   b. How do developing economies differ from developed economies? [6]
   c. Why are all economies seeking to become more developed? [4]
   d. Discuss whether rapid economic growth always results in more economic development. [7]
2. The US has a high real GDP per head but also an uneven distribution of income. Rwanda has a significantly lower real GDP per head but a much more even distribution of income.
   a. What is meant by an 'uneven distribution of income'? [2]
   b. How are the levels of absolute and relative poverty likely to compare in these two countries? [4]
   c. Explain **three** causes of poverty. [6]
   d. Discuss how a government can influence the distribution of income. [8]
3. a. What can cause an increase in the size of a country's population? [6]
   b. Explain three ways a government could influence the size of population. [6]
   c. Discuss **whether** an increase in the size of population will be beneficial for an economy. [8]
4. Between 2000 and 2008 absolute poverty fell in the United Kingdom. There were concerns, however, that the approaching recession would widen income inequality. Such concern did not stop the UK experiencing net immigration of workers.
   a. Identify **three** possible economic reasons why, despite fears about an approaching recession, the UK experienced net immigration in 2008. [3]
   b. Explain **two** advantages the UK could gain from the net immigration of workers. [4]
   c. Explain **three** reasons why a government would want to see a reduction in absolute poverty. [6]
   d. Discuss why a recession may increase absolute poverty and income inequality. [7]

 Homework assignments

1. The importance of remittances

More people are choosing to work abroad to take advantage of higher pay. It is becoming increasingly easy for them to send money back home to their relatives.

These changes are making remittances more important in a number of economies. Indeed, in many developing economies, more money is now coming from remittances than from foreign aid, foreign investment or even traditional exports. In 2006 migrants from developing countries sent back US $ 206.3bn which was almost seven times the figure for 1990.

Remittances are particularly important for the Philippines. In 2006 they accounted for 14.6% of the country's GDP. Filipinos work as domestic helpers, sailors, labourers, factory workers and nurses throughout the world.

Losing workers to other countries has both advantages and disadvantages. It can result in skill shortages and training can be wasted. For example, Jamaica has to train five and Grenada twenty two doctors to keep just one. The remittances can also push up the exchange rate which makes the country's exports more expensive.

On the other hand, they can reduce poverty. For instance, some of the money sent back may be used to educate the children of those who are working abroad. Remittances are also more reliable than foreign direct investment, fluctuating to a much lesser extent.

   a. Identify **three** sources of foreign currency available to the Philippines referred to in the passage. [3]
   b. Explain **two** reasons why someone from the Philippines may go abroad to work. [4]
   c. What evidence is there in the passage that training is a merit good? [2]
   d. Explain **two** factors that would attract foreign direct investment to a country. [4]
   e. Discuss whether the emigration of workers from developing countries promotes the development of those countries. [7]

2. Japan's falling population

In 2008 Japan had a population of 127m but its population was ageing and declining at such a rate that some economists were predicting that there would be only one Japanese person by 3000!

In 1947 5% of the country's population was aged over 65, by 2008 this had risen to 20% and it is predicted to increase by 25% by 2015. At the moment, there are four Japanese workers for every retired person. This will be two to one by 2030 and three to two by 2050.

The Japanese government is seeking to offset the effects of an ageing population by encouraging more mothers to enter the labour force.

The Japanese population is ageing because of a fall in the death rate and birth rate. In 1947 Japanese life expectancy was 50. This had increased to 82 by 2008. The birth rate fell below the replacement rate of 2.1 in the early 1970s and was as low as 1.26 in 2008.

Rural areas are being particularly affected by the changes in the birth and death rates as they are being combined with rural to urban migration.

a. Explain two effects of an ageing population. [4]
b. Identify two causes of a decline in population. [2]
c. What is meant by a 'replacement rate'? [2]
d. What may be happening to Japan's dependency ratio? [3]
e. Discuss the effects of a declining population. [9]

3. Water – the development issue of the twenty-first century

One of the United Nations' Millennium Development Goals (MDG) is 'to halve by 2015 the proportion of people without access to safe drinking water and basic sanitation. It has been estimated that out of a world population of approximately 6.5 billion about 1.1 billion people have no access to safe water and 2.5 billion are without basic sanitation.'

The basic water requirement per person per day is 50 litres although, for a short time, it is possible to get by on 30 litres. Whilst the average US citizen uses 500 litres per day and UK citizens 200 litres a day, in a number of countries people have to try to survive on less than 10 litres each. For example, in Mozambique it is 9.3 litres, Somalia 8.9 litres, Mali 8 litres and Gambia it is as low as 4.5 litres per person.

Water is used not just for drinking, washing and disposing human waste but also by industry and agriculture. Indeed, it takes 1,400 litres to produce a kilo of maize and a staggering 42,500 litres to produce a kilo of beef.

Whilst two-thirds of the earth is made up of water, 97.5% of this is salt water. The remaining 2.5% of the useable freshwater is available in lakes, rivers, ground water and rainfall runoff. The increasing shortage of this water is resulting in deaths and diseases. For instance, it has been estimated that diarroheal diseases results in 443 million school days being lost a year. One child dies from dehydration caused by diarrhoea every 14 seconds and half of the world's hospital beds are taken up with people with water borne diseases. It is also resulting in international disputes. There are conflicts between Botswana, Namibia and Angola over the water in the Okavango Basin and between Egypt, Sudan and Ethiopia over the water in the Nile.

It has been estimated that the money needed to meet the MDG on water and sanitation is US $ 15bn. This is a small proportion of the US $ 100bn that is spent in the west on bottled water.

Aid to improve access to safe water and sanitation has actually declined in recent years and, in addition, a higher proportion is now given in loans rather than grants which is pushing indebted countries further in debt.

a. What proportion of the world's population is without basic sanitation? [2]
b. Is water evenly distributed? Explain your answer. [2]
c. What is likely to happen to demand for water in the future? [3]
d. Explain how lack of water hinders development. [6]
e. Discuss the costs and benefits to developed countries of them providing grants to developing countries to improve the supply of their water. [7]

Section 8: International Aspects

 Definitions

Some of the definitions here are relatively long. Match each with the appropriate term, ensuring that all twenty fit.

1. Invisible balance
2. Portfolio investment
3. International trade
4. Trade restrictions
5. Absolute advantage
6. Comparative advantage
7. The terms of trade
8. The exchange rate
9. A floating exchange rate
10. Depreciation
11. Devaluation
12. Appreciation
13. Expenditure switching methods

a. The ratio of the average price of a country's exports to the average price of its imports
b. The ability of a country's firms to sell their products abroad
c. Speculative flows of money around the world taking advantage of changes in interest rates and exchange rates
d. A rise in the value of one currency relative to another due to market forces
e. A fall in the free market value of a currency in terms of other currencies
f. An action by the government or central bank to reduce the value of a currency under a system of fixed exchange rates
g. An exchange rate that is determined by market forces
h. International trade conducted without any government interference
i. Policies designed to improve a country's trade position by encouraging spending on domestic products and discouraging spending on foreign products
j. The purchase of shares and government securities
k. A newly established industry
l. Measures designed to protect domestic industries from foreign competition
m. Bans on the trade in particular products or with particular countries

14. Hot money flows
15. International competitiveness
16. Free trade
17. Protectionism
18. Quotas
19. Embargoes
20. Infant industry

n. Limits on the quantity of a product that can be traded
o. When a country or region can produce a product at a lower opportunity cost than other countries
p. When a country or region can produce a product with fewer resources than other countries
q. Trade in services
r. The exchange of products between individuals and firms in different countries
s. Restrictions on the exchange of products across national borders
t. The price of one currency in terms of another

Missing words

There are a number of sentences here which have only one word missing. Nevertheless, each sentence requires careful thought.

1. The four parts of the _____ account of the balance of payments are trade in _____, trade in _____, income and current transfers.
2. If a German firm buys a Namibian factory this will appear as a _____ item in the _____ account of Namibia's balance of payments.
3. International trade enables firms to take greater advantage of economies of _____ but changes in _____ rates may affect the revenue they receive from selling their products.
4. A country's firms are likely to export more if the country's inflation rate _____ and the productivity of workers _____ .
5. A current account deficit on the balance of payments may be mainly a cyclical or a structural deficit. A _____ deficit is more serious.
6. A possible benefit of an increasing current account deficit on the balance of payments is a fall in the _____ rate.
7. Higher world output but increased interdependency arises from countries _____ .
8. Two countries can both benefit from engaging in _____ trade even if one country has an _____ advantage in producing both products provided there is a difference in countries' _____ advantage.
9. A rise in a country's inflation rate may improve its _____ of _____ but lead to a deterioration in its trade in _____ and services.

10. A rise in a country's _____ rate will increase _____ prices but reduce _____ prices.
11. A government or central bank may raise the value of its currency by increasing the country's _____ _____ or buying its _____.
12. The value of a floating exchange rate may rise if speculators believe the price of the currency will _____ in the near future and if there is net foreign _____ investment.
13. Hot money flows will be attracted into a country by a rise in the _____ _____ or an expectation that the exchange rate will _____.
14. An increase in income tax may decrease a current account _____ by reducing consumer spending on _____.
15. A _____ economic growth rate and a _____ share of world trade may indicate a country's international competitiveness is declining.
16. A government may discourage imports by imposing _____ on a range of products. These are taxes on imports and are designed to make imports more expensive relative to _____ produced products.
17. Protectionism would be reduced by removing exchange _____ and reducing the _____ standards that imports have to meet.
18. The key argument for protecting sunset industries is to prevent an increase in _____. Over time, however, workers who retire or leave to take up employment in other industries will not be _____.
19. A country's workers may receive low wages but its products will not be internationally _____ if its workers have _____ productivity.
20. The removal of trade restrictions may benefit consumers by increasing _____ and lowering _____.

Calculations

1. Table shows the output of wheat and tractors in two fictional countries.

   Table 1. Output of wheat and tractors

	Output per worker per day	
	Wheat (tonnes)	Tractors
Erewhon	25	5
Utopia	75	10

   a. Which country has the absolute advantage in producing wheat?
   b. What is the opportunity cost of producing tractors in both countries?
   c. Which country has the comparative advantage in producing tractors?

2. The Kenyan exchange rate changes from 70 Kenyan shillings (KSh) equals 1 US $ to 100 KSh equals 1 US $. What will be the resulting change in the US price of a 210KSh Kenyan export and the Kenyan price of a US $ 20 US import?
3. A country exports 2,000 goods at an average price of US $ 5. It imports 3,000 goods at an average price of US $ 4. What is its terms of trade?

Interpreting diagrams

In analysing the causes and consequences of exchange rate changes, it is very helpful to use demand and supply diagrams.

a. Identify **two** possible causes of the change in the value of the pound sterling shown.
b. What effect is the change shown likely to have on the UK's trade in goods and services balance?

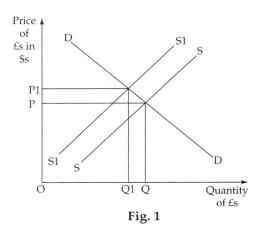

Fig. 1

Drawing diagrams

Use an exchange rate diagram in each case to llustrate the effect on the value of the Pakistani rupee of:

a. A rise in the value of Pakistani exports
b. Speculation that the value of the Pakistani rupee will fall
c. Pakistani firms buying out firms in India

Multiple-choice questions

1. Which change would increase international trade?
   - A An increase in the difference in production costs between countries
   - B An increase in the difference in health and safety regulations between countries
   - C A rise in tariffs
   - D A rise in transport costs
2. Which of the following is an item of invisible trade?
   - A Books
   - B Paper
   - C Printing presses
   - D Royalty payments

3. What would increase the debits on a country's balance of trade in goods and services?
- [ ] A Domestic firms buy more imported raw materials
- [ ] B Domestic insurance companies sell more policies to foreign residents
- [ ] C A foreign firm investing in the country
- [ ] D The government receiving a loan from a foreign bank

4. Which section appears in the current account of the balance of payments?
- [ ] A Capital
- [ ] B Financial
- [ ] C Income
- [ ] D Net errors and omissions

5. Which change may reduce a country's current account deficit?
- [ ] A An increase in the country's rate of inflation
- [ ] B An increase in the quality of imports
- [ ] C A rise in incomes abroad
- [ ] D A rise in the exchange rate

6. To increase world output, on what cost should countries base their specialisation on?
- [ ] A Average
- [ ] B Fixed
- [ ] C Opportunity
- [ ] D Variable

7. A country has a comparative advantage in producing paper. What must this mean?
- [ ] A The country produces more paper than any other country
- [ ] B The country produces more paper than any other product
- [ ] C The opportunity cost of producing paper in the country is lower than in other countries
- [ ] D The resources used to produce it are not available in other countries

8. Two countries are considering trading cars and TV programmes. The output per worker of these products in the two countries is shown in the table.

	Output per worker per month	
	Cars	TV programmes
Country X	20	60
Country Y	40	120

What can be concluded from this information?

- [ ] A Trade will benefit Country X only
- [ ] B Trade will benefit Country Y only
- [ ] C Trade will benefit both countries
- [ ] D Trade will not benefit either country

9. A country has a comparative advantage in producing sugar. Its government decides, however, to discourage its producers from specialising in sugar production. What could explain this decision?

- [ ] A The country lacks an absolute advantage in sugar production
- [ ] B There is an absence of foreign tariffs on sugar production
- [ ] C The government wants a diversified industrial structure
- [ ] D The government believes the productivity of workers in the domestic sugar production industry is increasing

10. A fall in the exchange rate reduces a current account deficit. What could explain this?

- [ ] A Export prices falling by less than export volume rises
- [ ] B Export prices rising by more than export volume falls
- [ ] C Import prices rising and import volume remaining unchanged
- [ ] D Import prices rising by more than import volume falls

11. What determines the value of a fixed exchange rate but not of a freely floating exchange rate?

- [ ] A Export revenue and import expenditure
- [ ] B Foreign direct investment
- [ ] C Government intervention in the foreign exchange market
- [ ] D Speculation

12. Which change would cause the value of the US dollar to rise?

- [ ] A US interest rates rising
- [ ] B US firms buying firms in foreign countries
- [ ] C US tourists spending more abroad
- [ ] D US inflation rate rising more rapidly than other countries' inflation rates

13. The UK pound falls in value against the US dollar from £1:US $ 2 to £1:US $ 1.8. What will be the effect of this change?

- [ ] A Dollars will become more expensive in terms of pounds
- [ ] B Fewer pounds will be exchanged for a given number of dollars
- [ ] C UK imports from the US will become cheaper
- [ ] D US imports from the UK will become more expensive

14. What does a deterioration in the terms of trade mean?

- [ ] A The country's exchange rate has risen in value

- B The country has a deficit in its trade in goods
- C The price of imports has risen relative to the value of the price of exports
- D The value of imports has risen relative to the value of exports

15. A country's terms of trade change from 90 to 120. What may have caused this improvement?
- A A fall in the country's exchange rate
- B A fall in the country's costs of production
- C A rise in the country's inflation rate
- D A rise in the quality of the country's imports

16. A government wants to protect domestic agriculture and to raise revenue. Which form of protection is it most likely to use?
- A Embargo
- B Quality standards
- C Subsidies to local producers
- D Tariffs

17. Which change would increase the level of protection to domestic industries?
- A A reduction in income tax
- B A reduction in quota levels
- C A reduction in subsidies to domestic producers
- D A reduction in tariffs

18. The Vietnamese government decides to increase tariffs on imported buses. Which two groups in Vietnam may benefit from this decision?
- A Bus travel companies and bus passengers
- B Bus producing companies and bus travel companies
- C Bus passengers and the government
- D The government and bus producing companies

19. What is a valid argument for protectionism?
- A To correct a long standing current account deficit
- B To increase the choice available for consumers
- C To prevent dumping driving out domestic producers
- D To protect employment overseas

20. Which item would be included in the current account position of South Africa's balance of payments?
- A The granting of a loan to a South African firm from an Italian bank
- B The payment of dividends to foreigners owning shares in South African countries
- C The purchase of a hotel in Madagascar by a South African citizen

☐ D The sale of a wildlife park in South Africa to a US company

Similarities

When you are considering a similarity between the two terms in each pair, remember you are doing this in an international context.
1. Exports and imports.
2. Invisible balance and trade in services.
3. Trade in goods and trade in services.
4. Inflation rate and exchange rate.
5. Revaluation and appreciation of the exchange rate.
6. Expenditure reducing and expenditure switching measures.
7. Speculation and foreign direct investment.
8. Voluntary export restrictions and quality standards.
9. Strategic industries and infant industries.
10. Less choice and retaliation.

Differences

Remember, what you are looking for here is differences in the meaning of the two terms in each pair.
1. Current account of the balance of payments and the financial account of the balance of payments.
2. Trade in goods surplus and trade in goods deficit.
3. Internal trade and international trade.
4. A cyclical current account deficit and a structural current account deficit.
5. Devaluation and depreciation of the exchange rate.
6. A fixed exchange rate and a floating exchange rate.
7. Free trade and protection.
8. Sunrise industries and sunset industries.
9. Hot money flows and foreign direct investment.
10. Credit items and debit items.

Data exercises

1. The rise of the rupee

The Indian rupee rose in value from 46.5 rupees to US $ 1 in January 2006 to 40 rupees to US $ 1 in December 2007. The rise had been the result of increased foreign direct investment in India (see the table given) and less confidence in the dollar. It had an adverse effect on India's exports, particularly exports of textiles which declined by 12% over this period and led some to expected job losses in the textile industry.

Table 2. Net capital flows to India

Year	US $ bn
2001	9
2002	8
2003	11
2004	20
2005	31
2006	22
2007	45

The Reserve Bank of India (RBI) did sell rupees in a bid to reduce the upward pressure on the currency but it was reluctant to push the value of the rupee down for fear of the effect it would have on inflation. Nevertheless, some Indian entrepreneurs have argued that the RBI should keep its currency low in order to promote export-led growth.

a. What was the percentage increase in net capital flows to India from 2001 to 2007? [2]
b. Explain how 'less confidence in the dollar' could raise the value of the Indian rupee. [5]
c. Using a demand and supply diagram, analyse how the sale of its currency by a central bank would influence the exchange rate. [6]
d. Discuss whether the Indian economy would benefit from a fall in the value of the rupee. [7]
e. Apart from the sale of its currency, explain one other way a central bank could influence the value of its currency. [4]
f. Discuss whether a decrease in exports will always cause unemployement. [6]

2. Differing UK and US trade performance

In September 2007 the UK had a record trade in goods deficit of £7.8bn compared with £6.9bn the previous month. Whilst imports, including imports of cars, rose in September 2007, exports to both the US and EU fell.

The overall goods trade gap was partly offset by a £2.7bn surplus on services, unchanged from the previous month. The growing deficit slowed down UK economic growth.

In contrast to the UK's trade performance, the US trade deficit fell to its lowest level of US $ 56.5bn in twenty eight months. This was largely the result of a rise in exports, including cars, computers and farm products, to a record level of US $ 140bn.

One of the causes of the difference in the trade performance of the two countries was the different movements in the value of the pound sterling and in the value of the US dollar. Whilst the pound rose in value, the value of the US dollar fell.

   a. Calculate the value of US imports in September 2007. [3]
   b. What is meant by a trade in goods deficit? [2]
   c. Explain how a widening trade deficit can slow down economic growth. [5]
   d. Apart from a change in the exchange rate, explain one other reason why the US may have exported more cars. [3]
   e. Discuss whether a fall in the exchange rate will always improve the trade in goods position. [7]
   f. Explain what factors influence the products a country exports. [4]
   g. Discuss whether a rise in imports is always a disadvantage for a country. [7]

3. China threatens to take action against US tariffs

In September 2007 the Chinese government threatened to report the US government to the World Trade Organisation (WTO) for imposing tariffs on its exports of paper.

The US government claimed its trade restriction was justified as favourable tax treatment and low cost loans from the Chinese government were making China's exports of paper artificially cheap. The US government also claimed that China was dumping, selling paper at a lower price in the US than at home.

The Chinese government argued that the help it was giving to paper producers was not excessive and that the US government had failed to show the extent to which it helped its exporters. It also threatened to impose import duties on US products in retaliation.

International Aspects

a. Identify two motives for imposing tariffs. [2]
b. What is meant by exports being 'artificially cheap'? [3]
c. Explain one advantage and one disadvantage to US consumers of Chinese firms dumping exports of paper. [4]
d. Explain one argument for the Chinese government giving help to its paper producers. [4]
e. The US government decides to impose tariffs on Chinese paper. You are a member of the Chinese government. Discuss whether you would recommend that the Chinese government should retaliate by imposing trade restrictions on US products. [7]
f. Explain whether if a country's firm's produce a product at a lower cost than firms in rival countries, they will always have higher sales. [4]
g. China has a current account surplus. Discuss whether a government should aim for a current account surplus. [6]

Structured questions

1. a. Explain three of the components of the current account of the balance of payments. [6]
   b. What are the consequences of a current account deficit? [6]
   c. In 2008 the US had a current account deficit whilst China had a current account surplus. Discuss what factors could explain the difference in the countries' current account positions. [8]

2. a. What are the benefits of free international trade? [6]
   b. Explain three arguments for protectionism. [6]
   c. Discuss the effectiveness of two other government policy measures, apart from protectionism, that could be used to correct a current account deficit. [8]

3. a. What are the benefits of a floating exchange rate? [4]
   b. Explain the factors that could cause a rise in a country's exchange rate. [7]
   c. Discuss the effects a rise in a country's exchange rate may have on a government's macroeconomic objectives. [9]

4. In 2008 Pakistan's economy was facing both an increasing current account deficit and a growing budget deficit. The value of the Pakistani rupee fell by more than 25%.
   a. Distinguish between a current account deficit and a budget deficit. [4]
   b. Explain the effect that a fall in the value of its currency is likely to have on a country's inflation rate. [6]
   c. Discuss what information you would need to assess the performance of Pakistan's economy in 2008. [10]

Homework assignments

1. Indian spice exports

India accounts for almost 50% of the global spice exports, even though only a small proportion, approximately 8%, of its annual production is traded internationally.

In March 2008 Indian spice exports hit record levels, particularly of chilli and pepper. Failed harvests in key growing countries, including China, growing demand in the West and improved quality controls in the country, helped to push up demand for India's spices.

Another factor affecting the sales of chilli was concerns about the levels of pesticide that might be contained in Chinese and Pakistani crops. Indeed, the European Union decided to ban imports from Pakistan because of quality concerns.

Whilst chilli exports increased by about a third, exports of pepper rose by a fifth. The harvest in Vietnam, the world's largest producer of pepper, had been hit by bad weather.

As a result of the rising demand for spices, Indian farmers were planning to devote more resources to growing crops not only of pepper and chilli but also garlic, ginger, turmeric and mint. They were concerned, however, about the volatility of global prices and the unpredictability of the weather.

    a. Identify from the passage four reasons why demand for Indian chilli increased. [2]

    b. Does India have the capacity to increase its exports of spices? Explain your answer. [3]

    c. Explain the impact that an increase in the sales of spices would have on India's balance of payments. [3]

    d. Using a demand and supply diagram, analyse the impact on the market for Indian pepper of a good harvest in Vietnam. [5]

    e. Discuss whether Indian farmers should devote more resources to growing spices. [7]

2. Mercosur

Mercosur is South America's largest trade bloc. A trade bloc is a group of countries which integrate their trade to differing degrees. The lowest level of integration is a free trade area. In this case, the member countries agree not to place any trade restrictions on each others' products. The most integrated form is an economic and monetary union. In this case, the member countries do not impose any restrictions on the movement of products, capital and workers between member countries and the governments follow the same fiscal and monetary policies and operate one currency.

Mercosur comes in between these two types of trade blocs. It has been described as an 'imperfect' customs union. A customs union is one in which member countries not only agree to remove any trade restrictions between each other but also agree to impose a common external tariff on non-members. The four founding members were Argentina, Brazil, Paraguay and Uruguay. Chile and Bolivia became associate members in the 1990s, entering into free trade agreements with Mercosur but not accepting its common external tariff. In 2006 Venezuela became a full member pending ratification from the other members.

Mercosur has been called an 'imperfect' customs union as there are more than 800 exceptions to the common external tariff and member countries have imposed tariffs on each others' products.

    a. What is the difference between a free trade area and a customs union? [3]
    b. Explain what will influence whether the economy of Venezuela will benefit from membership of Mercosur. [5]
    c. In what circumstances may it be disadvantageous for a government to follow the same fiscal and monetary policies in other countries? [5]
    d. Discuss how the existence of customs unions, such as Mercosur, affect non-members. [7]

3. International competitiveness

International competitiveness can be defined as the ability of a country's firms to compete successfully in international markets and so allow the country to continue to grow. Sometimes economists interpret international competitiveness narrowly in terms of price competitiveness. However, it is more usually taken to also include competitiveness in terms of quality and marketing as well.

There is a wide range of factors that influence an economy's international competitiveness. These include transport infrastructure, productivity, education and training and innovation.

Cuba in 2008 was seeking to make its tourist industry more internationally competitive. Its US $ 2bn a year tourism industry is a crucial earner of foreign exchange. Tourist numbers fell both in 2006 and 2007 largely due to high prices and poor facilities. The main visitors to the country are Canadians and Britons but not many return for a second visit. To boost tourist numbers and to encourage them to come back again, the Cuban government was considering a number of measures including building up to ten golf courses across the country, including several in the capital.

Becoming more internationally competitive is not all beneficial. For example, if the firms in an economy become more competitive, this is likely to push up the exchange rate.

   a. What is meant by 'price competitiveness'? [2]

   b. Explain how

      (i) international competitiveness and economic growth are linked. [5]

      (ii) productivity and international competitiveness are linked. [3]

      (iii) international competitiveness and the exchange rate are linked. [3]

   c. You are the tourist minister in your country. Discuss how you would seek to make your country's tourist industry more internationally competitive. [7]

Answer Key

SECTION-1

Definitions

1. i　　2. d　　3. g　　4. a　　5. h
6. c　　7. b　　8. j　　9. e　　10. f

Missing words

1. scarcity, wants
2. choices
3. occupationally, immobile
4. net
5. wage, profit
6. raising, lowering
7. production, productivity
8. uninsurable or uncertain
9. opportunity
10. two, technology

Calculations

1. The firms' total wage cost is 26 x US $ 75 = US $ 1,950.
2. Net investment is gross investment minus depreciation. In this case this is US $ 900m – US $ 620m = US $ 280m.

Interpreting diagrams

a. 10m capital goods.
b. 110m consumer goods.

Drawing diagrams

An increase in the quantity of resources will mean that more can be produced and so the PPC will shift to the right as shown in Figure 1.

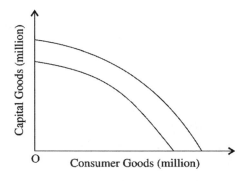

Fig. 1

Multiple-choice questions

1. A

    Scarcity arises because wants are unlimited whereas resources are finite. A reduction in resources would widen the gap between the two. In contrast, B, C and D have the potential to reduce but not eliminate the problem of scarcity.

2. C

    Investment in human capital involves the improvement in the quality of labour that arises as a result of the experience workers gain and the education and training they receive. A would increase the supply of the labour force, B may raise labour productivity and D is investment in capital goods.

3. C

    A tractor is a capital good. It is a factor of production as it is used to produce a product which in this case is food. A is the product. B is a non-monetary advantage the farmer gains and D is a payment to a factor of production.

4. B

    An economic good takes resources to produce it. Air from an air conditioning system has been processed. In contrast, A, C and D are free goods – they exist without any resources being needed to make them.

5. D

    Land is a natural resource. Water is an example of a natural resource. A and B are capital goods and C is labour.

6. D

    The next best use of the bus may be transporting a group of retired people on a day out. A is a change in revenue and B and C are financial costs.

7. B

    Labour is human effort used in producing products. A is defining only part of labour as it does not cover mental effort or physical and mental effort used in other sectors. C is a definition of land and D is a definition of enterprise.

8. A

    A production possibility curve shows the different combinations of two products that can be produced with existing resources and technology. A production point would indicate the combination the country is producing. This may reflect what people want to be produced. A PPC does not provide any information about prices or profitability.

9. D

    A PPC illustrates opportunity cost as it shows how much of one product has to be given up to gain some more units of the other product. It shows scarcity as it indicates that because resources are limited, there is a restriction on the amount that can be produced.

10. A

A point outside a PPC is currently unattainable as there are not enough resources, and technology is unchanged. B and D would be shown by a point inside the curve and C by a point on the curve.

Similarities

1. Both are examples of labour, one is involved in physical work and one in mental work.
2. Both are human resources.
3. Both are examples of land.
4. Both are free goods.
5. They are two different names for the same thing.

Differences

1. Capital goods are used to produce other goods and services whereas consumer goods are used by people for their own satisfaction.
2. Economic goods take resources to produce them and so involve an opportunity cost. In contrast, free goods do not take resources to produce them and so have no opportunity cost.
3. Capital is a human made resource whereas land is a natural resource.
4. Geographical immobility occurs when resources find it difficult to change their location whereas occupational immobility occurs when resources encounter difficulties changing their use.
5. Opportunity cost is cost in terms of the best alternative forgone whereas financial cost is cost in terms of money.

Data exercise

a. Three factors of production used in the making of cars are capital, enterprise and labour. Robotic machinery is used to produce cars and this is an example of capital. Enterprise is provided by the managers and the shareholders of Tata. Car designers are one of the forms of labour employed in car production.

b. The passage mentions that 100,000 rupees can buy a new Nano or a second hand 1993 Land Rover. So if someone buys a new Nano, the opportunity cost may be the second hand Land Rover.

c. The economic problem is that wants exceed resources. The passage mentions that many millions of people would like to buy a car but cannot afford one.

d.

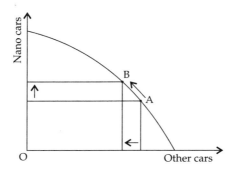

Structured questions

1. a. The basic economic problem is that whilst wants are unlimited, resources are not. This results in wants being greater than resources.
    b. An increase in the supply of labour in a country means that there are more people available for work. One reason for this may be immigration of people of working age. Another reason may be more women deciding to enter the labour force, perhaps because social attitudes to women working may have changed. A third possible reason is that the retirement age has been raised. This would mean that people would stay in the labour force for longer.
    c. (i) A worker in deciding whether to accept a new job would have to consider carefully the opportunity cost. This is what he or she is giving up in terms of his or her current job. This may include, for example, having a shorter distance to travel to work and good promotion chances.
       (ii) A family will consider where else it can go on holiday and what else it could do with the time and money. For instance, the opportunity cost of a family holiday abroad may be a holiday in the domestic economy or to purchase a second hand car. The family will weigh up the benefits of the choices, particularly its first and second choices.
       (iii) An entrepreneur will compare the expected revenue, costs and profitability of a number of products that could be launched. If a firm's resources are used to produce one product, they cannot be used to make something else. If during the period of consideration, the prospects of the proposed new product decline, the opportunity cost may become too high. In this case, the entrepreneur is likely to switch to the best alternative.
       (iv) The production of economic goods involves the use of resources. This means that that they involve an opportunity cost. For instance, the factors of production that are employed in the production of TV programmes cannot be used to educate university students.

2. a. An economic resource is a factor of production used to produce goods and services. The four economic resources are land, labour, capital and enterprise.

   b. The mobility of economic resources comes in two forms. One is occupational mobility. This refers to economic resources' ability to change their use. For instance, a farm worker may leave his job and become a factory worker and an office building's use may switch from providing insurance to producing TV programmes. If demand for housing is increasing, an area of land that had been used for farming might be built on. An entrepreneur who had been running a car company may take up a new position running an IT company.

   The second type of mobility is geographical mobility. This refers to the ability of economic resources to change their geographical location. Most land is geographically immobile. Some types of capital goods can be moved from one part of the country to another, or indeed from one country to another country. For instance, delivery vans and fax machines can be moved from one area to another. In contrast, office buildings and airports are geographically immobile. The extent to which labour is geographically mobile depends on a number of factors including the cost and availability of housing in different parts of the country and family ties. Entrepreneurs tend to be both occupationally and geographically mobile.

   c. One cause of an increase in the quality of labour is education. A more educated labour force will be able to undertake more tasks and will perform tasks more efficiently. A more educated labour force will be a more productive labour force.

   An increase in training should raise the quality of the labour force. Training workers to, for instance, use new capital equipment or work more efficiently in teams should again raise labour productivity.

   The quality of capital goods is regularly increased by advances in technology. Today's computers can perform tasks more efficiently and can undertake far more tasks than the computers of ten years ago.

   d. If more resources are devoted to producing cotton garments in Pakistan, the opportunity cost may be knitwear. Some of the workers, capital goods, land and enterprise used in producing knitwear may be switched to producing cotton garments. The output of knitwear, however, would not have to fall if the cotton garments industry makes use of resources that had previously been unemployed or if the country experiences an increase in the quantity or quality of resources.

Homework assignment

a. The passage mentions that not all families are able to go on holiday. This is likely because they do not have enough money.

b. Three factors of production involved in providing holidays in the Maldives are capital, labour and land. A wide variety of forms of capital are used including, for instance, aeroplanes and hotels. Among the forms of labour used are hotel staff and travel agents. Examples of land include beaches and the sea.

c. (i) An economic good is one which has an opportunity cost as it takes resources to produce it. These resources could be used for another purpose. In contrast, a free good occurs naturally. It does not have to be made. It does not have an opportunity cost as it does not use resources to produce it.

(ii) Beaches or sunshine.

d. A travel firm in deciding how to use its resources of, for instance, workers and premises, will take into account opportunity cost. In deciding whether to offer a new holiday, the firm will have to consider whether the profit it will gain from this holiday offer will be higher than the profit it would gain from what it considers to be its next most rewarding holiday offer. It will have to keep the position under review as profitability can change over time as demand for holiday destinations and their costs change.

SECTION-2

Definitions

1. q	2. l	3. k	4. f	5. m
6. n	7. b	8. p	9. j	10. a
11. s	12. i	13. c	14. r	15. g
16. d	17. e	18. t	19. h	20. o

Missing words

1. three, distributed
2. resources, price, government/state
3. consumer
4. ability
5. rise/increase
6. substitutes, complements
7. rise/increase
8. narrowly, substitutes
9. supply, price
10. disequilibrium, supply
11. allocative, competitive
12. fall, contraction
13. supply, demand
14. private, beneficial, third
15. public, free
16. external
17. subsidy, tax
18. failure, prices
19. high
20. public/government/state

Calculations

1. a. Price elasticity of demand = % change in quantity demanded/% change in price. In this case it is 6%/4% = (−1.5).
    b. The price elasticity of demand is greater than 1 and so demand is elastic.
    c. One reason why it is elastic may be because it has close substitutes in the form of other bars of chocolate. This would mean that if the price of the bar rose, a relatively high proportion of customers would be lost to other brands.
    d. To raise revenue, the chocolate manufacturer should lower price. This is because, with elastic demand, a percentage fall in price would cause a greater percentage rise in demand. People would be paying less for the product, but the greater rise in sales would mean that total expenditure and so total revenue would rise.

2. a. The percentage change in demand is − 60,000/200,000 × 100 = − 30%. The percentage change in price is US $ 3/US $ 6 × 100 = 50%.
    So price elasticity of demand = − 30%/50% = − 0.6.
    b. As the figure is less than 1, demand is inelastic.
    c. Demand is likely to be inelastic as cigarettes are addictive. If prices rise, some buyers may find it difficult to cut back or give up.
    d. Taxing cigarettes would be more effective in raising revenue than reducing smoking. As demand for cigarettes is inelastic, the rise in price resulting from a tax would cause a relatively small percentage change in demand. Tax revenue would increase but there is unlikely to be much impact on the quantity of cigarettes bought and sold.

3. a. The percentage change in supply of freshly cut roses is 25/500 × 100 = 5%. The percentage change in price is US $ 0.80/US $ 4 × 100 = 20%. So price elasticity of supply of freshly cut roses is 5%/20% = 0.25.
    In contrast, the percentage change in supply of plastic roses is 80/200 × 100 = 40%. So price elasticity of supply of plastic roses is 40%/20% = 2.
    b. The supply of freshly cut roses is inelastic whilst the supply of plastic roses is elastic.
    c. It is relatively easy to adjust the supply of plastic roses in response to a change in price. This is because they can be produced quickly and can be stored. In contrast, it is harder to alter the supply of freshly cut roses. This is because it takes time to grow roses and because roses cannot be stored.

Interpreting diagrams

a. See Figure 1.

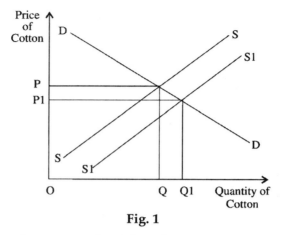

Fig. 1

b. A shift of the supply curve to the right is known as an increase in supply.

c. One possible cause of an increase in supply is a reduction in the costs of production. This would enable firms to supply more at each and every price.

Drawing diagrams

a.
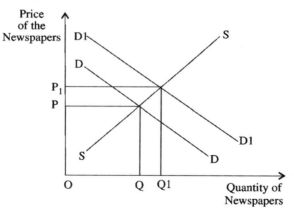

Fig. 2

Demand would increase, price would rise and supply would extend.

b.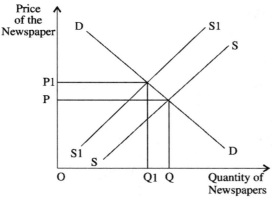

Fig. 3

Supply would decrease, price would rise and demand would contract.

c.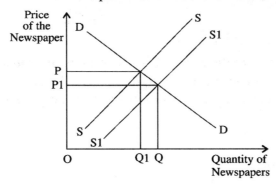

Fig. 4

Supply would increase. Price would fall and demand would extend.

d.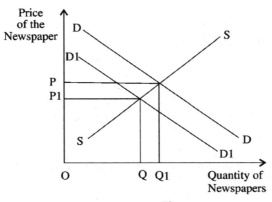

Fig. 5

Demand would decrease, price would fall and supply would contract.

e.

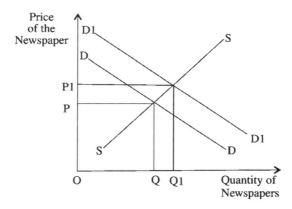

Fig. 6

Demand would increase, price would rise and supply would extend.

Multiple-choice questions

1. **B**

   In a market economy, producers should pick up on price signals to alter their production in response to changes in consumer demand. A, C and D are features of a planned economy.

2. **D**

   In a mixed economy, some output is produced by the state (in the public sector) and some by privately owned firms (in the private sector). A, B and C are features of most economies.

3. **A**

   In a market economy there will be less need for government officials as the operation of market forces will determine output. There will be an increase in the role of the price mechanism, a reduction in state ownership and in the output of public goods.

4. **B**

   An increase in the price of diesel may encourage some people to switch from driving vehicles that use diesel to those that use petrol. A, C and D would all tend to decrease demand for petrol.

5. **A**

   A contraction in demand is a fall in demand caused by a rise in the price of the product. A is a decrease in demand, C is an extension in demand and D is an increase in demand.

6. **C**

   A shift to the left of a demand curve represents a decrease in demand. Air travel is a complement to foreign holidays. If the price of foreign holidays rises, demand for foreign holidays would contract and demand for its complement would decrease. A and D would be likely to increase the demand for air travel. B would cause an increase in the supply of air travel and so a fall in price and an extension in demand.

7. A

Beef and leather can both be produced from cattle. B, C and D are in joint demand – they are complements.

8. C

The diagram shows a shift to the right of the supply curve. This is an increase in supply. This could be caused by a reduction in the cost of producing the product. A and B are the result, and not the cause of the decrease in supply. D would cause a decrease in supply.

9. C

Equilibrium price is the price at which demand and supply are balanced. At such a price, there are no pressures causing the price to change. The number of buyers could equal the number of sellers but the quantity demanded by buyers might exceed that being supplied by producers. In both cases, price will not be in equilibrium – it will be changing. The lowest possible price for a product is zero and this price will only operate in cases where the product is being given away free. The most profitable price for a product would be where the gap between revenue and cost is greatest.

10. C

The diagram shows an increase in demand and a decrease in supply. Higher incomes would increase demand for gold whilst an increase in the cost of mining gold would decrease supply. A, B and D would cause a decrease in demand for and an increase in the supply of gold.

11. A

Travel by private jet is expensive and so is seen as a luxury. A rise in the price of such travel would result in a greater percentage fall in demand. B, C and D would all tend to result in a product having inelastic demand.

12. A

The % change in quantity demanded is $-40/800 \times 100 = -5\%$. The % change in price is US $ 10/US $ 50 = 20%. So the price elasticity of demand is $-5\%/20\% = -0.25$.

13. A

A price elasticity of demand of -0.3 means that the product has price inelastic demand. In such a case, price and total spending (revenue) move in the same direction. B is incorrect as a fall in the price of a product with either inelastic or elastic demand will cause an extension in demand. C applies to elastic demand and not inelastic demand. For D to occur, price elasticity of demand would have to be zero.

14. D

Price elasticity of supply is the percentage change in quantity supplied divided by the percentage change in price.

15. B

Market forces are supposed to result in efficiency. If firms respond to what consumers demand and produce at low costs and hence low prices, they will be rewarded with high profits. If they do not, they will be punished by going out of business. A, C and D are all possible features of a planned economy.

16. C

Market failure occurs when the social cost of producing a product and the social benefit of producing it are not equal. If producers base their output decisions only on private costs, they are ignoring external costs. As a result price is likely to be below and output above the allocatively efficient level. A, B and D all represent the market working efficiently.

17. C

A monopoly may restrict output to push up price. This will mean that it will under-produce the product. The lack of competitive pressure may also mean that it does not produce at the lowest possible average cost. A and B would tend to lead market efficiency. High profit rather than low profit as in D may be a sign of abuse of market power.

18. B

It is not possible to exclude non-payers benefiting from flood defences and one person's enjoyment of the service does not reduce someone else's. In contrast, A, C and D are all both excludable and rival.

19. B

Public expenditure is spending by the government. One purpose of government spending is to enable the old, sick and other groups unable to earn a living to buy basic necessities. A government would want to decrease and not increase external costs, increase and not reduce the mobility of resources, and tax and not subsidise demerit goods.

20. A

A CBA (cost benefit analysis) is most likely to be used to decide whether to go ahead with a public sector investment project based on the relationship between the social benefits and costs which are estimated to arise.

Similarities

1. These are two of the fundamental economic questions.
2. Both show how much is demanded at different prices.
3. These are both terms for a price at which demand and supply are equal.

4. Both are influences on demand.
5. These are both ways a government can influence supply.
6. In both cases a change in price will have no effect on demand and supply.
7. Both are effects on third parties.
8. Both are examples of market failure.
9. They are the two key characteristics of a public good.
10. Both cases result in inefficiency.

Differences

1. Individual demand is the demand of one consumer whereas market demand is the total demand for a product.
2. An extension in supply is a movement along a supply curve whereas an increase in supply is a shift to the right of the supply curve. Whilst an extension in supply is caused by a rise in the price of the product itself, an increase in supply is the result of a change in an influence on supply other than a change in the price of the product itself.
3. A market surplus means that some products are unsold because supply exceeds demand. In contrast, a market shortage means that demand exceeds supply and so some consumers are unable to produce the product.
4. A complement is a product used with another product whereas a substitute is used instead of another product.
5. Price elasticity of demand measures how responsive demand is to a change in price whereas price elasticity of supply measures the responsiveness of supply to a price change.
6. Private expenditure is spending by the private sector and includes spending by consumers and firms. In contrast, public expenditure is spending by the public sector, that is the government.
7. Allocative efficiency is concerned with how resources are distributed among different uses. It is achieved when firms produce what consumers demand in the right quantities. Productive efficiency, however, is concerned with costs of production. It is achieved when firms produce at the lowest average cost and no resources are wasted.
8. Merit goods are under-valued and so under-consumed whereas demerit goods are over-valued and so over-consumed. Merit goods generate external benefits but demerit goods create external costs.
9. External benefits are benefits to third parties, that is those not directly involved in the production or consumption of a product. In contrast, social benefits are the total benefits that arise from the consumption or production of a product. Social benefits include both external and private benefits.

10. Conservation of resources involves preserving resources for future generations whereas exploitation of resources involves using up resources now.

Data exercises

1. a. The percentage rise in the price of tea was US $ 0.40/US $ 2 × 100 = 20%.
    b. Demand is the willingness and ability to buy a product.
    c. (i) The price of tea rose between 2006 and 2008 due to an increase in demand. This increase in demand shift the demand curve to the right as shown in Figure 7.

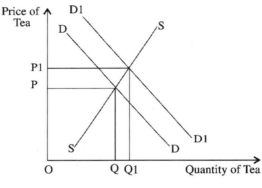

Fig. 7

   (ii) A drought affecting tea growing areas would result in a decrease in the supply of tea. Such a decrease would cause price to rise and demand to contract as shown on Figure 8.

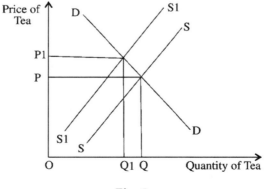

Fig. 8

    d. (i) Coffee is a substitute for tea. Most people tend to drink either coffee or tea.
        (ii) Two other influences on demand for tea are changes in population and advertising. A rise in population is likely to increase the number of

tea drinkers and so increase demand for tea. A successful advertising campaign for tea would also increase demand for tea. The adverts could provide information about the tea or be purely persuasive.

e. The price elasticity of supply of tea is inelastic. This is because it takes time for tea bushes to mature. As a result, it can be difficult to adjust supply in response to changes in market conditions. Tea producers may want to supply more if prices rises, but it would take them time to plant and grow tea bushes.

f. There are a number of factors which will influence whether a country would benefit from specialising in tea production. These include whether the country has a comparative advantage in the product, whether demand is increasing and whether other countries impose trade restrictions on tea imports. If a country's tea producers can produce tea at a lower opportunity cost than other countries, it will have the potential to sell a high value of tea. Good natural resources, including fertile land and a favourable climate, and well trained workers may give a country a comparative advantage. Ability to produce a product efficiently, however, is not sufficient. There would be no point in specialising in tea production if international demand for tea is decreasing. Import restrictions, such as tariffs and quotas, may also reduce the benefits of specialising in tea production.

2. a. The three costs are air pollution, noise pollution, congestion and accidents.

   b. (i) A rise in the tax on petrol would increase the cost of car travel. This will decrease supply, cause price to rise and demand to contract as shown in Figure 9.

      (ii) A subsidy given to bus travel would encourage bus companies to supply more services. Supply will increase, price will fall and demand will contract. This change in shown in Figure 10.

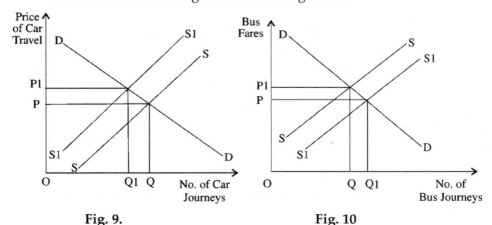

Fig. 9.   Fig. 10

   c. (i) A government could finance spending on an underground system by taxation or by borrowing. The government could introduce a new tax or raise rates on existing taxes. It could borrow from the banking sector or from the non-banking sector by selling government bonds.

(ii) Beijing officials could carry out a CBA (cost benefit analysis). This would measure all the costs and benefits involved in upgrading the underground system.

As well as private costs, including the labour costs and material costs, external costs such as noise and air pollution would be estimated. Similarly both private benefits, such as extra revenue raised, and the external benefits, including reduced car congestion, would be measured.

It is often more difficult to place a value on external costs and benefits than private costs and benefits. For instance, how can a value be placed on lost welfare habitats resulting from engineering works?

Once social costs and benefits have been estimated, they are then compared. If social costs exceed social benefits, Beijing officials should not go ahead with the upgrading. Even if there is a net social benefit, the project may be rejected if an alternative project would generate higher net social benefit.

d. There are a number of reasons why demand for car travel may have increased in Beijing. These include a rise in income and a rise in the price of public transport. As income rises, more households are likely to purchase a car and some may buy more than one car. They are also likely to use their car or cars more often. Train and bus travel are substitutes for car travel. If train and bus fares rise, some passengers are likely to switch to using their cars more frequently or to purchasing a car to use.

e. Whether a reduction in pollution will benefit a country will depend on whether the social benefit of reducing pollution exceeds the social cost of reducing pollution. If pollution is very high, the social benefit of reducing it is also likely to be high. Nevertheless, the social cost of pollution reduction must still be considered. When pollution is relatively low, the private cost of pollution reduction may be high in comparison to the benefits which will be gained. This is why governments do not aim for zero pollution. Resources can be put to better use than in lowering pollution from very low levels to zero.

3. a. In a planned economy it is the government which decides what is produced, how it is produced and who receives what is produced. The state owns most of the land and capital. In contrast, in a market economy, the allocation of resources is determined by the market forces of demand and supply. Capital and land in such a type of economy is owned by private firms and individuals.

b. A country with low unemployment will be producing close to its production possibility curve as shown in Figure 11.

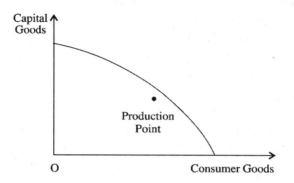

Fig. 11

c. (i) A benefit of a market economy mentioned in the passage is 'a wide choice of good quality products'.

   (ii) Another advantage of a market economy is productive efficiency which results in the lowest possible costs and prices. A market system provides both an incentive and the threat of punishment to be efficient. The incentive comes in the form of profit and the threat of punishment in the form of bankruptcy. For these pressures to work, however, there has to be actual or potential competition present.

d. (i) Market failure arises when the market forces of demand and supply do not achieve an efficient outcome.

   (ii) Air pollution may arise in a market economy because private sector firms are likely to base their production decisions only on private costs. They are not likely to consider external costs such as air pollution. Indeed, private sector firms may be reluctant to install new machinery which would reduce air pollution as it may increase their private costs.

e. There are three main types of economic systems. These are market, mixed and a planned economy. If I was Prime Minister of a country I would take into account the current economic system being operated, the stage of economic development and the advantages and disadvantages of the different economic systems. Changing an economic system can be rather disruptive and I would only recommend such a change if I thought the country would benefit and if the country has, or could quickly develop, the necessary institutions. For instance, a developing country may lack a developed banking sector, may not have a stock exchange and may not have a sufficiently strong legal system to protect private property.

Very few countries now operate a planned economy. If, however, I thought that market forces would not work well in the country and that state planning would operate efficiently, I would opt for a planned economy.

On the other hand, I could recommend a market economy if I believed that the market system would work well and there would be little risk of market failure. In a market economy the allocation of resources is determined by the forces of demand and supply. The price mechanism indicates to producers the products that consumers are willing and able to buy. This system has the potential advantages of consumer sovereignty, choice and efficiency. It does, however, have a number of disadvantages.

If I think that market failure is a significant problem, I would be likely to favour a mixed economy. I would want the economy to reap the advantages of a market economy whilst minimising its disadvantages. I would want the government to consider social costs and benefits, provide public goods, encourage the consumption of merit goods and discourage the consumption of demerit goods and protect vulnerable groups.

f. No economy is a pure market economy because all countries accept there is some role for the public sector. Most economists would argue that governments should control monopolies to prevent them exploiting their monopoly power. Many think that the government should support the poor and vulnerable by providing benefits and essential products. The nature of merit, demerit and public goods also provide a role for the government. In addition, some would also argue that government intervention may be needed to achieve the macroeconomic aims of full employment, price stability and balance of payments equilibrium.

g. It would appear that all consumers would benefit from a wide choice of good quality products. Competition can drive down price and increase the quality further. Firms will be rewarded with profit if they produce products that consumers want and at a price which is lower than their competitors. On the other hand, they will be punished if they are not competitive – they will be driven out of the market.

Nevertheless, not all consumers may benefit for a number of reasons. One is that despite prices possibly being low, some consumers may still not be able to afford the products. Other consumers may find a wide choice to be rather time consuming and confusing. A wide choice of quality products may also not necessarily be produced by a high number of competitors. Indeed, one or two firms may produce a range of products. In this case, whilst consumers may have choice, they may be charged high prices due to the lack of competition.

Structured questions

1. a. Demand and price are inversely related. A rise in price would cause a fall in demand, called a contraction in demand. This is because a higher price would reduce people's ability and willingness to buy a product.

A fall in price would cause an extension in demand as consumers would be able to buy more of a product and would be likely to switch a way from substitutes towards the product.

b. One of the main factors influencing demand for cinema tickets is price. A rise in the price of cinema tickets would be expected to cause a contraction in demand as shown in Figure 12.

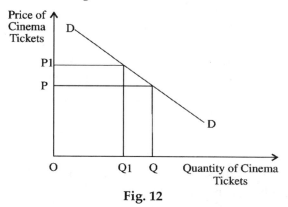

Fig. 12

Other influences would cause an increase or decrease in demand. An increase in income would usually be expected to increase demand for cinema tickets. On occasion, however, a decline in incomes can result in more people visiting the cinema as a form of escapism.

A change in the price of other forms of entertainment will affect demand for cinema tickets. Tickets to sports events, for instance, may be a substitute to cinema tickets. A rise in the price of tickets to cricket matches may encourage more people to visit the cinema. A fall in the price of a complement to visiting the cinema, such as transport may have a similar effect. A successful advertising campaign and the launch of a new popular film would also be likely to increase demand for cinema tickets. Indeed, sales of cinema tickets tend to be highest in the first three weeks of the release of a film.

A fall in population would cause a decrease in demand for cinema tickets as there would be fewer people to visit the cinema. This is shown by a shift to the left of the demand curve as shown in Figure 13.

c. A government could influence the market for cinema tickets in a number of ways, such as by regulating the industry, setting a maximum price, taxing cinema tickets, providing a subsidy and by altering income tax.

Regulating the industry may involve, for instance, stopping under 16s from watching certain films. This will reduce the potential number of tickets sold.

If the government decided to extend the ban to under 18s, the number of tickets sold would fall even more.

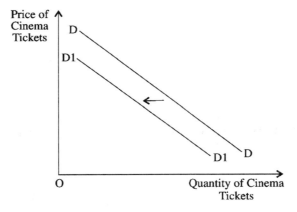

Fig. 13

A government might set a maximum price of tickets in a bid to make them more accessible to the poor. The problem with this measure is that it will create a shortage as shown in Figure 14.

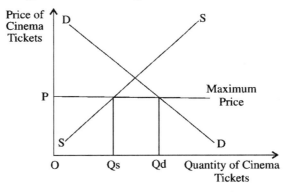

Fig. 14

It is more likely that a government may place a tax on cinema tickets. Such a measure would cause cinema operators' costs of production to rise. The supply curve would shift to the left, price would rise and demand would contract as shown in Figure 15.

To develop its own cinema industry, a government may provide a subsidy to its cinema operators. This would encourage them to raise their output. Supply would shift to the right, price would fall and demand would extend. The outcome is shown in Figure 16.

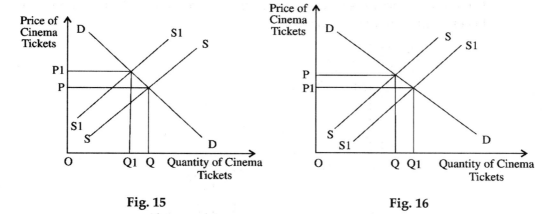

Fig. 15   Fig. 16

A cut in income tax would mean that people would have more disposable income. They may spend some of this on visiting the cinema more often. If they do so, demand would increase causing price to rise and supply to extend as indicated in Figure 17.

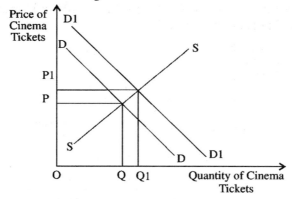

Fig. 17

2. a. Equilibrium price is a price at which demand and supply are equal. At this price, there is no pressure for price to change. In contrast, a disequilibrium price is one at which demand and supply are not equal. In the absence of government intervention, market forces will move a disequilibrium price towards an equilibrium price. Figure 18 shows an equilibrium price of P and a disequilibrium price of P1.

At P1, demand exceeds supply. This shortage will pull price up to P. A disequilibrium price above P would result in a surplus which would push price down to P.

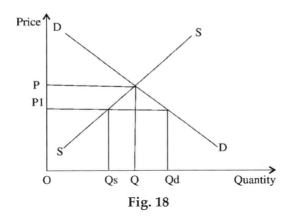

Fig. 18

b. The quantity of mobile phones being bought and sold in many countries continues to increase. They are becoming cheaper because supply is increasing at a more rapid rate than demand. Advances in technology have significantly reduced the cost of producing mobile phones. The lower costs are shifting the supply curve to the right to a greater extent than the demand curve is shifting to the right. This greater increase in supply is causing the price to fall as shown in Figure 19.

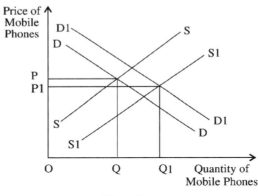

Fig. 19

c. Price elasticity of demand is a measure of the responsiveness of demand to a change in price. The main influence on the degree to which demand for a product will change when its price changes, is the extent to which it has close substitutes of a similar price. If a product does have close substitutes, it is likely to have elastic demand. If its price falls, consumers will switch to it from rival products.

Another influence on price elasticity of demand is the degree to which the product is a necessity or a luxury. Necessities tend to have inelastic demand whereas luxuries have elastic demand. A rise in the price of staple food such as bread may not have much effect on demand. In contrast, demand for a luxury apartment is likely to be much more responsive to a change in price.

Addictive products, such as cigarettes tend to have inelastic demand. People who find it difficult to give up smoking are unlikely to cut down the number of cigarettes they buy significantly if the price rises.

Two other influences on price elasticity of demand are the proportion of income spent on the product and whether the purchase can be postponed. Products where the purchase takes up a large proportion of income and where the purchase can be postponed, such as a new car, tend to have elastic demand.

The more widely defined a product is and the shorter the time period is, the more inelastic demand is. This is because, in the first case, there will be fewer substitutes available and, in the second case, there may not be enough time to find a substitute.

d. Knowledge of price elasticity of demand is likely to be of use to a firm selling a particular type of mobile phone as it will indicate the extent to which it has substitutes and will help it decide whether to raise or lower its price. If a firm finds that its products have elastic demand, this would suggest that it has close substitutes. This may encourage it to carry out an advertising campaign or improve on the quality of its products to attract consumers from rival firms.

It would also tell the firm if it wanted to raise revenue, it should lower the price of its products. This is because when demand is elastic, a fall in price will result in a greater percentage rise in demand. For example, if the price of a product is US $ 10 and 500 are sold a week, revenue would initially be US $ 5,000. If demand is elastic, a 10% fall in price to US $ 9 may result in a 20% rise in demand to 600. In this case, revenue would rise to US $ 5,400.

A firm, however, in making a decision on price would take into account not only the impact on revenue but also the impact on cost. Selling more in this case will not only raise revenue but also cost. If revenue rises by more than cost, profit will also increase.

If demand for a firm's products is inelastic, it could raise revenue by increasing price. In this case, a rise in price will cause a smaller percentage fall in demand. Inelastic demand would usually occur when there is a lack of substitutes. Such a situation would give a firm market power.

3. a. A mixed economy is one in which there is both a private sector and a public sector. Both the price mechanism and government directives are used to allocate resources. There are both private firms and state owned enterprises producing products.

b. A number of countries are moving from a mixed to a market economy in a bid to gain more of the advantages that can arise from the operation of free market forces. Consumers want more say over what is produced and a market economy should provide this. They also want low prices and good quality and if there are sufficient competitive pressures and incentives in a market economy, firms will be allocatively and productively efficient.

c. Three causes of market failure are a failure to consider the full costs and benefits of economic decisions, over-consumption and over-production of demerit goods and under-consumption and under-production of merit goods. Consumers and private sector producers take into account only the costs and benefits, known as private costs and benefits, that they experience. Failure to base their decisions on the full costs and benefits of their decisions means that resources will not be allocated in an efficient manner.

For instance, a firm may generate what are called external costs when it makes a product. These are costs on third parties, that is those who are not directly involved in the production or consumption of the product. These costs, such as noise and air pollution will not be taken into account when a firm decides the quantity it will produce. This failure can result in the social (full) cost exceeding the social benefit and so too many resources being devoted to the production of the product.

Over-production also occurs in the case of demerit goods. These are products that are more harmful for people than they realise and which create external costs. A lower output of these products would benefit society.

In contrast, if left to market forces, merit goods would be under-consumed and so under-produced. Some people may fail to appreciate the true value of, for instance, regular health check-ups and are unlikely to take into account the benefits other will gain from them being healthy.

d. There are a number of potential advantages in having a private sector company build an airport. The firm may have a financial incentive to keep costs low and complete it on time. In determining the location and size of the airport and designing it, the private sector company is likely to consider the level of consumer demand and the type of facilities consumers want and are willing to pay for. A private sector company may have experience in building airports and it may be able to make decisions quickly.

There is, however, the chance that a private sector company may be a monopoly. If it is the only company building airports in the country it may charge a high price and may not build a high quality airport.

The company may also suffer from information failure. It may not know, for example, where to buy the cheapest building material. An even greater risk is that it will not take into account external costs and benefits in determining whether to build the airport, where to build it and the size of the airport. External costs and benefits can be quite significant in the case of building and operating an airport. For instance, building and operating an airport is likely to cause noise and air pollution, traffic congestion around the airport, loss of wildlife habitats but also employment in the area.

One advantage of the government building a new airport is that may take into account social costs and benefits. A private sector company will carry out an investment appraisal and go ahead with the project if private benefits exceed private costs. In contrast, the government may carry out a CBA (cost benefit analysis). It may consider a number of sites and locate it where the net social benefit is greatest.

In some countries, private sector companies may lack the finance to build a new airport. The government may have sufficient funds or may be able to raise the finance through taxation or borrowing from abroad. There will, however, be an opportunity cost – the government could have used the money for some other purpose such as building more schools. Higher taxes would reduce tax payers' disposable income and may make the government unpopular. Borrowing from abroad could result in a high debt burden.

An alternative approach would be for government to pay a private sector firm to construct the airport. This would have the advantage that the expertise of a private sector company could be employed whilst the financial resources of the government could be drawn on and its concern with social costs and benefits could determine the size and location of the airport.

4. a. In a market economy, resources are allocated by means of the price mechanism. If demand for air travel, for instance, increases, its price will rise. The change in the price will signal to producers that consumers are willing and able to buy more of the product. The higher price will also provide a profit incentive to respond to this change in consumer demand. Existing firms producing air travel will put on more flights and new firms will be likely to enter the industry. This way more resources will be devoted to air travel.

   b. Education is a merit good as people do not appreciate the benefits to themselves and their children of being educated and because education provides external benefits. These two factors result in education being under-consumed if left to market forces. Children and adults may not realise the enjoyment they will gain from studying, the boost to their earning potential that they will experience and the need to be literate and numerate to be able to participate fully in today's society. Education also provides benefits to third parties, that is to people not directly involved in consuming or supplying education. The external benefits that would arise from an increase in the number of students going on to university, for instance, would include, in few years time, a rise in the quantity and quality of output.

   c. The two main reasons why some governments provide free primary and secondary education is to correct market failure and to promote equity. If left to market forces, education will be under provided because it would be under-consumed. By providing it free, a government will encourage its consumption. Some governments also believe that education should be provided free on grounds of fairness. If parents have to pay to send their children to school, some poor people would not be able to afford to educate their children. Since education is seen as so important, some governments are keen to ensure that all children go to school.

d. Health care is a private good rather than a public good. This is because it is both rival and excludable. If one person is being operated on, the doctors carrying out the operation and the equipment being used cannot be employed to operate on someone else at the same time. It is also excludable as hospitals and doctors could charge for their services, and indeed some do. In some countries, patients are not charged for their treatment. This, however, is not because charges cannot be imposed but because governments have decided to provide the service free. They may do this because health care is both a private good and a merit good. As with education, it provides more benefits to the consumers than they realise and it generates external benefits.

Homework assignments

1. a. (i) Private costs are the costs borne by those consuming or producing the product. In contrast, external costs are the costs borne by third parties, that is those not directly involved in consuming or producing the product.

   (ii) The information in the passage suggests the UK government believes cigarettes are over-produced. The evidence is that the government is seeking to reduce cigarette consumption and production.

   b. The ban on smoking in public and workplaces, is likely to result in people smoking less. This will reduce demand for cigarettes. The demand curve will shift to the left, causing price to fall and supply to contract as shown in Figure 20.

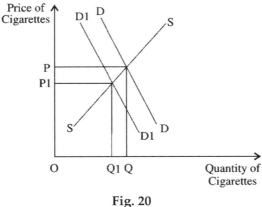

Fig. 20

   c. (i) An inferior good is one which does not have the usual relationship with changes in income. In this case, unlike with most products, people will buy less of it when their in come rises.

(ii) The passage indicates that smoking declined in the UK between 1974 and 2005. During this period, income rose in the UK. The passage also mentions that more of the poor smoke than the rich.

d. To assess what will happen to the market for cigarettes in a country in the future, it would be necessary to study information on demand and supply of the product, health reports and predictions of future government policy on smoking. For example, it would be useful to estimate what is expected to happen to the price of cigarettes in the future. If the price rise is anticipated to exceed that of other products, demand would be expected to fall. Estimates of future income, population size and change in age structure would all provide useful information on what might happen to the sales of cigarettes.

Trends in the amount of land devoted to tobacco production, any indication of technological development in the production methods and trends in wage rises would also be worth examining.

The most important influences on the market for cigarettes, however, are probably health and government policies. If it is known that more research is being undertaken on the effects of smoking cigarettes, it might be expected that demand would fall. Government future plans for a higher tax on cigarettes and possibly greater future restrictions on where people can smoke may have a significant impact on the quantity of cigarettes bought and sold in the future.

2. a. Whales are a natural resource. Economists classify natural resources as land.
   b. A sustainable catch of whales means that the catch does not permanently reduce the stocks of whales. The number of whales caught is small enough to be replaced by the birth of new whales.
   c. (i) A decrease in demand is a fall in demand caused by a change in an influence on the product other than the price of the product itself. Two factors that could cause a decrease in demand for whale meat are a fall in the price of other types of meat and consumers developing a greater concern about the welfare of whales. If other meat, such as chicken, becomes cheaper some people may switch away from buying whale meat. They may also buy less whale meat if they become more worried about any cruelty involved in capturing and killing whales or about the chance of whales becoming extinct.
   (ii) If the whaling ban were to be removed, more whales would be caught. This would increase the supply of whale meat. As Figure 21 shows such an increase would lower price and cause demand to extend.

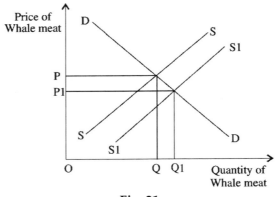

Fig. 21

d. To help assess the arguments for and against conserving whales, there is a range of information that would be useful. In judging the arguments against conserving whales it would be beneficial to consider the contribution that the industry makes to the output, employment and export earnings of the whaling nations. For some countries, whaling may make a significant contribution to output and employment and may help to reduce a current account deficit.

In assessing the arguments for conserving whales, the possibility of other industries growing and replacing whaling should be taken into account. One of these industries is tourism. The current income earned from tourism and predictions for future earnings should be considered as well as the extent to which whales will be endangered by whaling. Some people may be attracted to visit the countries by the prospect of going out in boats to see the whales. Conserving whales will protect the balance of nature and will permit future generations to see whales. Ensuring that whales survive into the future may also mean that more will be learnt about whales and it may be discovered, for instance, that whales can be harvested for medical purposes.

3. a. (i)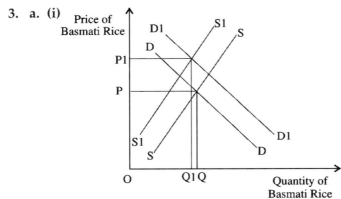

Fig. 22

(ii) Three reasons why the price of basmati rice rose in 2007 were an increase in its popularity, a poor harvest and some farms switching cultivation from basmati rice to wheat and other grains. Basmati rice is seen as a luxury product. As income increased in 2007 people sought out better quality products.

Whilst its increased popularity raised demand, supply was decreased by a poor harvest. The supply was further reduced by some farmers deciding to grow other, more profitable, crops.

b. (i) The cultivation of basmati rice being labour-intensive means that a relatively high number of workers are employed relative to the amount of capital used.

(ii) Another factor of production used in growing rice is the entrepreneur. In this case, this may be the farmer. The farmer is likely to bear the uncertain risks involved in growing and selling the rice and to organise the other factors of production. (Capital: ploughs and land: water).

c. (i) Growing wheat.
(ii) Basmati rice.

d. (i) Elastic supply means that the quantity of a product offered for sale can be adjusted relatively easily when there is a change in price. Specifically, it means that a percentage change in price results in a greater percentage change in quantity supplied.

(ii) Products have different degrees of price elasticity of supply because they are supplied under different conditions. Fresh agricultural products usually have inelastic supply. This is because it takes time for crops to grow and for animals to be bred and reared. If the price of wheat increased, for example, the supply could not be extended quickly.

Shoes, DVDs and other products which can be stored have elastic supply. Should their price fall, some items could be removed from the market and be kept in storage until prices rise again.

Products that take a short time to produce, such as mobile phones, have elastic supply. Producers would usually be able to produce more mobile phones quickly should price rise. Advances in technology can increase the price elasticity of supply of a range of products over time by making production easier and quicker.

SECTION-3

Definitions

1. r   2. l   3. m   4. i   5. j

6. k	7. a	8. h	9. g	10. b
11. q	12. f	13. n	14. p	15. e
16. d	17. c	18. s	19. o	20. t

Missing words

1. specialising, division
2. medium, standard, deferred
3. money, generally acceptable
4. central, notes, coins
5. Interest, borrowing, saving, lending
6. shares, securities/bonds
7. high, low
8. wage
9. benefits, short, holidays
10. skilled, more
11. low, above, equilibrium
12. raise/increase, extend
13. hours, force
14. supply, wage
15. power, low, highly
16. smaller, income
17. rises/increases, reduced/cut
18. income.
19. consume, save
20. inflation, direct

Calculations

1. US $ 250 x 8/100 = US $ 20. US $ 250 + US $ 20 = US $ 270.
2. Yield = dividend per share/market share price x 100. In this case it is US $ 2/ US $ 40 x 100 = 5%.
3. The total wages paid is US $ 2,700. There are nine workers, so the average wage is US $ 2,700/9 = US $ 300.

Interpreting diagrams

a. The equilibrium wage rate is the wage rate which equates the demand for and supply of labour as shown in Figure 1.

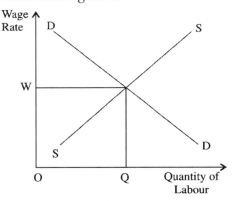

Fig. 1

b. The demand curve is downward sloping as the higher the wage rate, the less labour firms would be willing and able to employ. In contrast, the supply curve is upward sloping as workers would be more prepared to work and to work longer hours, the higher the wage rate.

Drawing diagrams

a.
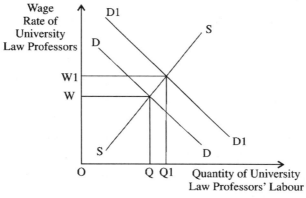

Fig. 2

More university law professors will be needed to lecture to students. As a result demand will increase, the wage rate will rise and supply will extend.

b. A lower wage rate for lawyers would be likely to decrease the number of students wanting to study law. This would reduce the need for law professors. At the same time, more lawyers may try to become law professors if the wage rate of lawyers falls below that of law professors. The effect of these changes would be to reduce the wage rate of university law professors.

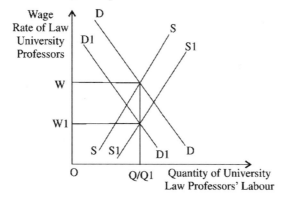

Fig. 3

c. An increase in the qualifications needed to become a university law professor would reduce the number of people who could undertake the job. This decrease in supply would raise the wage rate.

132 Cambridge IGCSE Economics Workbook

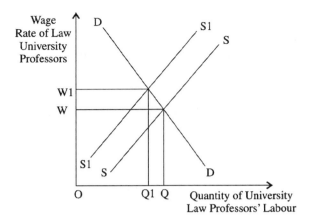

Fig. 4

 Multiple-choice questions

1. D

   A large market is likely to mean larger labour force. The greater the number of workers there are, the more they can specialise. A is the name for workers specialising. B is the definition for the best alternative forgone and C does not directly influence specialisation.

2. C

   If money keeps its value, it can be saved for future use. A is the function concerned with buying and selling products, B with borrowing and lending and D with measuring value.

3. A

   A central bank may lend to banks that are in financial difficulties.

4. B

   Workers may get bored doing the same job day after day and so may not stay in jobs for long. This will increase the cost of recruiting, inducting and training workers. A, C and D would all reduce unit cost.

5. A

   The main form of money used in Europe and indeed in most countries is bank accounts. The money is transferred from one person to another by a variety of measures including credit cards.

6. A

   For an item to act as money it has to be able to last for some time. It must have divisibility and not indivisibility and must be in limited and not unlimited supply. Whilst some forms of money, most noticeably gold and silver, have intrinsic value, most do not and it is not an essential requirement.

Answer Key

7. **B**

   An increase in the rate of interest would be likely to increase saving as it will raise the reward for saving. It would also be likely to reduce borrowing as it will increase the cost of borrowing.

8. **B**

   People either save or spend their income. A fall in saving would increase spending, presuming income has not changed. A, C and D would all be likely to lead to a fall in consumer expenditure.

9. **C**

   A commercial bank makes most of its profit by lending to its customers. A and D are functions of the central bank. B is a function of an investment bank.

10. **B**

    If it is difficult to replace workers with machines, a rise in wages will not have a significant impact on demand for labour. A, C and D would lead to elastic demand for labour.

11. **A**

    A craft union represents workers, such as engineers, who have particular skills. A general union represents a range of workers, an industrial union represents workers in a particular industry and a white collar union is formed by professional workers.

12. **B**

    If the wage rate is pushed above the equilibrium level, the demand for labour will contract and employment will fall. Fewer workers will be employed. Firms will seek to lower and not raise the wage rate. Increasing the output may or may not raise revenue. It will depend on price elasticity of demand. Even if it does raise revenue it will also increase costs as not only will they have to pay existing workers more, they may also have to hire more workers.

13. **B**

    If it is difficult to substitute workers, it would make demand for labour inelastic, as indicated in the answer to question 10. This would strengthen the ability of a trade union to push up the wage rate. A and D would make demand for labour elastic. This would weaken the power of trade unions and so would, an unwillingness to take industrial action.

14. **B**

    A labour market is in equilibrium when the demand for and supply of labour are equal.

15. **D**

    The diagram shows that the demand for bus drivers has increased. This could have been caused by an increase in demand for bus travel – a derived demand.

A, B and C would be likely to cause an increase in the supply of labour which would reduce the wage rate.

16. C

    An extension in the supply of labour can only be caused by a rise in the wage rate to the workers who supply that labour. A might increase the supply of labour. Each farm worker may work less but if more workers are attracted to the industry, the total number of hours worked could rise. B and D would be likely to increase the supply of farm workers' labour as they would both increase the rewards of the job.

17. D

    More on the job training would be likely to increase the skills of workers and so their earning potential in both that and other jobs. A, B and C would be likely to reduce the number of people willing to do the job.

18. B

    Doctors are likely to spend the most in total as they are likely to earn more than cleaners, factory workers and railway porters.

19. A

    Average propensity to save is saving/disposable income. In this case, the woman saved US $ 300 - US $ 270 = US $ 30. So APS = US $ 30/US $ 300 = 0.1.

20. D

    The very rich can buy food and other necessities and still have a considerable amount of income left to spend on luxuries such as leisure goods and services.

Similarities

1. Division of labour is a term for workers specialising on particular tasks.
2. Unit of account and standard for deferred payments are two of the functions of money.
3. A bonus and overtime payment are extra payments made to workers over the standard wage rate.
4. Working conditions and working hours are both non-wage influences on a person's choice of occupation.
5. Both trade unions and professional organisations are bodies that represent the interests of workers.
6. Both are central banks. The Federal Reserve is the central bank of the US and the Bank of England is the central bank of the UK.
7. Shares and bank loans are both examples of external finance.
8. Time rates and piece rates are both systems of paying workers.
9. Location and career prospects are another two influences on a person's choice of occupation.

10. Both work to rule and an overtime ban are forms of industrial action.

Differences

1. Specialisation involves concentrating on a narrow range of tasks or products. In contrast, diversification involves producing a wide range of products.
2. Commercial banks are high street banks which provide services for households and firms whereas investment banks concentrate on providing services for large firms.
3. A bullish market occurs when share prices are rising whereas a bearish market occurs when share prices are falling.
4. External finance and internal finance both relate to ways of financing an expansion in output. External finance is money raised outside the firm by arranging bank loans and selling shares. In contrast, internal finance is money raised inside the firm in the form of retained profit.
5. Wages refers to the basic amount paid to workers, whereas earnings is the total amount paid to workers. In addition to wages, earnings may include bonuses, overtime pay and commission.
6. Equilibrium wage rate is the wage rate that equates the demand for and supply of labour. In contrast, a disequilibrium wage rate is one at which the demand for and supply of labour are not equal. This wage rate is unlikely to last.
7. A craft union represents workers with particular skills whereas an industrial union represents workers in a particular industry.
8. Wealth is a stock of assets. In contrast, income is a flow of earnings.
9. Earned income is income received from working in a job whereas unearned income is income received in the form of profits, interest and dividends.
10. Saving occurs when people spend less than their income. In contrast, dissaving takes place when people spend more than their income.

Data exercises

1. a. An investment bank lends money to large firms and helps with the issue of new shares.
   b. There are three main reasons why a firm may pay a bonus to its staff. One is to encourage them to increase their performance. Bonuses can be linked to the output produced by a worker, the sales the worker makes or the contracts she/he gains. The other reasons are to attract and retain workers. Some workers may be encouraged to work for a firm if they believe that they can earn high bonuses. Workers, once recruited, may also be prepared to stay with a firm which pays generous bonuses.

c. One of the reasons why senior executives are paid more than cleaners is that the skills needed to be senior executives are in more limited supply than those required to be cleaners. Senior executives have to possess a wide range of skills, including the ability to manage people and to assess market conditions. The number of people with these skills is not very large whilst a high number of people have the ability to be a cleaner.

   Another related reason is that senior executives have more bargaining power than cleaners. A senior executive can ask for a high wage, often combined with high bonuses, knowing that she/he would be hard to replace. In contrast, cleaners can be replaced relatively easily by other people willing to do the job. They also do not usually belong to trade unions.

d. There are a number of factors which will influence whether cleaners will be able to raise their wages by taking industrial action. These include what proportion of cleaners are members of a union, whether any members work close together, the funds available to the union, whether cleaners can be replaced by non-unionised labour, the laws affecting unions and the funds available to those employing cleaners.

   As mentioned above the low degree of unionisation among cleaners in many countries weakens their ability to take industrial action. Even should membership be high, the fact that cleaners are widely dispersed would make it difficult for them to take industrial action.

   If a union representing cleaners has strong financial backing, cleaners could go on strike for a long period. This would have the potential of strengthening their case. If, however, employers could take on other people as cleaners during any industrial action or threat of industrial action, this would reduce their ability to raise their wages. If unemployment is high, replacing striking cleaners should be relatively easy as most people can do the work of cleaners.

   In some countries there may be limits placed on the industrial action workers can take. The more restrictive these limits are, the less power a trade union will have to pursue their claims.

   No matter how strong a group of workers is, it will not be able to obtain higher wages if the employer does not possess the funds to increase pay.

e. Favourable financial market conditions for an investment bank would involve a growing economy, a high number of firms engaging in mergers and takeovers and the issue of new shares. A growing economy would increase firms' profits. This would result in them depositing more money with investment banks and possibly borrowing more from them to finance their expansion. Demand for an investment bank's services may also be high if firms are asking them to help with mergers and issuing new shares. The higher the demand for an investment bank's services, the greater the profit it is likely to make.

f. High bonuses may prevent senior executives moving from Goldman Sachs to another bank as it may mean that the earnings the executives enjoy at Goldman Sachs are higher than those at rival banks. Of course, high bonuses may not mean that earnings are higher if another bank is paying higher bonuses or higher wages.

Senior executives may also move to another bank if it offers better non-wage benefits. For instance, senior executives may be attracted to another bank by greater job security, longer holidays and better working conditions. When deciding which firm to work for, people take into account a variety of factors and not just the size of any bonuses paid.

2. a. Opportunity cost is the best alternative forgone. What people forgo when they save, is the opportunity to spend.
    b. The passage mentions that people are not saving enough for their retirement. They are failing to appreciate the need to save, placing too much reliance on state provision and in some cases not having sufficient income to save.
    c. The passage mentions income as an influence on saving. The more income people have, the more able they are to save. When people are poor, they have to spend all of their income buying basic necessities.
    d. The level of saving might vary between countries for a number of reasons. These include differences in incomes and wealth, differences in government incentives to save, differences in the range of financial institutions, differences in attitude to saving, differences in age structure and differences in the rate of interest. Saving is likely to be higher in countries with high income and wealth and in which the government provides tax incentives to save. The greater the range and reliability of financial institutions, the greater the likelihood people will find a scheme that suits them and the more confident they will be in saving. Saving is also likely to be high in countries which regard saving as a virtuous activity and in which the population is relatively middle-aged. In addition, the rate of interest can have an impact with a high rate of interest providing a high reward for saving.
    e. Borrowing might be increased by a fall in the rate of interest. This is because it will be cheaper to borrow. Greater willingness of banks to lend, irrespective of the interest rate, would enable more people to borrow.

    If more people get into financial difficulties, there may be a rise in borrowing. If, for example, some people lose their jobs, they may borrow to maintain their living standards if they believe they will soon gain another job. Some people will borrow against future anticipated earnings. For instance, people who expect to gain promotion may start spending more now. So a rise in optimism about future prospects may encourage people to spend and borrow more now.

    People often borrow to buy particular products, including a new car, a house and a foreign holiday. So the more cars that are bought, the more houses purchased and the more foreign holidays they take, the higher borrowing is likely to be.

f. A government could encourage people to save more by providing a tax incentive. For instance, people could be allowed to save up to $5,000 a year without paying any tax on the interest earned. It could also set up savings banks. These may enable the poor to save by allowing them to withdraw cash without any penalties and by cutting down on the paperwork needed to be completed in order to open an account.

g. The effect the introduction of a generous state pension will have on saving is uncertain. This is because before the introduction, some people may have been saving up to provide an income for their retirement. These people may save less. However, a generous state pension by giving some people a higher income in their retirement may enable them to save more for medical treatment and residential care. It may also raise total saving by enabling people to live to a greater age and so increasing total population.

3. a. 44m Indian households had a colour TV set in 2008 (40/100 x 110m).

    b. A number of factors influence demand for TVs. As with many products, a key influence is price. A fall in price will cause an extension in demand for TVs. Other influences include disposable income, the rate of interest, advertising, prices of related products and population. As households become richer, they tend to buy more TVs and upgrade their TVs more frequently. Some homes in the USA, for instance, have four or five TVs. A successful advertising campaign for TVs, a rise in population and an increase in the price of alternative forms of entertainment may also increase demand for TVs. In addition, a fall in the price of complements to TVs, such as electricity and DVD players, may also increase demand for TVs.

    c. The increase in the number of TV channels would suggest that more TV programmes were being made. This would have increased demand for TV production staff. Such an increase would have pushed up the wage rate and caused supply to extend as shown in Figure 5.

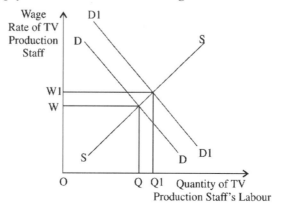

Fig. 5

d. **(i)** The likely relationship is that watching TV and going to the cinema are substitutes. Some people may watch TV rather than go to the cinema and vice versa. In a few cases, they may be complements. A successful TV series, for instance, may encourage people to go the cinema to see a film based on the series.

(ii) The most obvious way to increase the sale of cinema tickets is to reduce their price. A lower price would increase people's ability and willingness to buy the tickets. The impact that such a move would have on revenue would depend on the price elasticity of demand. If demand is elastic, a fall in price would raise revenue.

I may consider undertaking an advertising campaign. Such a campaign will cost money so I have to be confident that such a campaign would add more to revenue than to cost.

I would also seek to hire popular films to show. Of course, the film distributors are likely to charge more for what are expected to be popular films. I would, again, have to consider whether the higher cost would be outweighed by even higher revenue.

Another strategy I may try to attract more customers is to lower the price and/or increase the quality of complementary products such as food, drink and parking spaces.

If my cinema is regularly full, I could increase sales by building a larger cinema. An additional strategy would be to buy out another cinema.

e. Cinema attendance may increase due to a number of reasons. These include an increase in the quality of films being released to cinemas and the price of other forms of entertainment. More people will visit a cinema if more popular films are on show. A rise in the price of theatre tickets and tickets to music concerts may increase cinema attendance, This is because these forms of entertainment are substitutes for visiting the cinema.

f. A person may benefit from specialising as a producer of TV sports programmes if he or she has the skill to do the job, it is well paid and there is high and increasing demand for TV sports programmes. In such a situation, specialising may build up his or her skills and he or she may gain a good reputation as a producer of such programmes. If, however, the person lacks the appropriate talent he or she may find it difficult to get or keep a job as a producer. Specialising may also make the person vulnerable to a fall in the popularity of TV sports programmes. Producing a greater range of programmes may be more interesting and may provide the opportunity to apply skills and ideas gained in producing one type of programme to a variety of programmes.

Structured questions

1. a. Specialisation involves concentrating on particular tasks or products. Workers can specialise in carrying out particular tasks. For instance, a university lecturer may specialise in teaching nineteenth-century Chinese history. A firm may specialise in tourism and a country may specialise in agriculture.

    b. Money promotes specialisation because it makes it easy for people to buy and sell products. When people specialise they need to exchange some of what they produce for other products. They can sell some of their output for money and use that money to buy other goods and services. In this sense, money acts as a medium of exchange.

    c. Commercial banks carry out a range of functions. They may, for instance, look after their customers' legal documents and act as executors to their wills. Their main functions are, however, to accept deposits, lend and to enable their customers to make payments. People may keep some of their money in current (demand) accounts. They can withdraw money from these accounts when needed and can make payments from and receive money into these accounts. The other type of account that people may hold is a deposit (time) account. This enables people to save and to earn interest on their savings.

    Banks like lending as it is their most profitable activity. They lend by giving loans and permitting overdrafts on current accounts. Customers have to ask for a loan, explaining what they are going to use the money for. They may also be given permission to spend more than is in their current account up to a set limit. In both cases, interest will be charged. Banks charge more for the money they lend than the interest they pay to their customers with deposit accounts.

    The third main function is to provide a range of ways by which their customers can make and receive payments. Banks have developed a range of methods including cheques, direct debits, debit cards, credit cards and online banking.

    d. If a commercial bank specialises in the services it provides, it can develop expertise in its chosen area and build up a good reputation. For example, a bank may specialise in lending to farmers. This may enable it to develop a good understanding of the farming industry and the financial position and requirements of farmers. Concentrating on a particular area may save the bank money. Training costs, for instance, will be lower and the bank can focus its advertising in, for example, farmers' journals.

    There is a risk, however, in specialising. Should farming decline as an industry, demand for loans by farmers may decline. If farming gets into financial difficulties, farmers default on their loans. Diversification spreads risks. If a bank lends to a variety of customers and provides a range of services, it will not be too reliant on any one particular area. If one type of business is declining, a more successful area can be expanded.

2. a. Three influences on the supply of labour to a particular occupation are the wage rate paid, job satisfaction and the qualifications needed.

   The higher the wage rate paid, the more people will want to do the job. Indeed, a rise in the wage rate paid to a particular occupation would be expected to lead to an extension in supply.

   A job may not be particularly well paid but if it provides a high degree of job satisfaction, it is likely to attract a number of applicants. A number of people, for instance, gain much pleasure from gardening and are prepared to work for relatively low wages.

   The qualifications needed to do a job is another key influence on the supply of labour to a particular occupation. The higher the qualifications needed, the lower the supply will be. For instance, very few people possess the qualifications needed to be top surgeons. This is because it requires the willingness and ability to study and pass difficult examinations over a relatively long time.

   b. An increase in the occupational mobility of labour would mean that workers would find it easier to change from one occupation to another occupation. Improved education would mean that future workers would be qualified to undertake more types of jobs. This would increase the ability of people to switch from one job to another.

   More and higher quality training would also make it easier for people to change jobs. For example, training unemployed steel workers in ICT (information and communications technology) may enable them to move from a declining to an expanding industry.

   In addition, greater availability and greater accuracy of information should mean that workers move with greater ease and greater speed between different types of jobs.

   c. Dentists are paid more than waiters and waitresses because the supply of dentists relative to demand is lower than that of waiting staff, dentists have stronger bargaining power and because government policies and public opinion tend to favour dentists.

   The supply of dentists is relatively low as it requires high qualifications and a long period of training to qualify as a dentist. The supply of and demand for dentists is also relatively inelastic. In contrast, the supply of waiters and waitresses is relatively high. Waiting staff do not have to have any qualifications and do not need any particular skills. The supply of and demand for their services is elastic. An increase in the wage rate is likely to result in a greater percentage rise in supply as it would be likely to attract a relatively high number of applicants. Demand is elastic as the wage bill for waiting staff is likely to form a relatively high proportion of a restaurant's or cafe's total costs. Figure 6 compares the markets for dentists and for waiting staff.

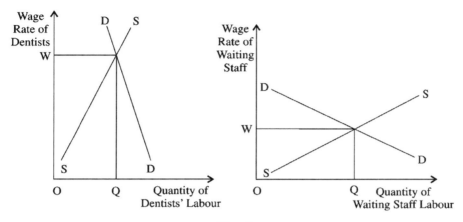

Fig. 6

Dentists in most countries have stronger bargaining power than waiting staff because they are more likely to belong to a labour organisation and one which is likely to have more funds. Waiters and waitresses do not tend to have much contact with waiting staff in other parts of the country. They often also do not stay in the job for long and so are less likely to join a trade union or professional body. With low membership, any labour organisation representing waiting staff is likely to have limited funds and power.

In some countries, governments will provide dental treatment free or at subsidised prices. Such an approach would be likely to lead to a relatively high demand for dental treatment. People also expect dentists to be paid more than waiting staff and this influences the wage claims the two groups make. In addition, waiting staff may be newly arrived immigrants who may be prepared to work for wage rates that are higher than in their country of origin but which are relatively low in the country they have moved to.

3. a. A trade union is an association of workers formed to represent their interests. They carry out a range of functions. One is to engage in collective bargaining. Union officials negotiate with employers on pay and working conditions and job protection. They provide information to their members and may help with their education and training. In some countries unions provide financial help to members in need. This may be in the form of sickness pay and unemployment pay. They may also have the funds to support members who are taking industrial action.

b. Three ways in which a trade union could seek to raise its members' wage rates are through collective bargaining, helping with training and taking industrial action. When workers negotiate as one body, as opposed to individually, they have stronger bargaining power. The higher the proportion of workers who are members of the union, the more powerful the union is likely to be. If a union has a hundred per cent membership, it will not be undercut by workers accepting a lower wage rate. When a union puts in a wage claim, it usually asks for more than it is prepared to accept whilst an employer will first offer less than she/he is willing to pay.

Encouraging members to participate in an employer's training scheme and putting on their own training schemes, should raise their productivity. Increasing their output per hour will increase their worth to an employer who may, therefore, be more willing to raise their wage rate.

Taking industrial action, such as striking or working to rule, may succeed in raising wages. This is more likely if most workers are members of the union, members cannot be replaced by non-union labour, the union has funds to support members during the industrial action and the employer has sufficient profit to raise the wage rate.

c. People may spend less, despite a rise in wages, if the tax rate increases by more than the wage rise. In this case, disposable income will fall and people will not be able to afford to spend as much.

Even if their disposable income rises, there are a number of reasons why they may spend less. One is that they may be pessimistic about the future. In this case, they may decide to save more. A rise in the rate of interest may also encourage people to save more.

Wages may rise but wealth may fall. Share prices and house prices may fall which would reduce some people's wealth. Falling house prices also reduce house sales. When people move house less frequently, spending on carpets, furniture and other household items tend to fall.

d. A more even distribution of income would transfer income from the rich to the poor by means of progressive taxes and state benefits. The effect that such a change would have on the pattern of expenditure in an economy would depend on the initial gap between the rich and the poor and how much the income of the two groups changes. If the poor become slightly better off, spending on food and other basic necessities as a percentage of total expenditure is likely to rise. If the rich lose a significant part of their income but the poor do not gain significantly as the income taken from the rich is spread thinly over a large number of poor people, expenditure on luxury goods and services may fall.

4. a. Demand for farm workers, as with other workers, is a derived demand. It is influenced by demand for the product. If demand for Bangladeshi

agricultural products is high, this will tend to result in a high demand for farm workers.

The higher the productivity of farm workers, the more farm workers are likely to be employed. If farm workers become better trained, their output is likely to rise. This will make them more valuable to employers.

The wage rate of farm workers and the price of rival factors of production also influences demand for farm workers. For instance, if the wages of farm workers are rising whilst the price of capital equipment, such as combine harvesters is falling, some workers may be replaced by machines.

b. There are a number of reasons why people may continue to be farm workers despite the offer of a better paid job in a factory. They may think that the wage paid to farm workers may increase in the future and that promotion chances in factory work may be limited.

Workers, in deciding what job to do, take into account not only the wage but also non-wage factors. Some farm workers may enjoy working outside and may derive job satisfaction from, for instance, looking after livestock. The working conditions and working hours may not be good in factories. In some factories people may have to work in cramped and noisy conditions. Factory workers may be required to work long hours and may have short holidays.

Some people may stay as farm workers because they are given living accommodation by their employer. It may be hard to find affordable homes near to factories. Indeed, even if they can be found, some people may not want to move because of family ties.

People also consider job security. They may not accept a better paid job if they think there is a risk that the job will not last.

c. A key benefit farm workers may gain from joining a trade union is that the union will bargain on their behalf for higher pay and better working conditions. A union may have considerable expertise in negotiating with employers. Bargaining on behalf of a group of workers also gives them considerable power.

Belonging to a union may enable workers to gain access to advice on a range of matters including pension rights. Some unions put on training sessions for their members and some even pay for some of their members to undertake degree courses.

In a number of countries, unions provide strike pay when their members are taking industrial action in pursuit of their claims. In some countries, unions also provide sickness and unemployment pay to their members.

Farm workers may benefit from their union or unions pressing the government for policies which benefit the farming industry. For instance, a union may persuade a government to provide a subsidy to farmers. Such a subsidy would encourage farmers to increase their output. This may result in the pay and job opportunities of farm workers increasing.

 ## Homework assignments

1. a. Indian banks became more cautious in their lending in 2008 because they became aware of the problems faced by US and UK banks resulting from them lending to high risk customers who were not able to repay them.
    b. Bank lending in India increased in 2008 but the rate at which it increased slowed in comparison to 2007.
    c. The functions of a central bank include to act as a banker to the government and to issue bank notes.
    d. Two factors that influence demand for loans are the rate of interest and the state of the economy. The lower the rate of interest, the more households and firms are likely to borrow. This is because they will have to pay back less.

    Households and firms are also likely to spend more when the economy is doing well. People may be more inclined to buy a more expensive home, a new car or take a foreign holiday when they expect their employment prospects to rise.

    e. As manager of a firm in India, or in another country, I would have a number of ways of financing new branches. These include borrowing from a bank, issuing new shares, obtaining a government grant and using retained profits. In considering these options, I would take into account their availability, their cost and the impact they may have on the business.

    I might decide that the firm should borrow from a bank if I believe that the rate of interest my firm will have to pay will be lower than the return it will gain from the investment. There are, however, disadvantages in this method of finance. It is likely that interest payments will have to be made on a regular basis. It may take some time to achieve a return from new branches and the firm's revenue may vary. In addition, should the firm experience a fall in profit, it may have difficulty making its repayments. This may mean that the bank may gain a stake in the firm. In addition, if the firm has a poor credit record or its prospects are uncertain, banks may not be willing to lend to it.

    Another option I would consider if I manage a limited company is to issue more shares. Such a measure would not cost the firm much and should the branches prove to be successful, more profit would be generated to pay additional dividends. There is a risk, however, that issuing more shares will drive down the share price as the supply of shares will be greater. This would not please existing shareholders. There would also be a risk that a rival firm could buy up the shares and use a larger shareholding to gain control of my firm.

I would investigate the possibility of obtaining a government grant. The government may be prepared to give my firm financial support to open branches in poorer areas or if my firm is in a new industry. If it does not matter where my branches are located and if a grant does not come with unreasonable conditions, I may take up the offer of a grant. It may, however, not provide all the finance I need.

The source of finance I am most likely to favour is retained profit. This is because I am more likely to want to expand the business when it is making a profit. Using retained profit will also mean that the firm does not have to make regular interest payments and I would be able to retain control over the firm. I would, however, consider whether the firm will earn more in profit from the expansion than it would receive in interest from placing the retained profits in a financial institution.

2. a. Public sector workers are people employed by the government.
   b. One of the arguments a union might advance in support of a wage claim is the need for workers' pay to rise in line with an increase in the cost of living. The passage mentions that the largest public union wanted a pay rise, in part, because of inflation. If the price level rises, workers need a pay rise just to be able to buy the same goods and services.

   Another basis for a wage claim is comparability with the pay of other workers. Workers often ask for a pay rise if workers carrying out similar jobs receive higher pay. If successful, such a claim would maintain their wage relative to similar workers. The passage mentions that workers in other industries had received a pay rise equivalent to the increase that the Verdi union was asking for.

   A third argument mentioned towards the end of the passage is that higher wages are needed to attract more workers to the industry. Evidence of unfilled job vacancies would strengthen this argument.
   c. Two other forms of industrial action a union could take are an overtime ban and working to rule.
   d. Arbitration involves a third party, often a government body, which seeks to get a union and an employer organisation to come to an agreement.
   e. There are many ways in which an employer could attract more workers. Probably the most obvious way is to offer higher pay if the firm has sufficient funds. It could do this by paying a higher wage rate, providing more generous bonuses and more opportunities to work overtime. This approach is likely to be successful if the total remuneration offered by the employer is higher than that offered by other rival employers.

   Among the non-wage ways it could seek to gain more workers is to improve working conditions, to shorten working hours, to increase the number of holidays given, to raise pensions, to increase fringe benefits such as free meals and to provide more job flexibility. All of these measures could cost a firm money but if they increase labour productivity and keep workers with the firm for longer, its unit labour costs might fall.

Providing more and better quality training may also raise labour costs, at least in the short run, but again should increase labour productivity and so reduce unit labour costs. The opportunity to take part in high quality training is likely to attract workers.

One possible way of attracting more workers which would reduce a firm's rent, heating and some other costs would be to allow workers to do at least some of their work from home. A number of people, including those with young children, may find home working attractive.

3. a. Borrowing means acquiring something with the obligation of returning it. In the case of borrowing money, as well as having to repay the sum borrowed, people usually also have to pay interest on the amount borrowed.

    b. One reason why a fall in unemployment may cause spending to rise is because incomes will increase. Those who had been unemployed will now be receiving income. Those who were already in employment, may enjoy higher incomes as there will be more competition for workers. As people get richer they may spend a smaller proportion of their income as they can now afford to save. Nevertheless, they usually spend more in total. For instance, when a person has a disposable income of US $ 90 a week she may spend a hundred per cent of her income i.e. US $ 90. When her income rises to US $ 400 she may spend only 75% of her income but this will be US $ 300.

    Another reason why a fall in unemployment may increase spending is that it is likely to increase confidence. People will feel a greater degree of job security and be more optimistic about their future earnings. The more confident people are about the future, the more they tend to spend.

    c. The passage mentions there was rising affluence in Poland. It then mentions that Poles were driving their cars more and using bus transport less. A normal good is one which has a positive relationship with income. As income rises, demand increases. This is the case with car travel. In contrast, an inferior good has a negative relationship with income. As income rises, demand decreases. The Poles were using bus travel less as their income rose.

    d. The wage rate of construction workers may rise if demand for houses increases. This would increase demand for construction workers' labour. Figure 7 shows that an increase in demand for construction workers' labour would increase the wage rate.

    The wage rate of construction workers may also increase if the supply of construction workers' labour decreases. If, for instance, the fringe benefits given to construction workers are reduced or their job security is reduced, fewer people may want to be construction workers.

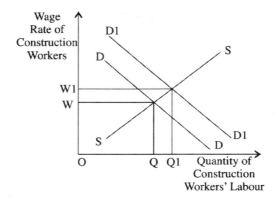

Fig. 7

Figure 8 shows that a decrease in the supply of construction workers' labour will increase the wage rate.

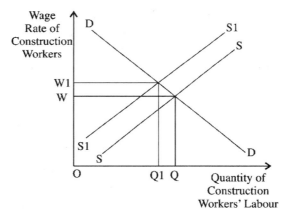

Fig. 8

e. A rise in the rate of interest is likely to reduce spending for several reasons. One is that it will encourage saving as people will earn a higher return by placing some of their disposable income in a financial institution.

A higher interest rate will also discourage borrowing as it will now be more expensive to borrow. People often borrow to buy new cars, houses and foreign holidays.

Another reason why spending may fall is that people who have borrowed in the past will have to pay back more on the loans and so will have less money to spend.

Of course, those who have net saving will gain extra income and may spend more but their extra spending will, in all probability, be more than offset by the fall in the spending of net borrowers.

SECTION-4

Definitions

1. f	2. e	3. g	4. j	5. p
6. t	7. b	8. o	9. a	10. q
11. c	12. d	13. h	14. s	15. r
16. l	17. k	18. i	19. n	20. m

Missing words

1. primary, secondary.
2. private, liability, shares.
3. public, private, privatisation.
4. primary, secondary, tertiary.
5. fixed, short.
6. total, fixed.
7. average, price.
8. profit, revenue.
9. market, entry, competitive.
10. barriers, supernormal/abnormal.
11. small, small size, market, finance.
12. average, economies.
13. risk bearing.
14. average or unit, discount.
15. growth/revenue.
16. fixed.
17. sole proprietor/trader.
18. production, supply.
19. capital, labour.
20. maker, average.

Calculations

1. The average product of labour is 2,210/85 = 26 units.
2. The fixed cost is US $ 400. The total variable cost of 2 units is US $ 900 – US $ 400 = US $ 500. The average variable cost is US $ 500/2 = US $ 250.
3. ATC = AFC + AVC i.e. US $ 10 + US $ 80 = US $ 90. ATC = TC/output. So US $ 90 = US $ 3,960/?, ? = US $ 3,960/US $ 90 = 44 units.

Interpreting diagrams

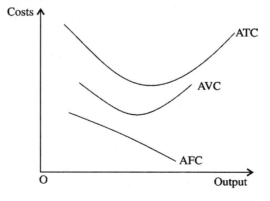

Fig. 1

Drawing diagrams

a.

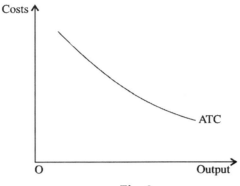

Fig. 2

Internal economies of scale are the benefits in the form of lower long run average costs resulting from an increase in output.

b.

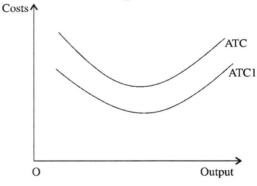

Fig. 3

External economies of scale are the benefits in the form of lower long run average costs arising from the growth of the industry. Whatever the firm's output, the average cost will be lower.

c.

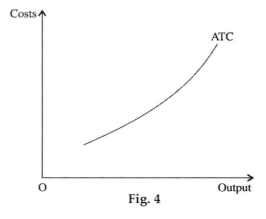

Fig. 4

Internal diseconomies of scale occur when long run average costs increase because the firm has grown too large.

d.
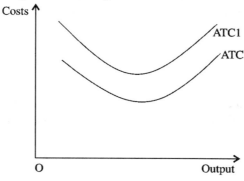

Fig. 5

External economies of scale are a rise in a firm's long run average cost resulting from the industry growing too large in size. Average total cost will rise at every level of the firm's output.

Multiple-choice questions

1. B

   House-building involves producing a good from raw materials and so it is in the secondary sector.

2. A

   A nationalised industry is run by the state and so is in the public sector. B, C and D are all in the private sector.

3. D

   A nationalised industry is most likely to suffer from diseconomies of scale as it is likely to be the largest business organisation. Sole traders, partnerships and private limited companies tend to be small business organisations.

4. B

   An ordinary partnership does not have shareholders. The other three do as multinational companies are usually public limited companies that produce in more than one country.

5. D

   AFC = ATC − AVC. In this case AFC is US $ 5 - US $ 3 = US $ 2. AFC = total fixed cost/output. So US $ 2 = US $ 4,000/?. Therefore ? = US $ 4,000/2 = 2,000.

6. A

   Fixed cost has to be paid even when the output is zero. In this case it is US $ 20. AFC is FC/output i.e. US $ 20/5 = US $ 4.

7. **D**

   A variable cost is a cost which varies with output. The higher the output produced, the more a firm will pay out in wages based on piece rates. This is because a piece rate system pays workers according to their output. A, B and C are all fixed costs in the short run.

8. **B**

   Fixed costs do not change with output in the short run. They do, however, alter in the long run as a firm changes all of its factors of production. For instance, rent will not change with output in the short run. This is because in this time period the number and size of the firm's offices or factories will not change. In the long run, the firm may have more and larger buildings.

9. **D**

   Privatising an industry involves selling a nationalised industry to the private sector. A government may do this to increase competitive pressure on the organisation to be efficient. A private sector firm will be likely to base its decisions on private, rather than social, costs and benefits. Selling a nationalised industry, also called a state owned enterprise, to the private sector will reduce and not increase state control. A nationalised industry will be a monopoly and so privatising it will increase rather than reduce competition.

10. **D**

    Profit is revenue minus cost, so revenue is cost plus profit. In this case, total revenue is US $ 600 + US $ 150 = US $ 750. Average revenue is total revenue divided by the quantity sold i.e. US $ 750/30 = US $ 25.

11. **B**

    The high barriers to entry into and exit from a monopoly market enable it to keep control of the industry. There is the highest degree of market concentration possible in a pure monopoly. This means that one firm sells 100% of all products sold. A monopoly has only one seller and there is unlikely to be perfect knowledge about market conditions. A, C and D are the characteristics of a perfectly competitive market.

12. **C**

    Research and development may improve the quality of products a monopoly produces and may lower the price charged. A and B would harm rather than benefit consumers. D would obviously benefit directors.

13. **B**

    The new firm will be larger and will have a greater market share. In the short term a takeover may reduce profit. As the firm is buying out another firm in the same industry it is not diversifying.

14. **D**

    A lower rate of interest will reduce the cost of borrowing to invest and high retained profit will provide it with the funds to invest.

15. C

    Recruiting more workers will increase a firm's total output. If they are less skilled, output per worker will fall. B and D would be likely to increase both production and productivity. Higher wages paid to the workers may improve their morale which may increase their productivity.

16. D

    Vertical integration forwards involves a move towards the market. A firm operating in the primary or secondary sector may buy out a retail chain to ensure that its products are sold.

17. A

    A conglomerate merger is a merger between two firms making different products. A local newspaper and a sweet manufacturer are not directly related businesses.

18. B

    An external economy of scale is a benefit available to the firms in an industry resulting from the industry growing in size. All the firms in the industry will be able to take advantage of their products. A, C and D are all examples of internal economies of scale.

19. D

    Small scale production is likely to be undertaken by a sole trader or a partnership. In such types of business organisations, decisions can be made quickly as there are few people to consult. A, B and C are more likely to be features of large scale production.

20. C

    Internal economies of scale result from the growth of a firm. A and B are connected with rising average costs whereas internal economies of scale lead to falling average costs. D may result in external economies or diseconomies of scale.

Similarities

1. Both are types of business organisations that do not have limited liability.
2. MNCs are often public limited companies.
3. Both are causes of an increase in investment.
4. In both cases, these are costs found by dividing a type of total cost by output.
5. Both are names for costs which do not change with output in the short run.
6. These are possible objectives of firms.
7. Both are barriers to entry.
8. Barriers to entry and exist are obstacles faced by new firms in non-competitive markets such as a monopoly.
9. Both are mergers between firms operating at different stages of production.
10. These are both types of internal economics of scale.

Differences

1. A firm is a business organisation such as a sole trader or a public limited company whilst an industry includes all the firms producing a given product.
2. Public limited companies are owned by shareholders whilst public corporations are owned by the state.
3. Fixed costs do not change with output in the short run whereas variable costs do.
4. The short run is the time period when at least one of the factors of production cannot be changed in terms of its quantity. This means there are both fixed and variable costs. In contrast, the long run is the time period when it is possible to change all the factors of production and so all costs are variable.
5. Revenue is the payment a firm receives for selling its products whereas profit is the difference between a firm's revenue and costs.
6. Both are examples of market structure but whereas perfect competition contains many sellers, a monopoly has only one seller.
7. Normal profit is just sufficient to keep a firm in the industry whereas supernormal profit is excess profit.
8. Internal growth involves a firm increasing the size of its market for its products or introducing new products. In contrast, external growth, which is quicker, involves a firm becoming larger by taking over or merging with another firm.
9. Vertical integration is the merger between firms at different stages of production whereas horizontal integration is a merger between firms at the same stage of production.
10. Internal economies of scale arise from the growth of a firm. In contrast, external economies of scale result from the growth of an industry.

 Data exercises

1. a. Profit is revenue minus cost. The more revenue exceeds cost, the greater the profit.
   b. Fuel is a variable cost for an airline. This is because the more flights an airline operates, the more fuel it will use.
   c. Ryanair could seek to attract workers by providing longer holidays and increasing the degree of job security. Workers like long, paid holidays. Increasing the length of contract given to workers will mean that they would have to be given a longer period of notice before they could be made redundant.
   d. (i) Price sensitive consumers mean people whose demand for products is elastic. If the airline were to raise its fares, demand for its tickets would fall by a greater percentage.

(ii) If all, or most, of its passengers are price sensitive, a cut in fares would increase demand by a greater percentage. In such circumstance, lower fares would increase revenue.

e. Profits can be increased by raising revenue and/or cutting costs. As well as cutting fares, if demand is elastic, there are a number of other ways, Ryanair could seek to raise revenue. One way would be for Ryanair to undertake an advertising campaign. If the campaign adds more to revenue than costs, it will increase Ryanair's profits. I would also recommend that Ryanair explores other routes. If there is sufficient demand for flights, for example from Dublin to Prague, and there are take off and landing slots available, it would be worthwhile for Ryanair starting a service.

Improving the quality of the service by, for instance, speeding up the check in process and ensuring luggage is not lost may attract more customers. Given sufficient demand on current flights, the firm could operate larger airplanes and might consider putting more seats on existing planes.

There are a variety of ways Ryanair could seek to cut its costs. It could try to reduce turn round times at airports, consider operating out of cheaper airports and either not serve any food on its flights or serve cheaper food.

Operating larger airplanes may enable the firm to experience economies of scale and cut its average costs. For instance, the takeover and landing slots would be spread over more passengers. Fewer cabin crew per passenger may be employed if, through training, the productivity of the cabin crew increases.

f. Ryanair could finance an expansion in its operations by using retained profits. If a firm is making high profits, it may want to expand to increase its profits further. Indeed, high profits provide both the incentive and means to expand.

An alternative to using internal finance, is to use external finance. Any type of firm could borrow and a public limited company could issue shares. Ryanair might decide to borrow from a commercial bank. As it is a well-known firm, it should find it relatively easy to obtain a loan. It will, however, have to pay interest on the loan.

g. Apart from profit maximisation, a firm such as Ryanair may decide to pursue growth. This will involve the firm increasing the scale of its operations, flying more passengers to and from destinations. This may enable a firm to take greater advantage of economies of scale and so reduce its long run average costs. For instance, it will buy fuel in bulk which may mean that it will receive a discount on the price it pays. Getting larger in size may also make it harder for other firms to takeover this firm and may result in an increase in the salary of managers and executives.

Growth, however, may come at the cost of profit. Getting larger may involve an initial rise in average cost if it involves taking over another firm or investing in new equipment. Average long run costs may also increase if the firm grows too large and as a result experiences diseconomies of scale. For instance, it can be hard to manage a large firm as there may be problems of co-ordination and communication.

2. a. The forms are sole trader, partnership, private limited company and public limited company.
    b. In the short run, the sale of state owned concerns will obviously increase government revenue. The effect in the long run is less certain. If the concerns are unprofitable, selling them to the private sector will improve the government's financial position. If, however, the concerns were unprofitable, selling them off may reduce government revenue over time.
    c. 'If market conditions are right' in this context means if the stock market is bullish. If share prices are rising, the government should be able to sell the shares at a relatively high price.
    d. Banks operate in the tertiary sector whilst shipbuilding operates in the secondary sector.
    e. It is difficult to determine whether the interest rate charged to borrowers by private sector banks would be lower than that charged by state owned banks. Private sector banks will seek to make a profit. They will be able to do this by charging borrowers more than they pay to customers who deposit money with them.

    A state owned bank may charge a lower rate of interest if it seeking to encourage the country's firms to expand. A lower rate of interest may make it profitable for firms to buy more capital goods. This would increase the country's economic growth rate and may raise employment.

    A state owned bank, however, may charge a higher rate of interest to discourage borrowing and spending if the country is experiencing inflation.

    In practice, however, banks tend to charge a relatively similar interest rate. This is because if one, for instance, charged a much higher rate of interest than other banks, no one would want to borrow from it.
    f. The key characteristic of a monopoly, that is a pure monopoly, is that there is only one firm in the industry. The firm will have control of the market. Another characteristic is that there will be high barriers to entry and exit. These will enable the firm to make supernormal profit in the long run as new firms will not be able to enter the market. A monopoly is also a price maker as a change in the quantity it supplies will influence price.
    g. Consumers may benefit more from perfect competition than monopoly. This is because they will have a wide range of producers to choose from and due to the high level of competition, price should be low and quality should be

high. In contrast, a monopolist may exploit its market power by charging a high price. It may also produce products of a low quality, knowing that consumers have no choice.

There is chance, however, that consumers may benefit more from monopoly than from perfect competition. A monopolist may use some of the profit it earns in improving the product, possibly also making it more difficult for new firms to enter the market. It may be able to earn a high profit and yet still be able to charge a lower price. This may be possible if economies of scale mean that its average costs are low. In addition, whilst consumers will not have a choice of producer, a monopolist may provide a range of products for consumers to choose from.

3. a. The percentage fall in Rentokil's profits from 2005 to 2007 was £70m/210m x 100 = 33.33%.

   b. The passage mentions that Rentokil has branches in more than forty nine countries. A multinational company produces in more than one country.

   c. One advantage of running a company with a 'diverse range' is that the firm is spreading its risks. Should one of the products cease to be profitable, it can switch resources to its other products. A possible disadvantage is that it is harder to maintain control and be an expert in a range of products.

   d. A fall in a company's share price will be unpopular with shareholders. This may result in them selling their shares which would further reduce the share price.

   It would also make it more difficult for the company to raise finance by selling new shares. If, for instance, it wanted to raise US $ 800,000 for expansion and the share price fell from US $ 5 to US $ 2 it would have to sell 400,000 shares rather than 160,000.

   In addition, a lower share price may make it easier for another company to buy out the company.

   e. The expansion of a company will not necessarily reduce its profits. Indeed, a company is likely to expand when it is doing well. If demand for the company's products is increasing, its revenue may be increasing by more than its costs. As a company grows it may be able to take advantage of economies of scale which will reduce its average costs. For instance, it may be given larger discounts when it buys in greater bulk and may be able to use machinery more efficiently. A larger firm is also more likely to be able to operate a research and development department which could raise the quality and reduce the cost of products produced.

   If, however, the company becomes too large it may experience diseconomies of scale. These are the disadvantages of being too large in the form of higher average costs. A larger company may be more difficult to control and industrial relations may not be very good. There is also the risk that a company may expand just as market conditions change. If demand for the company's products falls, its revenue will decline.

f. A firm may make a loss if either its revenue falls or its costs rise. A decrease in revenue will result from a fall in demand for the firm's products. This may be due to, for instance, a fall in consumers' income or a rise in the popularity of rival firms' products. A rise in costs may be caused by a rise in raw material costs or an increase in wages paid to workers which is not matched by a rise in productivity.

g. There are a number of reasons why a firm may benefit from producing in more than one country. Costs of production may be lower in other countries. For instance, raw materials may be in more abundant supply and wage costs may be lower. Corporation tax may also be lower in other countries and there may be fewer rules and regulations that the firm will have to comply with. In addition, there may be a strong and growing market for the firm's products in other countries. Producing within the countries will reduce transport costs and may get round import restrictions.

However, costs may not necessarily be lower in other countries. For instance, whilst wages may be lower in some other countries, average labour costs may be higher if labour productivity is lower. It may also be difficult and expensive to co-ordinate a number of overseas branches.

Nevertheless, the increase in the number of multinational companies and the increasing globalisation suggest that the benefits of operating in more than one country are significant.

Structured questions

1. a. A firm may become large either through internal or external growth. Internal growth involves a firm opening new factories, offices or, in the case of farms, purchasing more land.

   External growth occurs when a firm takes over or merges with another firm. Such growth is quicker but does not guarantee that the firm reaches its most efficient size.

   b. A variety of factors may attract a multinational company (MNC) to set up in a country. One is high demand for its products in the country. Producing in the country will enable the company to keep in closer contact with changes in consumer demand and will reduce transport costs. China's recent strong economic growth has been attracting multinational companies from throughout the world.

   Another key influence is labour costs. A MNC will be attracted to a country with low unit labour costs. These low labour costs may arise as a result of low wages or high productivity. Indeed, workers with good ICT (Information and Communications Technology) and language skills is one reason why a number of MNCs have recently set up in India.

The availability and low cost of raw materials may also attract a MNC to set up in the country. For instance, a number of MNCs from the UK and USA produce in Australia and South Africa because of their mineral deposits. Government policy can influence the location of MNCs in a number of ways. Government grants to MNCs can be a key factor in encouraging them to set up in a country. Low rates of corporation tax and a lack of government rules and regulations can also persuade a MNC to set up in a country. In recent years, a number of east European countries including Slovenia have reduced their corporate tax rates and simplified their tax systems.

c. An entrepreneur is someone who bears the uncertain risks of the business and organises the factors of production. These functions are split in the case of a public limited company. Shareholders bear the uncertain risks – should the company go out of business, they could lose their financial investment. The organisation of the factors of production is undertaken by the chief executive, directors and managers of the MNC.

d. A MNC may not maximise profits because it may be uncertain what the profit maximising output is. Profit is maximised when the gap between revenue and cost is greatest. This level of output can be hard to estimate.

A MNC may also be pursuing another objective, at least in the short term. For example, it may place most emphasis on growth, especially as the pay of those running the company may be more linked to the size of the MNC rather than its profitability. A larger firm is likely to have more market power, may be able to take greater advantage of economies of scale and is less vulnerable to a takeover. To grow larger may, however, in the short term reduce profit. Buying more equipment, hiring more workers or possibly buying out another company may add more to costs initially than to revenue.

A MNC may also seek to improve its image in terms of social responsibility and concern for the environment. It may decide not to buy raw materials from countries employing child labour or workers experiencing poor working conditions that endanger their health and may spend money cleaning up its production process. These measures will increase the company's costs and may lower its profitability in the short term. In the longer term, however, it may raise its profitability if they increase demand for its products.

The difficulty of deciding exactly what is the profit maximising output and the fact that a company may want to pursue a range of objectives, may mean that it will aim for satisfactory rather than maximum profits. A certain level of profit will be needed to pay out dividends that will keep shareholders happy. Achieving such a level may enable the company to pursue other objectives including improving the training of workers which would enable it to earn higher profits in the longer term.

2. a. Total cost is the full cost of producing a given output. It includes both fixed and variable costs. In contrast, average cost is total cost divided by output. It is sometimes known as average total cost.

    b. If an insurance company moves into a larger rented office it will be paying out more rent. This will increase its fixed cost. Rent is a fixed cost as it will not change with output in the short run. Replacing temporary staff with permanent staff will also increase fixed cost. In addition, it will lower variable cost. This is because permanent staff have to be given a period of notice. If output should fall, these staff will still have to be paid in the short run. In contrast, the number and pay of temporary staff will change with output.

    c. An insurance company's choice of resources to employ will be influenced by which resources are needed to provide insurance, the productivity of those resources and their cost. The insurance company will need to employ labour as workers will be required in face to face meetings with customers. Capital will be used in terms of the offices, computers and equipment.

    Entrepreneurs, in the form of shareholders and managers, will respectively bear the uncertain risks and organise the other factors of production. Over time, with advances in technology, insurance companies have tended to reduce the amount of labour they employ and increase the amount of capital. This is because the productivity of capital has increased whilst its cost has fallen.

    d. The growth of the insurance industry may reduce this insurance company's average cost if it leads to external economies of scale that it can take advantage of. As the insurance industry grows, a skilled labour force may build up. This may enable this company to hire trained workers from other insurance companies. If the insurance industry grows large enough, it may be worthwhile for colleges and universities to put on courses for the industry's staff. Sending its workers on such courses, perhaps on day release, may reduce its training costs.

    As an insurance industry grows in size, a specialist market may develop. In the UK much insurance, including maritime insurance, is traded in at Lloyds of London. London has also developed a good reputation for insurance. Firms may also set up to supply the insurance industry with the equipment and services it needs.

    If the insurance industry grows too large, however, this and other insurance companies' average cost may rise. The major diseconomy of scale likely to be experienced is increased competition for resources. For instance, the wages of the most talented insurance sellers may be pushed up as insurance companies compete with each other for their services. It is thought that diseconomies of scale are not that significant in the insurance industry and that it can grow very large without experiencing such disadvantages. This means that the growth of the industry is likely to reduce the company's average cost.

3. a. There are a number of reasons why so many firms exist in the car repair industry. People will not travel far to have their car repaired and in a given area demand for the service may be somewhat limited. The service is not a standardised one. A variety of cars with different problems are likely to be taken to a car repairer. This means that it would not be advantageous to be large. Indeed, a car repair firm would benefit from being flexible. Small firms can build up a relationship with their customers, getting to know their cars and their requirements.

   It is also relatively easy to set up a small car repair firm. Not much capital equipment is required and the premises may be small. The owner of a car repair firm may also want it to stay relatively small so that she/he can keep control of the firm.

   b. Many car manufacturing companies are large because they can take significant advantage of economies of scale. Technical economies of scale are important in the manufacturing industry. Large car companies use large scale equipment which mass produce cars. They are likely to experience research and development economies as they can operate research and development departments which develop new car designs and new features.

   They can also benefit from buying, selling, managerial and financial economies of scale. They can buy tyres, for instance, in bulk. As important customers, they are likely to be charged a discounted price. Transporting a high number of cars out to car dealers can be relatively cheap per car as the delivery vehicles can carry a number of vehicles.

   A large car manufacturer, employing a relatively large labour force, can take advantage of managerial economies of scale by allowing its labour force to specialise. Some of its workers can be accountants, some can be paint sprayers and some can be human resource managers.

   A large car manufacturer can reap financial economies of scale. Banks may be more willing to lend to a car company they have heard of and which has considerable collateral than a small, unknown car manufacturer. As a large company is likely to borrow a large amount of money, it may be charged a relatively low rate of interest. This is because the administrative costs of processing and managing a large loan per dollar lent are lower than those involved with a small loan. A large firm may also find it easier to sell its shares as again it is likely to be better known.

   c. There are both potential benefits and costs for a car manufacturer from both merging with another car manufacturer and with a company selling cars.

The merger with the car manufacturer might, in practice, prove to be more beneficial.

A merger with another car manufacturer may reduce average costs if the new, merged company can take greater advantage of economies of scale. A larger company should be able to make use of larger, more technologically advanced equipment and exploit division of labour to a greater extent. It will also have greater buying power, may be able to gain more loans on more favourable terms from banks and may face greater demand for its shares.

One reason why people may want to buy shares from a new, larger merged car manufacturer is because they may expect it will make more profit. This is because a horizontal merger, such as that between two car manufacturers, will increase the company's market share. Having more market power can enable a company to widen the gap between the cost per unit and the price it charges.

A horizontal merger can also reduce average costs as a result of rationalisation. The new company may be able to reduce costs by cutting out any unnecessary duplication.

There is a risk, however, that the merger between two car manufacturers may increase average costs. This may occur if the new company is too large and so experiences diseconomies of scale such as problems of managing the new company. These problems are more likely to arise if the two companies were located some distance apart, although advances in information and communications technology are reducing this problem.

There is initially likely to be some extra costs involved in seeking to harmonise, for instance, wage rates and accounting systems in the two companies.

Management problems may be more serious in the case of a vertical merger forwards, such as that between a car manufacturer and a car dealer. This is because of the different nature of the firms and the different skills required in running them. There may also be a problem if the size of the two companies does not match. For example, if the car manufacturing part does not produce enough cars for the car dealers, there will be a waste of resources in the car dealing part.

There would, nevertheless, be some advantages which could be gained from such a merger. One is that it will guarantee a market outlet for the cars. The car manufacturer will know that the cars it produces will get into car showrooms. It will be able to control how its cars are sold, seeking to ensure that they are well presented and that the sales staff are fully informed about the advantages. Having the direct link to the sale of the product should also mean that it will receive feedback from its customers. It could use this information in the design of new models. The merged company is also likely to use its control of car dealers to stop them selling rival companies' cars.

4. a. A reduction in the number of Chinese tourists visiting Indonesia may result in fewer people staying in Indonesia's hotels. This would reduce the total revenue received by the hotels. Catering for fewer guests would also lower their total costs. In the short run, it would be their variable costs which would fall. For example, the hotels would buy less food and may dismiss some temporary staff. For a period of time, they will not be able to lower their fixed costs such as rent and the pay of permanent staff. In the long run, however, the owners of the hotels may move to smaller premises or close their hotels.

    The impact on profits will depend on the relative change in revenue and costs. If revenue falls by more than costs, profits of Indonesian hotels will fall. As it is difficult to cut some costs, it is likely that revenue will fall by more than costs and so profits will fall.

    Of course, there is a chance that the reduction in tourism from Indonesia may be offset by a rise in tourists from elsewhere.

    b. Fewer Chinese people might have gone on holiday in Indonesia because the price of holidays there may have increased. The hotels may have charged more and/or the flights might have become more expensive.

    Real income per head might have fallen in China. Tourism is a normal good. As income falls, demand for tourism, especially foreign tourism, declines. People do not cut back on necessities but they do reduce demand for luxuries such as foreign holidays.

    A fall in the price of, or rise in the quality of a substitute, may also reduce demand for a product. Substitutes for holidays in Indonesia include holidays in other countries and holidays at home. One of the reasons why fewer Chinese people went abroad in 2008 was because they wanted to stay at home to visit or watch on television the Olympic games which were held in the country.

    It might have become more fashionable for the Chinese people to holiday in other countries. Closer contact between China and Europe in recent years, has seen more Chinese tourists visiting Europe.

    A successful advertising campaign by another country's tourism industry may have persuaded some Chinese people to decide to change their choice of holiday destination.

    Reports of bad weather, natural disasters and political unrest in a country may also dissuade some people from visiting it.

    c. Whether a decline in the Indonesian tourism industry will result in an increase in unemployment in Indonesia will depend on how many workers the tourism industry makes redundant, whether other Indonesian industries are expanding and how mobile workers are.

    The tourism industry is a labour-intensive one and so if it declines, there is a chance that a high number of workers may lose their jobs.

Of course, the number of workers affected in this adverse way will be influenced by how much the industry declines and whether it is thought that the decline is temporary or permanent. If it is only a small decline which is considered to be only temporary, employers may try to keep most of their staff.

If the tourism industry does reduce its demand for labour, unemployment may not rise if the workers no longer required by the tourism industry move into jobs in other industries. For them to do this, there must be job vacancies elsewhere. The workers must be able to take up the jobs. Their ability to do this will be influenced by their occupational and geographical mobility. The chances of unemployment will be greater if workers are occupationally immobile because of, a lack of skills and qualifications. Geographical immobility, because of, for instance, differences in the price and availability of housing and family ties, would also increase the risk of unemployment.

Homework assignments

1. a. A conglomerate merger is a merger between two companies that produce different types of products. The passage mentions that Tata had previously taken over both a steel maker and a tea producer. Both steel and tea are different from cars.

   b. Three types of economies of scale that Tata may gain from taking over Jaguar and Land Rover are buying economies, research and development economies and risk bearing economies. A larger car manufacturer will become an even more important customer of firms producing windscreens. This means that they are likely to be able to strike a good deal on how much they have to pay.

   A larger car manufacturer will also be able to support a larger, better equipped and better staffed research and development department. This may result in it developing more and better quality cars.

   In addition, by taking over two companies producing different models, Tata will be spreading its risks. The more models it makes, the less it will be affected by any one model becoming less popular.

   c. The passage suggests that whilst the UK based branches are expected to generate more revenue, the positive gap between revenue and cost is greater in India than in the UK. This is because it implies that the India based branches are more profitable.

   d. A multinational company (MNC) should locate in a country if it believes that producing there will be profitable. The profitability or otherwise of an overseas branch will be influenced by a number of factors. If demand for the product is high and growing in the country and there is limited competition, the revenue might be expected to be high.

There may be a number of reasons why average cost of production may be low in a country. A MNC may find out information on the standard of education in the country. If it is good it may expect that the productivity of workers will be high and so unit labour costs may be low. Unit labour costs may also be low if wage rates in the country are low. The MNC should research raw materials costs and the cost of buying or renting premises.

The MNC should also consider how the policies of the government of the country may affect its profit. A low corporation tax would mean that the MNC would be able to keep a relatively high proportion of its profit. Government grants to set up in depressed areas and subsidies to train workers may increase potential profit. In contrast, a high level of rules and regulations may mean that costs of operating in the country are relatively high.

2. a. Ocado is a smaller and more specialised firm than Tesco. Being smaller may mean that it can make decisions more quickly and have closer contact with its customers. Both of these factors should mean that it can respond more quickly to changes in market conditions.

   Being more specialised on just home delivery means that it can gain expertise and can build up a reputation for reliability. The expertise should lower average cost and the improved reputation should increase average revenue.

   b. Ocado's price for the basket of goods shown was £0.98 higher than Tesco's (£10.77 - £9.79). So overall it was not achieving its objective of matching Tesco's prices or undercutting them. It was only selling one product cheaper – the cleaning fluid. It was charging the same price for tinned beans but a higher price for three goods, wholemeal loaf, biscuits and batteries.

   c. A firm could finance the expansion of its business by borrowing from a bank or by using retained profit. It may borrow from a bank if it believes that the profit it will earn from the expansion will be greater than the interest it will have to pay on the loan. It may also use profit that it has earned on previous sales if it thinks that it will receive a higher return from ploughing back profit rather than by placing the profit in a financial institution.

   d. Ocado could seek to attract more workers by advertising, speeding up its delivery times, delivering free, stocking a greater variety of products, introducing loyalty cards and even running competitions.

   Advertising will make its service better known and may encourage more people to use the service. Delivering orders more quickly than its rivals may persuade more people to switch from using delivery services from supermarkets and a speedier service may encourage more to obtain their products this way rather than by visiting a supermarket.

   Most supermarkets charge for delivery, so if Ocado can deliver free, they may gain more of the market. The greater volume of products they sell may mean that the difference between their revenue and costs grows even without charging for the delivery.

Stocking a greater variety of products may mean that customers can get all the products they want from Ocado and this may encourage them to use it.

Introducing loyalty cards and running competitions may not only encourage more customers to use the company but also to use it on a more regular basis. Loyalty cards reward customers for staying with the firm and competitions can require customers to buy on a regular basis.

3. a. A co-operative is owned by individuals, called members, whereas a public corporation is owned by the state.

   b. Two factors that would increase the chances of a strike being successful are the workers having public support and their organisation having sufficient funds. If the public think workers are underpaid or have poor working conditions and so are justified in going on strike, this may put pressure on employers to settle in the workers' favour. Private sector employers may be reluctant to alienate the public as it may affect their sales. The state, as an employer, may also be worried about losing popularity.

   Having adequate funds would enable a labour organisation to pursue a strike over a long period of time. This would enable it to severely disrupt production. An employer, worried about permanently losing customers may be more likely to agree to the organisation's demands.

   c. A co-operative does not seek to make high profits, just a reasonable return for its members. This, combined, with large scale production and bulk buying should mean that it can sell food cheaply. Giving buyers the power to influence the decisions of the business, including what food it produces and what food products it buys to sell, would be likely to keep the quality high.

   d. The benefits of diversification include spreading risks, enabling a firm to explore new areas and to provide its staff with variety. A firm producing a range of products will not be very vulnerable to a fall in demand for one of those products. Moving into new areas of production may enable a firm to discover new strengths. It will also enable staff to gain experience in a number of different areas which may make their job more interesting.

   e. Introducing an ethical policy, for instance only buying raw materials from suppliers who provide good working conditions for their staff, may increase costs in the short run. If this is the case, profits are likely to fall. They may not, of course, if the good working conditions raise productivity and so cut unit labour costs.

   The same may also be true of providing better living conditions for livestock. Whilst this may raise costs of production, it may not if it means that fewer animals are lost through ill health.

Even if costs are raised, profits may increase in the long run. This is because revenue may increase by more than costs if the ethical policy proves to be popular with consumers.

SECTION-5

Definitions

1. p	2. t	3. s	4. h	5. i
6. l	7. b	8. d	9. e	10. m
11. r	12. k	13. c	14. q	15. o
16. j	17. n	18. a	19. f	20. g

Missing words

1. monopoly, private
2. low, inflation
3. potential, production possibility
4. aggregate, consumption, exports, imports
5. rich, poor, taxes
6. deficit, tax
7. fiscal, aggregate, taxes, government spending/expenditure
8. elastic
9. shortage, below
10. tax
11. customs duties
12. multiplier
13. increase, decrease/reduce
14. progressive, percentage
15. automatic stabilisers
16. monetary, reflationary/expansionary, fiscal
17. base, burden
18. inflation
19. right, actual, potential
20. increase, subsidise

Calculations

1. The unemployment rate is the number unemployed divided by the labour force. In this case, this is 2m/12.5m x 100 = 16%.
2. US $ 8bn (40% of US $ 20bn).
3. The total tax which will be deducted will be US $ 7,000. (US $ 5,000 x 0% = 0, + US $ 5,000 x 20% = US $ 1,000, + US $ 20,000 x 30% = US $ 6,000 = US $ 7,000).

Interpreting diagrams

a. Unemployment of resources.
b. Economic growth.

Drawing diagrams

1. a.

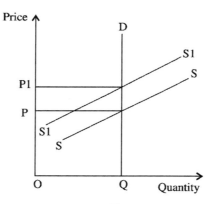

Fig. 1

b. As demand is perfectly inelastic, the whole of the tax can be passed on the consumer without reducing the quantity sold. The consumer bears all of the tax.

2. a.

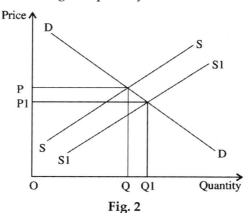

Fig. 2

b. The more elastic supply is, the more of the subsidy will go the consumer and the less to the producer. With elastic supply, firms will be able to produce significantly more which will drive the price down and benefit consumers.

Multiple-choice questions

1. B

   Public goods have to be financed by the state as the private sector has no financial incentive to produce these products. This is because people can enjoy such goods without paying for them. The government would only finance unprofitable goods if it believes they are beneficial or would be under provided if left to market forces. It would not want to finance goods that have higher social costs than private costs as these will be generating negative externalities. Luxury items will be produced by the private sector if there is sufficient demand. If there is not sufficient demand, the government will not feel obliged to finance them.

2. A

   Increasing employment will raise incomes, output and bring other benefits. B may be a microeconomic policy objective. Whilst a government may seek to reduce inflation, it is unlikely to try to lower the price level. A government is also more likely to want to increase rather than reduce economic growth.

3. B

   An increase in savings will be accompanied by a fall in consumption, given an unchanged level of income. A will directly increase aggregate demand. C may increase aggregate demand if it is the result of the government cutting taxes. D will increase net exports and so contribute to aggregate demand.

4. B

   A subsidy will shift the supply curve to the right which in turn will cause price to fall and demand to extend.

5. B

   Fiscal policy covers government decisions on taxation and government spending. Cutting the rate of taxation will increase disposable income which, in turn, is likely to increase consumption and so aggregate demand. Increasing the budget surplus (the positive gap between tax revenue and government spending) is a fiscal policy measure but one which will reduce aggregate demand. A and D are monetary policy measures.

6. A

   A limit on bank lending will influence the money supply and may act to reduce aggregate demand. B is a monetary policy measure but one which will be likely to increase aggregate demand. C and D are fiscal policy measures.

7. D

A government's budget position is concerned with government spending and taxation. For instance, if government spending exceeds tax revenue, a government is said to have a budget deficit.

8. C

Supply-side policy measures are always designed to increase the maximum potential output a country can produce and so increase the country's AS curve and PPC.

9. D

Fiscal policy is concerned with government decisions on taxation and government spending. A and B are examples of monetary policy and C is a direct control measure.

10. B

A cut in taxation would be expected to increase aggregate demand. Higher total spending should reduce cyclical unemployment as such unemployment is caused by a lack of aggregate demand. A, C and D would all be likely to benefit from a rise rather than a cut in taxation.

11. D

A decision on government spending can be classified as fiscal policy. If it is designed to increase AS, it may also be classified as a supply-side measure. C is a fiscal policy measure but one which would be more likely to reduce rather than increase AS – and so would not be classified as a supply-side measure. A and B are monetary policy measures.

12. A

A budget surplus would mean a government is receiving more in tax revenue than it is spending. In the other cases, it is not possible to determine the relationship between government spending and taxation without more information.

13. B

A maximum price is the highest price that can be charged as laid down in law. For instance, a landlord may wish to charge US $ 50 a week for renting a room. If a law is then passed stating that no more than US $ 70 a week can be charged, the landlord would not have to change the amount he is charging.

14. A

The incidence of taxation is concerned with who bears the cost of a tax.

15. D

A regressive tax falls more heavily on the poor. This is because it takes up a higher percentage of their income than of the income of the rich.

The poor are likely to pay less as tax in total but nevertheless a higher percentage with such a tax. For instance, a tax which takes US $ 2 from a poor person spending US $ 10 and US $ 4 from a rich person spending US $ 40 is regressive. In this case, the poor person is paying 20% in tax whilst the rich person is paying 10%.

16. C

Income tax is a progressive tax. It takes not only more in total in tax from the rich than the poor but also a higher percentage. Such a tax is likely to reduce income inequality. A and D are likely to be regressive taxes. In the case of B, the impact of the tax will depend on what type of product the import duties are imposed.

17. D

A progressive tax may act as a disincentive to work as some people may be reluctant to take promotion or work long hours, knowing that a higher percentage of their income will be taken in tax, the more they earn.

18. A

A good tax is one that is easy to pay and collect. B, C and D are some of the characteristics an item needs to possess to act as money.

19. B

Most sales taxes are regressive, falling more heavily on the poor. Therefore, their removal should reduce the gap between the rich and the poor. The removal would increase rather than reduce aggregate demand. It would reduce the tax base as there would be fewer sources of tax revenue. Disposable income is income minus direct taxes rather than indirect taxes.

20. C

Labour productivity is output per worker hour. If each worker can produce more, the maximum potential output of the economy will increase.

Similarities

1. Both may be produced or financed by a government.
2. They are both macroeconomic aims.
3. Both seek to influence aggregate demand.
4. They are both microeconomic policies.
5. Both are direct taxes.
6. In both cases, price will change by more than quantity.
7. These are two qualities of a good tax.
8. Both measures would be expected to increase aggregate demand.
9. They are both supply-side policy measures.
10. Both are designed to reduce spending.

Differences

1. Employment involves the use of resources, whereas unemployment means that resources are not being used.
2. Aggregate demand is the total spending on an economy's products. In contrast, aggregate supply is the total output of an economy.
3. The budget position is a comparison between government spending and tax revenue whereas the balance of payments is a record of a country's economic transactions with other countries.
4. Macroeconomic policies are designed to influence the whole economy. An example would be fiscal policy which may be used to alter total employment in the country. In contrast, microeconomic policies are intended to influence particular industries and products.
5. Actual economic growth is how much an economy's output is increasing by whereas potential economic growth is how much it is capable of growing by.
6. With progressive taxes, the tax rate increases as income rises and so these types of taxes take a higher percentage of the income of the rich. Regressive taxes, however, fall more heavily on the poor as with these taxes, the tax rate falls as income rises.
7. Fiscal policy covers government decisions on government spending and taxation whereas monetary policy covers government and central bank decisions on the rate of interest, the money supply and the exchange rate.
8. Subsidies are government payments to producers and sometimes consumers. In contrast, taxes are government charges on producers, workers and savers.
9. Income tax, as its name suggests, is a tax on income whereas inheritance tax is a tax on wealth.
10. Direct taxes are a tax on income or wealth whereas indirect taxes are taxes on spending. Another difference is that the burden of a direct tax cannot be shifted on to anyone else. In contrast, the burden of an indirect tax, or some of the burden, can be shifted from the seller to the consumer.

 Data exercises

1. a. Increased travel time, pollution, road rage.
   b. A congestion charge is, in effect, a tax. This will increase the cost of driving which should reduce the number of journeys motorists undertake. With less traffic on the roads, the remaining drivers should not be delayed as much and so should reach the destinations more quickly.

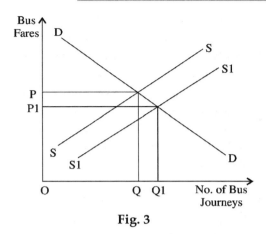

Fig. 3

c. A subsidy is a payment given this time to bus companies to encourage them to increase their services and so carry more passengers. The subsidy will increase the supply of bus travel. The supply curve will shift to the right, causing price to fall and demand to extend as shown in Figure 3.

d. Education and health care.

e. The congestion charge and the green tax may reduce the output of cars in Italy and may change the type of cars demanded in France.

Having to pay more to enter the city of Milan by car whilst public transport is made cheaper, may persuade some people to switch from using cars to using public transport. If people buy fewer cars, car production may fall in Italy. The extent of the fall, and indeed whether it occurs at all, will depend on a number of factors. One is the size of the charge and how much the price of public transport falls by. Another is the price elasticity of demand for both forms of transport. If demand is inelastic for both forms, there may not be much effect on demand for car travel and hence on demand for cars. The charge is also only affecting one city and so may not have much of an impact. In addition, people driving in Milan may be buying their cars, or at least some of their cars, from other countries and so the impact may be more on car production in other parts of the world.

The green taxes in France are being combined with a subsidy given to the buyers of small cars. This is likely to encourage people to switch demand from cars that use a large amount of fuel to smaller, more fuel efficient, cars. Of course, again, it will depend on the size of the taxes and subsidies and the price elasticities of demand for the two types of car. In addition, the impact may be on car production not only in France but also in other countries as the French purchase their cars from a variety of countries.

f. A congestion charge may not apply at night because the volume of traffic is likely to be much lower at that time. With fewer vehicles on the road, there is likely to be less of a problem in terms of the external costs that car travel may cause. In such a situation there may not be overconsumption of car travel and the social costs of car travel may equal the social benefit of car travel.

g. Two measures which could reduce traffic congestion are increased charges for car parking and the introduction of bus lanes. Car parking is, in effect, a complement to car travel. If it is more expensive to park a car, some people may be discouraged from driving into city centres where traffic congestion may be high. One possible disadvantage of this measure is that it will be regressive as both rich car drivers and car drivers with less income will pay the same amount.

The introduction of bus lanes may encourage some car drivers to switch to using buses and so reduce traffic congestion. Bus lanes should cut down bus journey times and increase the reliability and punctuality of buses. Building bus lanes in some city centres, however, may be difficult and expensive if it is necessary to buy and demolish buildings in order to construct the bus lanes.

2. a. Two supply-side policy measures are improving education and privatisation.
    b. The Accelerated and Shared Growth Initiative involves spending on public sector projects. Such spending increases aggregate demand. With more demand for goods and services, firms are likely to take on more workers. Unemployment will fall if the growth in the number of jobs exceeds any increase in the number of people in the labour force.
    c. Raising the economic growth rate means increasing the rate by which a country's output increases. For example, a country's economic growth rate may increase from 2% to 5%.
    d. The aim of the Accelerated and Shared Growth Initiative (ASGI) is to reduce unemployment. After it was introduced in 2007, unemployment fell from 28% to 26%. In 2008 it did, however, remain constant at 26%. It is, of course, difficult to determine whether the fall was the result of the ASGI and whether the failure of unemployment to fall further reflects a failure of the ASGI. This is because a range of other factors influence unemployment. For example, a rise in incomes abroad might have increased demand for South African products. More exports would be likely to increase output and so raise demand for workers.
    e. Supply-side policy measures may raise a country's output and reduce unemployment. Education and training, by raising workers' skills and mobility, may make employers more willing to employ them. Cutting direct taxes and state benefits will provide a greater incentive for people to take up the jobs on offer. This is because the gap between earned income and benefits will have widened. Reforming trade unions may increase employment if unions had been pushing the wage rate above the equilibrium level and imposing restrictive practices. Privatisation and deregulation may also raise

employment if they result in firms producing more efficiently and attracting more customers.

How successful supply-side policy measures are in reducing unemployment will, however, depend on the cause of unemployment and how well designed the policy measures are. If the cause of unemployment is a lack of aggregate demand, supply-side policy measures will not necessarily work. If there are no job vacancies, improving the quality of labour and increasing the incentives to work will not work. Indeed, cutting unemployment benefit in such circumstances may increase cyclical unemployment. This is because the unemployed will have less money to spend. If reform of trade unions involves reducing their power when trade unions are doing a good job by counterbalancing the power of employers, providing training and acting as a channel for communication, they may again increase unemployment. There is no guarantee that privatisation and deregulation will increase output and employment. Selling firms to the private sector and removing rules and regulations may not reduce unemployment if such measures increase rather than reduce inefficiency.

    f. Two government aims, other than full employment and economic growth, are price stability and a balance of payments equilibrium. Price stability involves keeping inflation at a low and stable level. A number of governments now set a target for inflation and charge their central banks with ensuring the target is met.

A balance of payments equilibrium is often interpreted as a balance on the current account of the balance of payments. This involves export revenue, income and current transfers coming into the country equalling import expenditure, income and current transfers leaving the country.

    g. It would be expected that a reduction in unemployment would cause economic growth. If it involves more people being in employment, firms should be able to produce more goods and services and demand for that extra output should increase.

Unemployment, however, can fall without employment rising and in this case, economic growth may occur. Unemployment may decline as a result of the unemployed retiring, emigrating, entering education or giving up seeking employment. If unemployed adults enter education, output may not rise in the short run but may increase in the long run. Net emigration may result in a fall in potential output especially if some of the unemployed who leave are skilled workers.

3.   a. The passage mentions that most of Brazil's tax revenue comes from sales tax. Such a tax is an indirect tax as it is a tax on expenditure.

    b. One way in which taxes place a burden on Brazilian firms is through the administration, time and effort their workers have to spend filling out tax forms. Indeed, the passage mentions that the average firm in the country spends 2,600 hours to process the tax. A second way is that the high level of taxation discourages investment. A higher rate of corporation tax, in particular, would reduce both the ability and willingness of firms to invest.

c. Regulations, such as a restriction on the amount of pollution a firm can emit and the ages till which children have to attend school, have the advantage that they have the force of law behind them. This may ensure that they are followed. A disadvantage, however, is that a cost is likely to be involved in ensuring that the regulations are being followed.

d. Three reasons why a Brazilian may prefer to work for the government rather than a private sector firm are better pay, a more favourable pension and better working conditions.

e. As a Brazilian government minister, I would consider a number of factors before deciding whether the government should cut taxes. These include the state of the government's finances, the state of the Brazilian economy, how firms and households will react to the change in taxation and other countries' tax rates.

If the government has a budget surplus, it would reduce tax rates or remove some taxes and still raise enough in tax revenue to cover its spending. I might be reluctant to recommend a cut in taxes if the government has a large budget deficit. In this case, a cut in taxes would increase the size of the budget deficit and may put pressure on the government to cut its spending on, for instance, education and health care. In the longer term, however, a cut in taxes may lead to a balanced budget or even a budget surplus if it stimulates an increase in economic activity. For instance, a cut in income tax will lower revenue from this source in the short term. In the longer term, even with people paying less in tax per US $ earned, if more people are working and earning higher wages, more will be received in income tax revenue.

Indeed, I would be likely to recommend a cut in taxes if the economy is experiencing high unemployment and slow economic growth or a recession. This is because a cut in income tax, for instance, would increase disposable income and so would be expected to raise consumption and so increase aggregate demand. Higher spending in such circumstances would raise the country's output as shown in Figure 4 and could be expected to increase employment.

The passage mentions that the tax burden is high and is discouraging investment. I would do a survey of entrepreneurs. If I find that the tax rates are discouraging firms from spending on capital goods, I would cut corporation tax. Such a cut would be expected to raise investment which, in turn, would be expected to increase both aggregate demand and aggregate supply as shown in Figure 5.

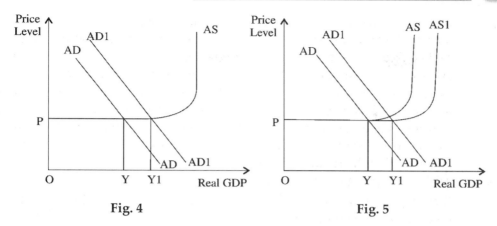

Fig. 4   Fig. 5

I would also recommend a cut in income tax if I believed it would provide an incentive for workers to work more hours and more people to enter the labour force. There is, however, a risk that if people are satisfied with their current level of disposable income, they may work fewer hours if tax rates are cut.

In addition, I would recommend a cut in Brazilian taxes if the tax rates are above other countries and the difference is discouraging foreign direct investment, tourism and the sales of domestic products. A number of countries have recently been cutting their tax rates and simplifying their tax systems to encourage multinational companies to set up in their countries.

Lower indirect taxes may attract more tourists, particularly those on shopping trips and may encourage the country's consumers to buy more domestic products rather than imports.

f. A government may impose a national minimum wage in order to reduce poverty. One reason why people are poor is because they receive low wages. Low paid workers may have little power in negotiating with their employers. They may not be members of trade unions and are likely to be unskilled workers. An employer may be able to pay low wages knowing that if the current workers are not happy, they can be replaced by other unskilled workers. In this situation, the imposition of a national minimum wage may be needed to drive up the pay of those whose labour is in high supply and as a result have weak bargaining power.

g. A budget deficit arises when government spending is higher than tax revenue. In the short run, an increase in government spending on education will increase a budget deficit as the gap between government spending and tax revenue will rise. In the long run, however, it may reduce a deficit. This is because a more educated labour force should be more skilled and productive. This should increase real GDP and reduce unemployment. As a result tax revenue should increase. People will be earning more and spending more and so both direct and indirect tax revenue should increase. With lower unemployment, government spending on unemployment should fall.

Structured questions

1. a. Income tax is a tax on the income people earn. It is a direct tax. The tax has to be paid by the people on whom it is levied. In contrast, a sales tax is a tax on spending. It is an indirect tax. The people selling products on which a sales tax is levied are legally responsible for paying the tax. They can, however, shift some all of the burden on to consumers.

   b. The qualities of a good tax are equity, certainty, convenience, economy, flexibility and efficiency. A good tax should be seen as fair with those most able to pay or those benefiting the most from government spending, paying the most in tax. For instance, in many countries the rich pay the most in income tax and university graduates sometimes pay a tax based on how much they earn after their studies have been completed.

   Certainty means that it should be clear how much people and firms will have to pay in tax. A convenient tax is one which is easy to pay and an economical one is one which collects noticeably more revenue than it costs to administer.

   Flexibility is useful because the level of economic activity changes and government aims alter. It can take time to change income tax rates, for instance, but at least the revenue earned from income tax adjusts automatically to offset economic booms and downturns. During a period of rapid economic growth, income tax revenue will rise which will help to slow down the growth of aggregate demand.

   A good tax should also aim to improve the efficiency of markets or, at least, have a neutral effect on markets.

   c. A progressive tax is one which increases in both absolute and percentage amounts as income rises. For example, it may take 10% of the income of someone earning US $ 10,000 or less but 20% of the income of someone earning US $ 30,000. Such a tax falls more heavily on the rich.

   In contrast, a regressive tax places a greater burden on the poor. This is because, this time, the tax rate falls as income rises. For example, whilst someone earning US $ 10,000 may pay 30% in tax, someone earning US $ 20,000 may only pay 15% in tax.

   d. Relying less on direct taxes and more on indirect taxes may increase incentives for people to work and firms to invest. Lower income tax may persuade existing workers to work longer hours and accept promotion and encourage some homemakers and retired people to seek work. There is a risk, however, that with higher disposable income per hour, some workers may choose to work fewer hours.

Lowering corporation tax may increase firms' spending on capital goods as they will be able to keep more of any profits earned. Investment may also be stimulated by lower income tax as firms are likely to expect spending to rise.

Reducing taxes on the income earned on savings may be seen as being fairer as such income is effectively taxed twice. Taxes on income may also be difficult to collect if there is a large informal sector and if levels of literacy are low. Indirect taxes are more difficult to evade and can be cheaper and quicker to change.

There are, however, possible disadvantages of shifting the tax burden from direct to indirect taxes. One is the regressive nature of indirect taxes which means that the burden of taxation is likely to fall more heavily on those least able to pay.

A high sales tax may discourage consumption and tourism and high tariffs may lead to retaliation with other countries raising their tariffs.

2. a. A minimum price is a lower limit to a price. For example, sellers may be instructed that they cannot charge less than US $ 3 or employers may not be permitted to pay workers less than US $ 4 an hour. In contrast, a maximum price is an upper limit with sellers being told they cannot charge more than, for instance, US $ 6.

   b. A government may impose price controls if it believes that the market equilibrium price will not result in the best possible outcome. It may set a maximum price if it believes that market forces will push the price too high for the poor to afford the product. The motives behind a minimum price will be different. The three key ones are to encourage production, to raise the income of producers and, in the case of a minimum wage, to raise the income of low paid workers.

   c. The government produces products for three main reasons. One is that a product would not be produced by the private sector. This is the case with public goods, such as defence, which the private sector has no incentive to produce as it cannot exclude non-payers from consuming the products. Another could be that a product, for example education, would be under-produced by the private sector as it would be under-consumed. Merit goods are under-consumed as people fail to appreciate the benefits for themselves and for other people. A third reason could be that a product is considered to be essential, such as health care, and may not be available to the poor if it is sold at the market price.

   d. In assessing whether an industry should be privatised or not, I would consider whether the industry would perform better in the private sector, how much money would be raised and whether the government needs the money.

If an industry is not working well in the public sector, perhaps because of too much red tape and lack of competition, it may increase economic growth and employment by selling it to the private sector. Subjecting the industry to market forces may make it more responsive to changes in consumer demand and more determined to keep its costs low. This may be particularly the case if the industry is broken down into several firms, thereby generating competition.

Another reason why I might recommend privatisation is if a large amount of revenue could be raised from the sale and the government is in need of the money. A government may, for instance, want to spend more on education and health care but may be reluctant to raise taxation. In such a situation, privatisation may be a possible option especially if the industry has been making losses.

If, however, the industry is making a regular profit for the government and is expected to do so in the future, I might not recommend privatisation. As well as considering the relative profitability of the industry in both the private and public sector and whether the government needs to raise a large amount of money, I would also consider what type of products the industry is making. If it produces a public good, a good of strategic importance or a merit good, I might suggest that the industry should stay in the public sector. A public good has to be financed by the government and to ensure that this money is used efficiently, the state may wish to maintain control. A government may also wish to control an industry that is vital for the economy and one that would under-produce or charge too high a price.

3. a. Full employment does not mean zero unemployment but the lowest level of unemployment possible. This may be, for instance, 3%. Even in periods of very high aggregate demand, some people will be unemployed as they will be in between jobs.

   b. Investment is spending on capital goods. These goods include machinery, other equipment and buildings. If investment increases, unemployment is likely to fall. This is because firms are likely to take on more workers to work with the extra capital goods to produce more products.

   There is a chance, however, that labour may be a substitute to rather than a complement to capital. New machinery, incorporating advanced technology, may reduce the need for labour. In this case, unemployment will rise.

   c. Two other government macroeconomic objectives are price stability and economic growth. Price stability is usually taken to be a low and stable rate of inflation. Most governments would be content with an inflation rate of around 2%. They do not aim for zero inflation as measures of inflation tend to overstate the rate at which the price level is rising.

Governments also want steady and sustainable economic growth. Economic growth occurs when a country's output increases. Governments want to avoid fluctuations in output, with economic booms and downturns, and want to ensure that the growth is achieved in a way that does not endanger future governments' ability to grow.

d. The unemployment of any factors of production can be serious but the unemployment of labour is probably the most serious. The unemployment of any factor of production involves an opportunity cost in the form of forgone output. When all resources are not used, a country will be producing less than its potential output and so its inhabitants will not be enjoying as high a standard of living as possible.

Not using some parts of land for a period of time may, in fact, be beneficial. It may give time for agricultural land to regain its fertility and for fishing stocks to build up. If capital equipment is not used, it may deteriorate and become obsolete.

Entrepreneurs who are made redundant tend to find work again relatively quickly. This is because they are usually resourceful and both occupationally and geographically mobile. Some may set up new businesses and others may move to take up jobs in other types of business or in other countries.

Unemployed workers can lose touch with developments in training and technology. They can also lose the work habit. The longer people are out of work, the harder they usually find it to gain another job. The reason why the unemployment of workers may be considered to be more serious than the unemployment of other resources is the human cost involved. The unemployed experience a fall in income and may experience a number of other problems including a deterioration in their physical and mental health.

4. a. Corporation tax is a tax on firms' profits. Firms would want a reduction in corporation tax as it would enable them to keep more of the profits they earn. This, in turn, will enable them to pay out higher dividends to shareholders and/or to buy more capital goods.

b. Firms might benefit from an increase in government spending on education and infrastructure in a variety of ways. One is that some of the extra spending may go directly to private sector firms. The government may order, for instance, books from some of the country's publishers and computers from some of the country's producers. In the majority of countries, most government spending on infrastructure goes to domestic producers. For example, governments often hire private sector firms to build roads.

Improved infrastructure reduces firms' transport costs. Lower costs of production can increase firms' profits. They also increase firms' price competitiveness. Capturing more demand away from rival foreign firms can enable them to expand.

If the increased government spending on education results in a more educated labour force, firms will be able to employ more productive workers. These more productive workers are likely to be able to work with more advanced technology and produce more, and higher quality output. The rise in productivity is likely to lower costs of production and enable the firms to lower their prices. Lower prices and higher quality products should enable firms to sell more products.

A more educated labour force may also reduce firms' training costs and make their training more effective.

c. A government may impose rules on private sector firms in terms of what they produce, how they produce it, how they sell it and in terms of their dealings with the workers they employ. A government may stop firms producing products that are regarded as harmful such as non-prescription drugs. It is likely to impose some limits on how much pollution firms are allowed to emit, and health and safety standards on the production of, for instance, food. Firms may not be permitted to sell certain products to children and shops may have to close on certain days. A government may make it illegal for firms to get together to fix prices and may not allow firms to merge if it will give them too much market power.

There may be a range of rules relating to the employment of labour. A government may make it illegal for firms to discriminate against minority groups when employing workers, may set a limit on the number of hours a week people can work and may set a minimum wage.

A central bank may influence the private sector by changing the rate of interest. A rise in the rate of interest, for instance, is likely to harm private sector firms. Those private sector firms that have taken loans will experience an increase in their costs.

A higher interest rate may make it more difficult for public limited companies to sell their shares. This is because those people planning to make a financial investment might now be more inclined to place their money in a bank account rather than to buy shares.

An increase in the rate of interest is also likely to reduce demand for firms' products. This is because it will encourage households to save more and take out fewer loans. Firms selling highly priced products, such as houses and cars that people often buy, will be particularly hard hit.

In addition, a rise in the interest rate may raise the exchange rate as it is likely to attract hot money flows. A higher exchange rate will raise export prices and lower import prices. This will have an adverse effect on firms that export a significant proportion of their output and on firms that compete with imported products. Of course, those firms which use imported raw materials may gain.

Homework assignments

1. a. The information suggests plastic bags are over-produced. This is because the disposal of plastic bags imposes costs on society which are not always taken into account in the price, which in some countries is still a zero price. If consumption and production were based on the full costs, output would be lower.

   b. External costs are costs imposed on those not directly involved in the production or consumption of a product. In this case, two external costs are litter and the death of wildlife.

   c. One advantage of a ban is that it is easy to understand. Shops would know, for instance, that they are not allowed to give out plastic bags.

   A ban, however, has to be enforced. Government resources would have to be used to check that plastic bags are not being given out.

   d. An increase in the production of fabric bags will reduce the agricultural land, machinery and workers available to grow crops and rear animals for food. This will decrease the supply of food which, in turn, will raise the price of food and result in a contraction in the demand for food. This is illustrated in Figure 6.

   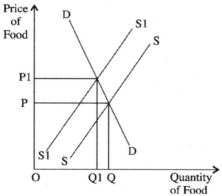

   Fg. 6

   e. Charging for plastic bags may raise shops' profits. It will bring in more money if people buy the same amount in the shops and purchase some bags.

   If, however, people resent paying for plastic bags, they may bring their bags with them when they visit shops. This may leave the shops' profits unchanged.

   There is also the possibility that the measure may reduce shops' profits. Some people may reduce the quantity of products they buy in order to economise on the number of bags they have to buy. Shopping and bags are complements.

In practice, though, the price of plastic bags is likely to be relatively low and so the impact on profits is likely to be minimal.

2. a. The two government macroeconomic aims referred to in the passage are economic growth and low inflation (price stability).

    b. The Argentinian government was intervening in the country's agricultural market to raise tax revenue. The Cambodian government was seeking to ensure adequate food supplies in the country.

    c. A tax on soya, which is an important Argentinian export may adversely affect its balance of payments. By raising the price of soya in foreign markets, the tax will reduce exportre venue if demand is elastic. A fall in export revenue may result in a current account deficit.

    d. The last paragraph indicates that demand for rice was, or would soon be, exceeding the supply of rice. Figure 7 the demand for rice outstripping the supply of rice.

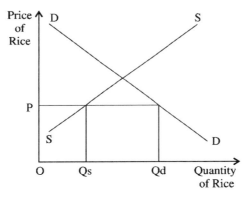

Fig. 7

There is a shortage of rice of Qd – Qs amount. Such a shortage would be likely to push up the price of rice.

    e. A government should not subsidise food production if there is a surplus of food and/or if farmers are making large profits. A subsidy is a government payment designed to encourage production or consumption of a product. If there is a surplus of food, the government would not want to encourage further production. If farmers are making large profits, it would suggest that they do not need government assistance.

    If, however, farmers are facing financial difficulties or there is a lack of agricultural output in the country, a government may want to subsidise food production. Agriculture is seen as a strategic industry as governments want to ensure that there is a sufficient amount of food produced in the country so that they are not too reliant on foreign food supplies which could be cut off in the event of a war or natural disaster.

A government may also want to subsidise food to lower the price of food and so enable the poor to purchase an adequate amount. Figure 8 shows a subsidy shifting the supply curve to the right, price falling from P to P1 and demand extending from Q to Q1.

There is a risk, however, in subsidising food production. The extra payment may reduce the pressure on farmers to be efficient. They may become too reliant on the subsidy, pay less attention to changes in consumer demand and be less concerned about the quality of their output.

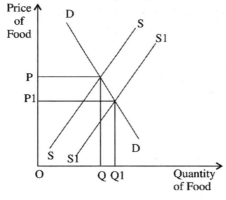

Fig. 8

3. a. The objectives of a petrol tax do conflict. One is to raise revenue and this objective would benefit from people buying a large quantity of petrol. The second motive is to discourage the consumption of petrol. This objective would obviously be helped by people buying less petrol.

b. Diesel-powered cars and petrol-powered cars are substitutes. A rise in the price of petrol-powered cars would be likely to increase demand for diesel-powered cars.

c. A tradeable permit is a licence issued by a government organisation which permits a firm to pollute up to a set level. If the firm does not need to use up all of its allowance, it can sell part to another firm.

d. The price of diesel may fall in the future if oil companies increase their investment in oil production. Such a move would increase supply as shown in Figure 9 and cause the price of diesel to fall from P to P1.

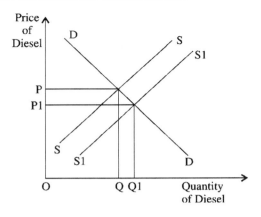

Fig. 9

e. Price elasticity of demand influences how the burden of an indirect tax is shared out between consumers and producers. If demand is elastic, most of the tax will be borne by the producers. Figure 10 shows that the price rises from P to P1 which is a relatively small proportion of the tax per unit (P1Z).

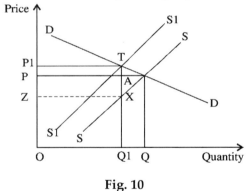

Fig. 10

The reason why producers bear most of the tax in this case is because they know that if they sought to pass on most of the tax to the consumer, there would be a significant fall in demand and revenue. In contrast, if demand is inelastic, producers can pass most of the tax on to the consumers. Figure 11 shows the consumers bearing most of the tax, PP1TA out of the total tax burden of ZP1TX.

When demand is inelastic, producers know that they can raise price without having much impact on demand.

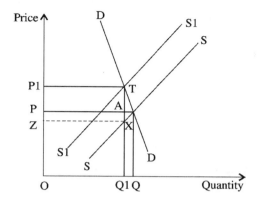

Fig. 11

SECTION-6

Definitions

1. b	2. i	3. e	4. j	5. t
6. g	7. f	8. s	9. p	10. q
11. a	12. h	13. d	14. k	15. c
16. r	17. l	18. n	19. m	20. o

Missing words

1. base, weights
2. inflation, capacity/employment
3. borrowers, weak, strong
4. shoe-leather
5. temporal, locational
6. rise/increase, reduction/fall/decrease
7. benefits, labour force
8. cyclical, frictional/structural, structural/frictional
9. higher, longer
10. deficit, fall/decrease, umemployment benefits
11. constant, inflation
12. increase/rise, decrease/reduction
13. increase, sustainable
14. living standards, unevenly
15. demand-pull, cost-push
16. government/state, private

17. long, technology, methods
18. reduce/decrease, increase/raise
19. life expectancy/span, schooling
20. sustainable, welfare, expectancy

 ## Calculations

1. The rate of inflation is 3/150 x 100 = 2%.
2.

Category	Weight		Price change		Weighted price change
Food	½	x	5%	=	2.5%
Clothing	¼	x	10%	=	2.5%
Leisure goods	¼	x	16%	=	4.0%
					9.0%

The change in the price level is 9%.

3. The unemployment rate is: unemployed/labour force x 100. The labour force consists of both the unemployed and the employed. In this case, the labour force is 3m + 21m = 24m and the unemployment rate is 3m/24m x 100 = 12.5%.

 ## Interpreting diagrams

a. AD is aggregate demand which is the total demand for the country's products at a given price level. Aggregate supply is the total output of a country's producers at a given price level. Real GDP is a measure of the country's output which has been adjusted for inflation.
b. Two possible causes of a shift in the AD curve are an increase in business optimism and a cut in income tax. An increase in business optimism would be likely to result in firms undertaking more investment. A cut in income tax would raise people's disposable income and so would probably result in an increase in consumption.
c. Figure 1 shows an economy operating at less than full capacity but relatively close to full capacity. In such a circumstance, an increase in AD would be likely to raise employment as output would increase. It would also be likely to result in inflation as the economy would be experiencing shortages of labour, raw materials and capital equipment. Figure 2 shows both real GDP and the price level increasing.

Answer Key

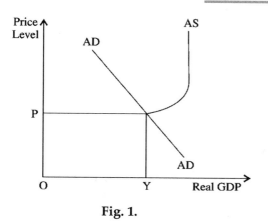

Fig. 1.

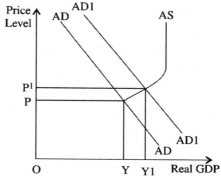

Fig. 2

Drawing diagrams

a. An increase in unemployment will move a country's output further away from its maximum possible output. Figure 3 shows the production point moving from A to B which results in a fall in output of both capital goods and consumer goods.

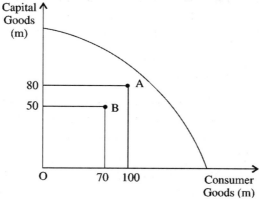

Fig. 3

b.

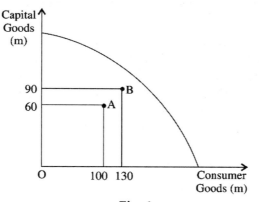

Fig. 4

Actual economic growth occurs when a country's output increases. Figure 4 shows the output of both capital and consumer goods increasing as the production point moves to the right from A to B.

c.

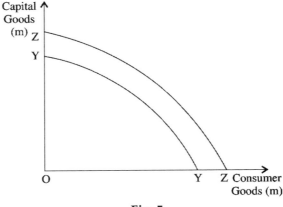

Fig. 5

Potential economic growth occurs when the productive capacity of an economy increases. Figure 5 shows the output potential of the economy increasing from YY to ZZ.

Multiple-choice questions

1. B

   A consumer prices index measures the price change of a sample of products that people spend most on.

2. A

   Money loses its value with inflation. Each US $ will buy less. Property, land and shares are likely to lose less of their value with inflation and may even gain value.

3. C

   When there is a low level of spare capacity in the economy, an increase in AD will be likely to push up the price level as firms will be competing for scarce resources.

4. D

   Cost-push inflation is caused by an increase in the costs of production. A, B and C may cause demand-pull inflation.

5. C

   A rise in the budget deficit would mean that the gap between government spending and taxation is increasing. It could be the result of a rise in government spending and/or a fall in taxation. In either case, aggregate demand would increase. B and D would reduce aggregate demand and A would increase costs of production.

6. **B**

   If other countries' price levels rise at a more rapid rate, this country's products will become more internationally price competitive. A, C and D would all reduce the country's price competitiveness.

7. **C**

   People are said to be economically active if they are in the labour force, that is working or seeking to work. A, B and D are economically inactive.

8. **C**

   Frictional unemployment occurs when people are in between jobs sometimes because of a lack of information about job vacancies. A is a cause of cyclical unemployment and B and D are a cause of structural unemployment.

9. **A**

   If people are ashamed to admit they are unemployed, they will not register as unemployed and this will mean the official figures will give a lower than accurate figure for unemployment. B, C and D would all give an artificially high figure for unemployment.

10. **B**

    As noted before frictional unemployment arises when people have left one job but have not yet taken up another job. A occurs because of a lack of aggregate demand and C and D because of changes in the structure of the economy.

11. **D**

    If consumers switch from buying domestic products to buying imports, demand for home produced products will fall. This is likely to result in a loss of jobs. A, B and C will increase AD and so are likely to reduce unemployment.

12. **A**

    If there are more people in work, AD will rise and there will be greater competition for workers which may bid up their wages. Both factors may push up the price level. The first effect may result in demand-pull inflation and the second effect, cost-push inflation.

13. **A**

    Structural unemployment is caused by the decline of particular industries and occupations. Increased government spending on training should make labour more occupationally mobile. This should make it easier for them to transfer from one occupation or industry to another.

14. **C**

    The payments which are included in the measurement of GDP are those made in return for producing a good or service and which are declared to the authorities. A would not be recorded and B and D are transfer payments.

15. C

    An economy may be able to produce a higher output with higher unemployment, if the existing labour force produces more per head. If occupational mobility increases, better use can be made of those in employment.

16. D

    Economic growth brings about change. Such change may result in some industries declining whilst others are expanding. Those workers who lack the skills to switch to a new industry may become unemployed.

17. B

    There are three ways of measuring GDP. These are the expenditure, income and output methods.

18. B

    A lack of skilled workers may prevent an economy from being able to produce more goods and services. A may slow down but will not prevent economic growth and C and D are likely to stimulate economic growth.

19. D

    Real GDP per head has been adjusted for inflation and takes into account population. GDP and GDP per head may be high but if inflation is also high, people may not be enjoying many goods and services – just more expensive products. Real GDP may also be high but if there is also a higher population, living standards may be low. If real GDP per head is high, it suggests that, on average, people are able to enjoy a high living standard.

20. B

    Higher national output may result in a decrease in living standards if it is accompanied by an increase in pollution, congestion or other negative externalities. A and D would increase living standards. C would increase GDP per head and so would be expected to increase living standards.

Similarities

1. Both are weighted price indices.
2. Each is a harmful effect of inflation.
3. These are two measures of unemployment.
4. Both groups are likely to benefit from inflation.
5. These are two forms of frictional unemployment.
6. Both are costs of unemployment.
7. These are two of the three ways of measuring GDP.
8. Both will lead to potential economic growth.

9. These are both transfer payments.
10. These are different terms for money GDP, that is GDP unadjusted for inflation.

Differences

1. Cost-push inflation is a sustained rise in the general price level caused by an increase in the costs of production. Monetary inflation is also a sustained rise in the general price level but this time caused by an excessive growth of the money supply.
2. The organised sector covers people working in the part of the labour market where they have employment protection, access to social security benefits and may be members of unions or professional organisations. The unorganised sector, in contrast, covers workers who are not in organisations and do not have employment protection and access to social security benefits.
3. Private sector employment covers those working for privately owned firms whereas public sector employment covers those working for the government.
4. The labour force participation rate is the proportion of people of working age who are either in employment or seeking employment. The employment rate only includes those who are of working age and are in employment. In other words, it does not include the unemployed.
5. Structural unemployment affects part of the economy whereas cyclical unemployment affects the whole economy. Structural unemployment is caused by a decline in particular industries and occupations whereas cyclical unemployment arises due to a lack of aggregate demand.
6. The employed work for someone else whereas the self-employed work for themselves.
7. Both are measures of living standards. The HDI takes into consideration GDP per head, life expectancy and education whereas the Index of Sustainable Economic Welfare considers personal consumption, income distribution, social and environmental costs, net capital investment, the value of housework and volunteer work and government spending on the infrastructure.
8. Cost of living is a measure of the price of products purchased by the average consumer whereas the standard of living reflects the products enjoyed by people.
9. Economic growth is an increase in a country's output over a period of time whereas a recession is a fall in a country's output over a period of six months or more.
10. The velocity of circulation is the number of times a stock of money changes hands to finance a level of expenditure in a given time period. In contrast, the circular flow of income is the circulation of expenditures and incomes throughout an economy.

Data exercises

1. a. Stockpiles are stocks of unsold products, in this case stocks of food.

   b. A rise in the rate of inflation means that the price level is increasing at a more rapid rate. For instance, in one year it may increase by 5% and then the next year it may increase by 8%.

   c. A multinational supermarket may set up in a foreign country if it believes there will be a high demand for its products in that country. In the UAE demand is high and growing because of the booming economy and rising population. A multinational supermarket may also seek to expand abroad if there are limits on the market share it can gain in its home country.

   d. A limit on food prices in the context of rising food prices is likely to be set below the equilibrium price. Figure 6 shows that this will result in a shortage with demand Qd exceeding supply Qs.

   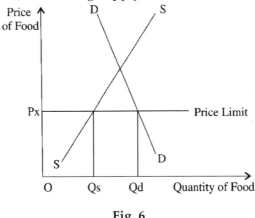

   Fig. 6

   e. An increase in government spending will not always cause inflation. It will depend on the initial level of economic activity and what the government is spending money on.

   Government spending (G) is a component of aggregate demand(AD) and so a rise in G will increase AD. Higher AD will not cause inflation if the economy was initially producing with considerable spare capacity. Figure 7 shows that an increase in aggregate demand from AD to AD1 increases real GDP but has no impact on the price level. A government may increase its spending specifically to raise the level of output in such a circumstance. In contrast, if the economy was initially producing close to full capacity, an increase in AD is likely to result in inflation. Such an outcome is shown by the shift in the AD curve to the right from AD1 to AD2.

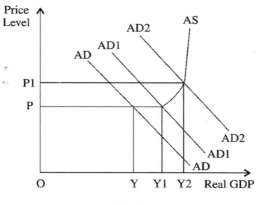

Fig. 7

Even if the economy is operating at or close to full capacity, an increase in AD may not cause inflation in the long run if the government spending also results in an increase in AS. For example, if the government increases its spending on training, labour productivity and potential output should increase. This outcome is shown in Figure 8.

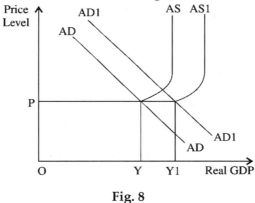

Fig. 8

f. A 'booming' economy is one which is growing very rapidly. Consumer expenditure will be increasing and unemployment will be falling. There may be demand-pull inflation as aggregate demand is likely to be increasing at a more rapid rate than aggregate supply.

g. Whether inflation is more harmful than deflation will depend on its rate and its cause. Hyperinflation will be more harmful than a low rate of deflation. If the price level is rising by more than 50%, the country's products are likely to be becoming less internationally competitive, purchasing power will be falling if wages do not rise in line with the price level and menu and shoe leather costs will be high. There is also the risk that if inflation is very high and accelerating, people may stop using the country's currency as money.

If inflation is caused by increasing aggregate demand whilst deflation is caused by decreasing aggregate demand, inflation may be less harmful than deflation. Demand-pull inflation may be accompanied by rising output and employment. In contrast, a sustained fall in the price level caused by a decrease in aggregate demand is likely to be accompanied by decreasing output and rising unemployment.

High rates of inflation and deflation can both cause uncertainty and may result in households and firms making inefficient choices. This is why governments aim for price stability.

2. a. A reduction in a budget deficit means that the gap between government spending and revenue is being reduced. A high proportion of government spending will be financed by taxation.

   b. VAT is an indirect tax. It is a tax on spending.

   c. A cut in government spending will reduce aggregate demand. This is because government spending (G) is a component of AD which comprises $C + I + G + (X - M)$.

   d. (i) $AD = C + I + G + (X - M)$. So $72\% + ? + 12\% + (49\% - 51\%) = 82\% + ? = 18\%$.

      (ii) The Philippines had a trade deficit in 2008 as the value of its imports exceeded the value of its exports.

   e. Monetary policy may be more effective in increasing economic growth in the short run if there is spare capacity in the economy but supply-side policy measures are likely to be more effective in the longer run.

   A cut in the rate of interest would be likely to raise both consumption and investment. Households may spend more as saving would be less rewarding and borrowing would be cheaper. Firms would find it cheaper to borrow and would expect higher sales. An increase in AD, if there are unemployed resources in the economy, will raise real GDP and so cause economic growth. This is shown in Figure 9.

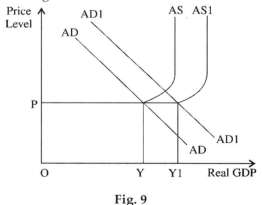

Fig. 9

Once full capacity is reached, however, an increase in AD resulting from an expansionary monetary policy will be ineffective in generating economic demand.

Some supply-side policy measures may take some time to have an effect but, if successful, they cause potential economic growth and so should enable real GDP to increase over time. For instance, extra government spending on education may in ten years time increase productive potential as a result of increasing labour productivity. If increases in AD can keep pace with increases in AS, the economy can experience both actual and potential economic growth, as shown in Figure 10.

f. Among the factors that influence consumption are disposable income and the rate of interest. People with higher disposable income tend to spend more than those with lower disposable income although they often spend a smaller proportion of their income. If the rate of interest increases, people are likely to spend less. This is because saving will become more rewarding, borrowing to buy items such as cars and houses will become more expensive and anyone who has borrowed in the past will have less money to spend.

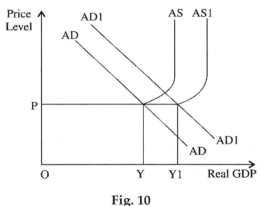

Fig. 10

g. Whether an increase in consumption will benefit an economy will depend on whether the higher spending goes on foreign or domestic products and on the initial state of the economy. If the spending goes on imports, it is other countries which will benefit from the higher demand. If the higher spending is devoted to domestically produced products and the economy has spare capacity, the economy will benefit. Output and employment will rise. If, however, the economy is operating at or close to full capacity, higher consumer expenditure will cause demand-pull inflation. Of course, if the higher consumer expenditure stimulates higher investment, in the longer run both aggregate demand and aggregate supply may increase, causing the economy to benefit from economic growth.

3. a. The three components of AD referred to in the passage are consumption, investment and government spending.

b. A decline in economic growth means that the country is continuing to produce more but the increase in output is less than the year before. For instance, real GDP may have increased by 5% in 2008 but only by 2% in 2009.

c. One economic consequence of unemployment would be forgone output. If the unemployed were in work, the country's inhabitants would be able to enjoy more goods and services. The higher the number of people unemployed, the more serious the opportunity cost would be.

Another economic consequence of unemployment is lost tax revenue. The more people are in work, the more direct and indirect tax revenue the government would receive as income and expenditure would be higher.

d. If economic growth rates and unemployment rates are inversely related, it would be expected that the countries with the highest growth rates would have the lowest unemployment rates and those with the lowest growth rates would have the highest unemployment rates. The information in the tables does not generally support this view. The countries with the five highest rates of economic growth all have relatively high rates of unemployment. Indeed, they have the first, third, fourth and fifth highest rates. The country which provides most support for the stated view is Spain. Out of the countries shown Spain has the lowest economic growth rate and the second highest unemployment rate.

It does, however, have to be remembered that data on only seven countries and for only one year is shown. If information on more countries was examined and the impact of changes in economic growth rates and unemployment rates over time were examined, more support for the argument might be found.

e. To assess whether cutting tax rates would increase the economic growth rate, I would examine a range of information. This would include what type of tax rates are cut, the state of the economy, government spending, how much the rates are cut by and people's expectations.

A cut in corporation tax would be likely to increase the willingness and ability of firms to invest. Higher investment would increase both aggregate demand and aggregate supply and so would lead to both actual and potential economic growth. A reduction in income tax may also lead to higher aggregate demand and higher aggregate supply as it will increase people's disposable income and the incentive to enter the labour force. A cut in indirect taxes may increase consumption and so result in higher aggregate demand.

If the economy has spare capacity, an increase in aggregate demand, resulting from lower indirect tax, would increase real GDP and so cause actual economic growth. If, however, the economy is operating at full capacity, an increase in AD will result in inflation but will have no effect on output and so economic growth will not occur. A cut in direct tax, however, might be expected to increase economic growth as it would raise both spending and potential output.

A cut in any type of tax, however, may have no effect on economic growth if it is accompanied by a fall in government spending. Lower government spending on, for instance, education would reduce both AD and AS and may offset the effects of a cut in taxation. A small cut in taxation would obviously have less effect than a large cut. A cut in taxation may also not have much effect on AD, AS and so economic growth. If consumers and firms are pessimistic about the future, they may not spend more and may not invest more, despite lower taxation.

f. A recession involves a fall in real GDP over a period of six months or more. Falling output will be likely to cause a rise in unemployment. Firms producing less will make some of their staff redundant. A recession is also likely to be accompanied by a fall in the price level. If output declines, incomes will fall. This will reduce aggregate demand and put downward pressure on the price level.

g. House-building and economic growth are usually directly related. An increase in house-building will add directly to output. It will also increase consumer expenditure as when people buy a new house they usually buy new carpets, curtains and furniture. Higher consumption will be likely to increase output further.

Economic growth, in turn, is likely to encourage an increase in house-building. Higher output will lead to higher incomes. Demand for new houses tends to increase as incomes rise. Some people will buy a first house and others will move from a less expensive older house to a more expensive new house.

Changes in house-building often indicate what is happening to confidence in an economy. When households and firms are pessimistic about future economic growth, house-building usually declines.

Structured questions

1. a. Unemployment arises when either there is a lack of job vacancies or when people are unable to fill the vacancies. A lack of job vacancies may arise due to an economic downturn. People may not be able to take up any job vacancies on offer because they lack the skills available, and so are occupationally immobile, or because they lack geographical mobility. They may also lack information about the job vacancies.

    b. The main disadvantage of unemployment to an economy is lost output. When people are out of work, they are not producing. The economy will be producing inside its production possibility curve as shown in Figure 11.

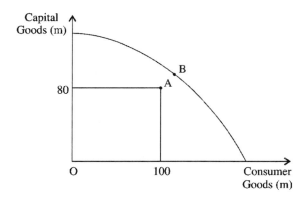

Fig. 11

Output and living standards would be higher if the economy moved towards, for instance, production point B. With lower than potential output, tax revenue will be lower than possible. People and firms will be earning and spending less than if more people were in work. With more tax revenue, the government could spend more on education, health care, reducing poverty and on other areas.

As well as lowering tax revenue, unemployment places a burden on government spending. Governments of many countries pay out unemployment benefits, such as housing benefits, claimed by the unemployed. This involves an opportunity cost – the money could have been spent on, for instance, education.

Unemployment can also give rise to a range of social problems. These include increased crime, mental and physical health problems and family breakdowns. These in turn can place a burden on government spending and lower living standards.

c. Two ways a government could increase spending by households is by cutting income tax and by raising the wages it pays to public sector workers. Cutting income tax will raise households' disposable income. This will increase their ability to buy goods and services. The more income tax is cut, the more disposable income will rise.

Raising public sector pay will also increase the ability of some people to spend more. Of course, the more public sector workers there are and the more pay is raised, the greater the impact on spending.

d. An increase in spending will usually be expected to increase employment. Higher demand should encourage firms to take on more workers and so increase employment.

There are, however, a number of reasons why higher spending may not increase employment. The first is that the higher spending may not be expected to last. If this is the case, firms will not take on extra workers.

They will cope with what they expect to be a temporary higher demand by asking workers to work overtime.

A second reason is that firms may be able to increase their output by making greater use of machinery or by replacing existing machinery by more technologically advanced equipment.

Firms may also want to take on more workers to produce more products but if the economy is operating at full employment, they may not be able to do so. Even if there is unemployment, firms may have difficulty taking on more workers, if the unemployed are occupationally and geographically immobile.

In addition, whilst higher spending may increase the number of people employed, it may not increase the employment rate. If the size of the labour force grows at a more rapid rate than the numbers employed, the employment rate will fall.

2. a. A consumer prices index is a measure of changes in the price of a representative sample of consumer products. It is a weighted price index. This means that more is attached to changes in the price of products that people spend most on. For instance, if people spend US $ 20 out of a total weekly spend of US $ 100 on a particular category of products, that category will be given a weighting of 1/5.

b. The costs of inflation are influenced by its rate, whether it was anticipated or not and how it compares with the inflation rate in other countries.

If a country's inflation rate is higher than that of rival countries, its products will become less internationally competitive. Its firms will sell fewer exports whilst its inhabitants will buy more imports. This will harm the current account of the balance of payments. If the country's current account position was originally in balance, it will move into a deficit.

An unstable inflation rate will make it difficult for firms and households to plan. Firms' staff will have to spend time and effort estimating future costs and prices. The uncertainty created by the instability may discourage investment. It can also make it difficult for both firms and households to judge whether a product is expensive or not. This may result in people and firms paying more for products and raw materials than necessary.

If inflation is unanticipated, it can result in a random redistribution of income with certain groups losing and certain groups gaining. The losers are likely to include savers and workers with weak bargaining power. This is because the rate of interest and the wages of workers with weak bargaining power do not tend to rise in line with inflation. In contrast, borrowers and workers with strong bargaining power tend to gain. Taxpayers may also lose and the government gain, if higher money wages take people's income into higher tax brackets.

A high rate of inflation, whether anticipated or not, will create menu and shoe leather costs. Menu costs refer to the costs involved in changing prices in catalogues, on products and indeed on menus, as a result of inflation. The quicker and greater the extent to which prices rise, the more frequently firms will have to change prices. Shoe leather costs will also be greater. These are the costs involved in moving money around in search of the highest interest rates. When inflation is higher, firms cannot afford to leave money lying idle.

One cost that is always experienced with inflation is a fall in the value of money. With rising prices, each US $ will buy less. During periods of hyperinflation, this fall in the value of money may be so great that money may stop being acceptable as a method of payment.

c. In deciding how to reduce inflation, a government would first consider the cause of the inflation. If its demand-pull inflation, it will seek to reduce the growth of aggregate demand. It may do this by raising income tax. This will reduce people's disposable income and so their ability to buy goods and services. The government, or the country's central bank, may also raise the rate of interest to slow down the rise in the price level. A higher interest rate may reduce consumption as it will be more rewarding to save and it will be more expensive to borrow. It may also reduce investment as it will be more expensive for firms to borrow, may encourage firms to save their retained profits and may reduce their expectations of future consumer demand. Figure 12 shows that keeping the growth of aggregate demand to AD1 will cause a smaller rise in the price level than allowing it to increase to AD2.

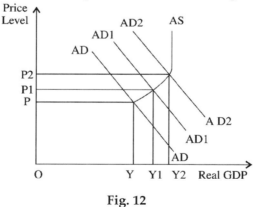

Fig. 12

If it is thought that inflation is caused by cost-push factors, a government may consider reducing corporation tax and any regulations which push up firms' costs. It may also introduce supply-side policies. For instance, if a privatisation programme may reduce inflation if firms work more efficiently in the private sector. A training programme may also lower inflationary pressure if it raises labour productivity and so cuts unit labour costs. Indeed, successful supply-side policies can reduce inflationary pressure over time by allowing AD to rise without encountering a supply constraint.

3. a. Economic growth is measured by the percentage change in real GDP. For instance, real GDP was US $ 20bn last year and is US $ 21bn this year, the economic growth rate is 5%.

   b. A more rapid rate of economic growth may result in balance of payment problems for two main reasons. One is that firms seeing rapidly rising demand in the home market, may switch products from foreign markets to the home market. Such a switch would reduce exports.

   With rising incomes, the country's population, as well as buying more domestically produced products may also buy more imports.

   A fall in export revenue and a rise in import expenditure would increase a current account deficit or may turn a surplus into a deficit.

   c. The traditional way of measuring living standards is by measuring real GDP per head. A high real GDP per head would indicate that people, on average, are able to enjoy a relatively high number of goods and services. Of course, there are a number of shortcomings with this measure. Real GDP per head may be high but if income is very unevenly distributed, pollution is high and working hours are long, for example, most people may not be enjoying high living standards.

   Another measure of living standards, which takes into account more influences, is the Human Development Index. As well as considering GDP (GNI) per head, this measure also takes into account health and education. Health standards are measured in terms of life expectancy at birth and education in terms of mean years of schooling and expected years of schooling. Mean years of schooling are the average number of years of education received by people aged 25 and older. Expected years of schooling are the number of years of schooling a child of school entrance age can expect to receive. This measure is thought to give a truer picture of living standards but it does not include everything, for instance, it does not include pollution and working conditions, both of which affect people's lives.

   d. Economic growth is usually, but not always, considered to be desirable. Economic growth has the potential to raise the living standards of the population, increase employment, raise tax revenue, reduce poverty and improve health care and education.

   An increase in a country's output makes more products available for its inhabitants. Over time, economic growth has changed the quality of people's lives in many countries. It has provided them with more and better quality products.

   Economic growth, especially actual economic growth, may be accompanied by a rise in employment. A higher output may require more workers to produce that output.

With rising incomes and expenditure, more tax revenue will be earned. Some of this can be spent on benefits to the poor and on measures to reduce poverty. In the absence of economic growth, a government wanting to help the poor would either have to raise taxation or switch government spending away from some other area.

Some of the higher tax revenue, resulting from economic growth may be spent on health care and education. This should improve living standards and raise economic growth in the future.

Economic growth, however, may not be desirable if it is unsustainable, the benefits are restricted to a few and it is imposing stress on workers. Unsustainable growth which results in the depletion of non-renewable resources and creates pollution will threaten future economic growth and may reduce the quality of people's lives.

If income is unevenly distributed, only a few people may benefit from economic growth. Economic growth can be associated with a widening in the gap between the rich and the poor and this may result in social unrest. Economic growth involves change and may involve longer working hours. Both effects may place stress on workers and so reduce the quality of their lives.

4. a. Real GDP is a country's output in a particular year whilst its economic growth rate is the percentage change in its output from the previous year. A country may have a higher output than another country but its output may be rising more slowly. The country may even be experiencing a negative economic growth rate, that is its output may be falling. Its economic growth rate may also be less stable which can discourage investment.

    b. A country's inhabitants may have a higher average life expectancy than another because they enjoy better health care. If, for instance, there are more doctors per head and more advanced equipment in hospitals, more illness may be prevented and any medical problems treated more efficiently.

    Better education can also result in higher life expectancy. If people are more educated, they are likely to be more concerned with hygiene, take greater care of their health and be able to undertake less physically hard work.

    In addition, better quality housing can allow people to live longer. With adequately heated and spacious accommodation with good plumbing, people should be less prone to a range of illnesses.

    Of course, better health care, better education and better housing are more likely to be found in a country with high GDP per head than one with a low GDP per head.

    c. On the surface, it would appear that an economy experiencing 8.1% inflation would face more serious problems than one facing 1.7%. This is because it would mean that the value of money in the country would be falling more rapidly. The difficulties associated with inflation such as loss of international competitiveness, menu costs and shoe leather costs may be greater.

The situation, however, is somewhat more complex. An economy with an 8.1% inflation rate may actually have a more stable inflation rate than one with a current 1.7% inflation rate. If this is the case, it would be easier for firms, households and workers to adjust to the inflation rate and plan ahead.

In deciding which economy would face the more serious problems, the cause of the inflation in both countries would have to be considered. Cost-push inflation tends to be more harmful than demand-pull inflation. This is because it is often associated with a fall, or slowdown, in economic growth whilst demand-pull inflation is often combined with positive economic growth.

It also has to be remembered that too low an inflation rate can cause some major economic problems. As measures of inflation tend to overstate price rises, a very low rate of inflation may mean that the price level is actually falling. If deflation is occurring, a downward spiral of economic activity may be setting in. Households, seeing that prices are falling, may delay their purchases. The fall in aggregate demand may lower employment and the price level which again would push down aggregate demand.

It is interesting to note that whilst inflation caused by increases in the costs of production tends to be more harmful than that caused by aggregate demand increasing too rapidly, the opposite is true with deflation. A fall in the price level may be beneficial if it is due to lower costs of production.

For example, advances in technology can make a country's products more internationally price competitive. As a result, such deflation may be associated with rising economic activity. In contrast, as mentioned above, deflation caused by falling aggregate demand is likely to be accompanied by a reduction in economic activity.

Homework assignments

1. a. I would assess its economic growth rate and its unemployment rate. I would consider that its economic performance has improved if its economic growth rate has increased and become more steady and sustainable. It is important to avoid fluctuations in economic growth and endangering future generations' ability to grow. I would also assess that its performance has improved if its unemployment rate has fallen and people were being unemployed for shorter periods of time.

   b. Two supply-side policy measures used by the Georgian government were privatisation and reform of the tax system.

   c. The two recommendations I would make to attract investment are to cut corporation tax and to improve education. Lowering corporation tax would mean that firms, including foreign firms, would be able to keep more of any profits they earn. Improving education would also tend to attract foreign firms. This is because the firms would expect labour productivity to rise which, in turn, would reduce unit labour costs.

d. As the Georgian economy develops, the size of its agricultural sector would be expected to decline. The size of the secondary and tertiary sector would be expected to increase in terms of both output and employment.

e. A cut in tax rates would be expected to reduce tax revenue in the short term but may increase it in the longer term. When tax rates are first cut people will not have to change their spending, the hours they work and whether they work or not and firms will not have had sufficient time to alter their scale of production. With the same level of expenditure, output and income, tax revenue will fall.

A cut in indirect taxes and a rise in disposable income resulting from lower income tax, is likely to encourage people to spend more. If people pay less tax per unit but purchase significantly more products, indirect tax revenue will rise.

The higher spending is likely to increase demand for labour and the greater incentive to work and work longer hours should encourage people to take advantage of greater work opportunities. With more people working and some people working longer hours, income tax revenue should rise. Of course, there is the chance that some workers, who are content with their living standards, may work fewer hours as a result of lower income tax.

A cut in corporation tax would probably encourage firms to use retained profits to expand their business. Higher output and higher profits in the future would increase revenue from corporation tax.

2. a. The basket of 650 goods and services is used to attach weights to price changes. The basket is a representative sample of products that households buy. The greater the proportion of total spending that goes on an item, the more importance is attached to any change in its price.

b. Items are removed from the basket when the amount spent on them by a representative sample of households falls to a low level. Whilst items that have become less popular are removed from the basket, items which have become more popular are included.

c. UK households devoted a higher proportion of their spending to transport. This can be concluded as it had a greater weighting than household fuel, water and related bills.

d. The weighting of audio, visual and related products will probably increase in the future. This is because people are likely to devote a higher proportion of their expenditure to such items as they get richer. There is a small chance that the weighting might fall. This would occur if, with advances in technology, the price of these products falls by more than the rise in demand for them.

e. An increase in the cost of living means that the price level has increased. If people's incomes have remained unchanged or risen by less than the price level, they will not be able to buy as many goods and services. This will result in a fall in material living standards.

Those people whose incomes rise by more than the inflation rate, will experience a rise in their real incomes and so in their material living standards.

A number of workers and recipients have their incomes index linked to a measure of the price level. These people will maintain their real living standards, provided the measure of inflation is an accurate one.

It is possible that people may experience a fall in their real income as a result of an increase in the cost of living and yet still experience an increase in their living standards. This could occur as a result of, for instance, a cut in working hours or a reduction in pollution.

3. a. A country may enjoy a higher HDI ranking than other countries because it has better health care. This would enable its population to enjoy a higher life expectancy. The HDI is based on GDP per head, education and life expectancy.

b. A fall in unemployment would be expected to increase output. If more people are in work, more should be produced. Higher output will enable people to enjoy more goods and services.

Another advantage of a fall in unemployment is increased tax revenue. With more people working and spending, the government will receive more revenue from both direct and indirect taxation. The extra tax revenue could be spent on, for instance, education and state pensions.

c. The change in the economy of Barbados may result in structural unemployment. One of the country's major industries, sugar, was expected to experience a decline in demand. This would be expected to lead to redundancies among workers in the industry.

d. A fall in the unemployment rate is likely to push up the wage rate. With fewer people out of work, firms wanting to expand may have to attract workers away from other jobs by offering higher wages. Workers, knowing that employers may have difficulty replacing them, may also be more prepared to press for wage rises.

e. The Chilean economy had a relatively high economic growth rate in 2008 but its rate was exceeded by both Argentina and Venezuela. Its inflation rate was rather high but was significantly below that of both Argentina and Venezuela. The inflation rate of Venezuela, at 19.8%, was particularly high. Chile had the second lowest unemployment rate out of the four countries shown, but at 7.3% it was still relatively high. From the information given, Mexico appears to have performed best in 2008. It had virtually full employment and an inflation rate that was a little high but reasonable. It had the lowest economic growth rate but 2.8% might be more sustainable than 6.2%.

In judging the economic performance of the Chilean economy relative to other Latin American economies, however, far more information would be needed. Data on the economic growth rate, inflation rate and unemployment rate over time is required. For instance, unemployment may be falling in Argentina whilst it is rising in Chile. Other economic data would also be useful on, for example, the position of the current account of the balance of payments and the countries' HDI ranking over a number of years.

It would also be necessary to check that the same measures have been used in measuring inflation and unemployment in the other countries and whether there is any difference in the size of the informal economy between the countries.

SECTION-7

Definitions

1. g	2. r	3. h	4. i	5. o
6. n	7. l	8. k	9. a	10. p
11. q	12. b	13. j	14. d	15. s
16. c	17. t	18. m	19. e	20. f

Missing words

1. saving, high
2. investment, productivity, income
3. development, reduced, uneven
4. income, income
5. minimum, income, uneven
6. absolute, relative
7. deciles/quintiles, quintiles/deciles
8. high, majority, expensive/costly
9. increase, dependency
10. Malthusian, food
11. decline/fall, fewer
12. raise/increase, greater/higher
13. below
14. rise, falls
15. import, domestic
16. World, multilateral
17. absolute/relative, relative/absolute
18. few, limited
19. high, developing, developed
20. developing, developed

Calculations

1. The natural increase is the change in births minus the change in deaths i.e. 2m − ½ m = 1½m.
2. 24m do not live in absolute poverty, so 6m (20%) do.

3.

Cumulative percentage of the population	Cumulative percentage of income
20	7
40	18
60	36
80	58
100	100

Interpreting diagrams

Country B is likely to be a more developed economy than Country A as it is capable of producing more products and is devoting a higher proportion of its resources to producing luxuries.

Drawing diagrams

Country A has the more even distribution of income. Figure 1 shows that the Lorenz curve for Country A is closer to the line of equality than Country B's.

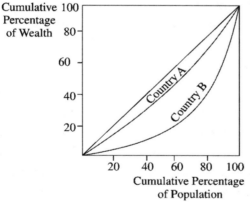

Fig. 1

Multiple-choice questions

1. B

    A natural decrease can arise from either a fall in the birth rate or a rise in the death rate or a combination of the two.

2. A

    Absolute poverty arises when people do not have sufficient income to purchase adequate food, clothing and housing.

3. **B**

   Improved education of the poor should raise their skills. This should increase their choices, job opportunities and the quality of their lives. It should also increase the output of the country. A and C may reduce economic development. D may slow down economic growth, but it will depend on what is done with the tax revenue.

4. **A**

   The term 'optimum population' relates to the highest output per head. This is a definition question.

5. **C**

   Overpopulation occurs when population has grown above the optimum level. Given available economic resources, output per head would be higher with fewer people. B is only referring to one factor of production. A – a country may have a high geographical density of population but may also have considerable economic resources. D – a country which is below optimum population would benefit from net immigration.

6. **A**

   Economic development involves an improvement in people's welfare. A reduction in adult illiteracy would mean more people can read. This would increase their employment chances and their ability to participate fully in society. A reduction in infant mortality would reduce distress and improve the health of mothers. An increase in life expectancy would obviously improve the quality of people's lives.

7. **B**

   If patients are treated more efficiently, they are likely to stay in hospital for a shorter period of time. This implies fewer beds are needed.

8. **A**

   Economic development is associated with an improvement in people's lives. A fall in the death rate would mean that people are living longer. C and D would reduce the quality of people's lives. The effect of B would depend on its cause.

9. **B**

   As an economy first develops, workers tend to move from the primary to the secondary and then the tertiary sector.

10. **B**

    A resistance to change may stop workers moving from declining to expanding industries. It may also stop firms from adopting new management techniques and using new equipment, and may prevent the country's institutions adapting to changing economic conditions. Such resistance to change would restrict economic growth. A, C and D would all tend to promote economic growth.

11. **A**

    The 45 degree line on a Lorenz curve plots an equal distribution of income or wealth. For instance, it would show that 20% of the population earn 20% of income, 40% of the population earn 40% of income, 60% of the population earn 60% of the income and so on.

12. **C**

    If, on average, income is lower but it is more evenly spread, there may be fewer people in absolute poverty. A and B can be rejected as inflation and population size have been taken into account in real GDP per head. D would tend to be a cause of low income rather than an offsetting factor.

13. **A**

    As an economy develops, health care, nutrition and the quality of housing usually improve. All of these factors tend to reduce the death rate. Better health care, improved education and more job opportunities for women is likely to reduce the birth rate.

14. **C**

    A reduction in job opportunities for women may mean that women do not postpone or reduce the number of children they have. A, B and D would all tend to reduce the birth rate. Improved health care would reduce infant mortality and so may mean that families, knowing more of their children will survive, may reduce the number of children they have. A rise in the school leaving age would increase the cost of having children and so may limit the number of children people have. An increase in the school leaving age would also delay the age of marriage and thus motherhood. This would lower the number of births. The introduction of a generous state pension scheme may mean that parents need fewer children to support them in their old age.

15. **A**

    A higher wage rate paid to people in the Philippines should increase people's living standards. It should also increase the tax revenue of the Philippine government. The extra revenue could be spent on education and health care which would promote economic development. B would tend to reduce the economic development of the Philippines and C and D would tend to promote the economic development of the USA rather than the Philippines.

16. **D**

    Untied, multilateral aid will give a country more choice on how it uses the aid and is more likely to be given with the motivation of improving economic development rather than for political or commercial reasons.

17. **B**

    Changes in the size of a country's population are influenced by both natural changes and by migration.

18. D

A virtuous circle arises when a process is set under way which leads to higher and higher income. Higher productivity will stimulate a rise in income, which in turn will raise saving and investment. A and B may restrict economic growth and the impact of C will depend on its cause and nature.

19. C

Low real GDP per head must mean that, on average, income is low. It does not, however, mean that everyone in the country is poor. Indeed, some countries with low real GDP per head contain a number of very wealthy people. Government spending and benefits depend on a number of factors. A country may have low real GDP per head but if tax revenue is low, spending on welfare benefits may also be low.

20. A

A fall in the death rate of males would mean that men live for longer and so there would be more men in the population. B, C and D would increase the proportion of women in the population.

Similarities

1. Both are measures of economic development.
2. Both influence the size of the population.
3. Each is a characteristic of developing countries.
4. They are both designed to reduce poverty.
5. Each involves the movement of people between countries.
6. Both are proportions of the total.
7. They will both increase population/dependency ratio.
8. Each is a consequence of an ageing population.
9. Both are problems faced by developing countries.
10. Each is a possible cause of poverty.

Differences

1. Economic growth is an increase in the output of a country or an increase in the country's productive potential. Economic development occurs when the economic welfare of the population increases. This may be the result of economic growth but it is influenced by a range of other factors including life expectancy, education and the choices available to people.
2. A developed country tends to have higher real GDP per head than a developing country.

3. A natural change in population occurs as a result of a change in the birth rate and/or death rate. In contrast, migration involves people entering or leaving the country.
4. Emigration is the departure of people from the country to live elsewhere whereas immigration is the arrival of people from other countries to live in the country.
5. Positive checks and preventive checks both limit population growth. Positive checks describe those factors which result in a rise in the death rate whereas preventive checks restrict the birth rate.
6. Import substitution and export promotion are different policies to promote economic development. Import substitution relies on government intervention to encourage the growth of industries to make products that replace imports. In contrast, export promotion relies on market forces to increase the efficiency of domestic firms and so their ability to export.
7. A vicious circle involves a downward spiral in GDP whereas a virtuous circle involves an upward spiral in GDP.
8. The distribution of income is how income is shared out between the population. The distribution of wealth is how wealth is shared out between people. Income is a flow of money whereas wealth is a stock of assets.
9. Overpopulated and underpopulated both mean that the best use cannot be made of resources. Whereas overpopulated means that there are too many people to make the best use of the other resources, underpopulated means there are not enough people to exploit the other resources.
10. A growing population is a population that is increasing in size. Its average age may be increasing or falling. It will, for instance, be falling if the growth is caused by a rise in the birth rate. An ageing population is one where the average age is increasing. If the rise in the average age is caused by a fall in the death rate, the population will be both ageing and increasing. If, however, the change is caused by a fall in the birth rate, the population may be ageing but declining.

Data exercises

1. a. The quality of overseas aid means how useful is the assistance given to one country by another country or groups of countries.
   b. Investment can promote development in a number of ways. One is that it should cause economic growth. The purchase of more capital goods increases aggregate demand and the use of more capital goods increases productive capacity. Higher output can increase employment and material living standards. It can also generate extra tax revenue which can be spent on education, health care and reducing poverty.

   Investment in new capital equipment can also make work less physically arduous and safer. If it does so, this should improve workers' health and reduce accidents. For example, advanced technology has made steel production safer and less physically demanding.

c. Developed countries can hinder the development of developing economies by imposing trade restrictions on their exports and subsidising their own exports. If the USA, for instance, places higher tariffs on steel imported from Malaysia, this will make the Malaysian steel less competitive on the US market. This would make it more difficult for Malaysian producers to sell the steel in the USA. If the USA subsidises its steel production, it would mean that Malaysian producers would also find it more difficult to sell to other countries and even to firms in its own country. Reducing Malaysian sales of steel will slow down the country's economic growth and so lower its material living standards.

d. The growth of the Chinese economy is likely to promote economic growth in other countries. A stronger Chinese economy may provide stronger competition in export markets and may push up the price of commodities. The higher incomes arising from the growth of the Chinese economy and resulting higher demand, however, are likely to have a bigger impact on the world economy.

China has a large population and as it is growing, its inhabitants are buying more goods and services from throughout the world. For example, Brazil is selling more sugar and the UK is selling more educational services to China. Those economies which can respond most appropriately and quickly to the growing and changing Chinese demand will obviously be the main beneficiaries.

Firms from China and the Chinese government are also investing more abroad, most significantly in Africa. Foreign direct investment can increase output and employment especially if the firms introduce new technology and methods to the countries.

As China gets richer, it may also provide greater aid to developing countries. If this aid is well designed and untied, it may help countries break out of the vicious circle of poverty.

e. 'Openness to poor countries exports' means the extent to which richer countries are not imposing trade restrictions on their products. Complete openness would mean that no trade restrictions, such as tariffs and quotas, are imposed on the exports of poor countries. In such a situation, there would be free trade between the poor and richer countries. This would enable countries to specialise in those products in which they have a comparative advantage.

f. There is not a fixed number of jobs in any country. If more people enter a country, they are likely to increase both demand and output.

Indeed, there is a possibility that more immigration will reduce unemployment. If the immigrants are skilled workers, firms may be able to produce at lower average costs. This will increase their international competitiveness which, in turn, would be likely to increase their output. As a result, they may employ more workers.

If a developed country is experiencing a decrease in its labour force, it may welcome more immigration so that it can sustain its economic growth. If, however, its population is above the optimum level and there is a shortage of natural resources and social capital, more immigration especially of dependants may not be welcome.

2. a. A poverty line is a level of income below which households are said to be living in poverty. This line varies between countries and over time.

   b. India's population may be less than predicted as the natural increase of population may be less than what forecasters have anticipated and the pattern of migration may not be what they expect.

   India's death rate is likely to fall in the future as living standards improve. Its birth rate, however, may decline more rapidly than expected. A desire for higher living standards and an increase in the cost of raising children may result in families choosing to have fewer children.

   It is particularly difficult to forecast future immigration and emigration. This is because migration depends on relative economic performance, restrictions on the movement of people between countries and political conditions.

   c. A government could increase literacy rates by increasing its spending on education. Such an increase may result in more children receiving an education, children being in education longer or children having better quality education. The lower the literacy rate, the more the government would have to spend. It may also have to make education compulsory up to a certain age, in those countries where it is not already so, to ensure families take advantage of the extra spending.

   d. There are a number of benefits of educating girls. One is that the country would be likely to gain a more productive and larger labour force. The increase in the quality and quantity of labour would raise the country's productive potential. This will allow an economy to grow without experiencing inflationary pressure.

   Educated women can help educate their own children which will help to improve the educational attainment and productivity of the future labour force.

   Educating girls should also improve their health. They will learn more about nutrition, will be able to read about government health campaigns, will be likely to undertake regular medical check ups and have their children inoculated. Healthier women and healthier children should reduce the burden on the country's health service.

More educated women can participate in society to a greater extent, becoming more involved in politics and making the decisions made more representative of the whole population.

In addition, educating girls can reduce population growth. Staying in education will delay the age at which girls marry and this will reduce their child bearing years. Being educated, girls are also more likely to want to pursue a career for at least a period of time, This, plus being better informed about contraceptive methods, is likely to limit the size of their families.

e. Economic progress implies that an economy is developing its industries and is performing better in terms of its macroeconomic objectives. A lower proportion of its output and employment is likely to be accounted for by the primary sector. The economy will be growing at a more stable and sustainable rate with real GDP per head increasing. Unemployment will be falling, inflation will be becoming more stable and the economy may be becoming more internationally competitive.

f. A space programme may promote economic progress. If the space rocket and equipment are built in the country, it will directly create employment and generate income. It may also give rise to industries which provide services for the space programme and which develop technological offshoots from the programme. In addition, it may be taken as a sign of economic strength which may encourage multinational companies to set up in the country.

There is a risk, however, that if a space programme is financed or in part financed by domestic government revenue, the money might have been put to better use to promote economic progress. For instance, tax revenue spent on education might be more effective in increasing economic growth, lowering inflation, unemployment and increasing exports. In addition, if a developing economy is spending money on a space programme, it may discourage developed economies providing it with foreign aid.

3. a. The share of Brazil's total income received by the richest 50% in 2006 was 88.1% (100% – 11.9%).

b. The type of poverty being discussed in the second paragraph is absolute poverty. This is because it is discussing people lacking basic necessities including adequate food and health care.

c. The cycle of poverty refers to people growing up in poverty, becoming poor themselves and then their children experiencing poverty. Poor children tend to have less and poorer quality education than the average population and lower expectations. This often results in them either being unemployed or in unskilled jobs.

d. One problem caused by rural to urban migration is a pressure on housing. People will be leaving accommodation in rural areas and coming to towns and cities that may lack an adequate supply of accommodation. This may result in slums developing.

Another related problem is that of unemployment. People move to urban areas in search of a better standard of living. There is, however, no guarantee that there will be jobs available for them. If they do not find employment, they may not have relatives living near by to support them.

e. There would be many benefits which could be gained from an increase in government spending on education. Improved education and greater accessibility to that education should raise labour productivity and increase labour mobility. Higher output per worker and greater labour flexibility should increase a country's international competitiveness. This would increase its exports, raise aggregate demand and increase real GDP. Higher output will raise tax revenue and some of the extra revenue could be spent on improving education further. Raising the educational performance of its population may also attract more foreign direct investment as foreign firms will expect the quality of output produced in the country to be higher and unit labour costs to be lower.

More spending on education may make income more evenly distributed in Brazil. If targeted at the poor it could help to break the cycle of poverty.

There are a number of other ways in which such a policy may increase economic development. These include improved health and more people exercising choice over some key aspects of their lives.

However, despite the desirability of spending more on education, the Brazilian government would realise that such a choice would involve an opportunity cost. To spend more, the government would either have to spend less on other areas (e.g. health care) or raise taxation or borrow, which would pass the opportunity cost on to taxpayers or lenders. The government may consider that switching spending from health care to education may currently lower economic development. It may also be reluctant to incur political unpopularity by raising taxation or to incur interest rate charges as a result of borrowing.

Of course, if the economy is growing, the government could devote some of the extra tax revenue to education but again it would have to consider carefully what would be the best use for such funds. In addition, the government would recognise that spending more on education is no guarantee that it will improve educational performance. It will depend on the quality and appropriateness of the education provided.

f. Improved health care should make people fitter. This should mean that they will lose fewer days off work and so lose less pay. They should be able to perform better at work and be more productive. With a more productive labour force, firms' costs should fall and their revenue should rise. The resulting rise in revenue may enable them to pay higher wages.

g. There are arguments for and against reducing income inequality although most governments do move at least some income from the rich to the poor. This is because there are vulnerable groups who have difficulty earning any income. These groups are likely to gain a considerable benefit from receiving financial help from the government. The rich may not lose much satisfaction as a result of a proportion of their income being taken in tax. Moving income from the rich to the poor can also help the poor to have access to health care and education. This is why the redistribution of income can raise productivity and increase economic growth.

There is a risk, however, that the provision of state benefits and progressive taxation may act as a disincentive to effort and enterprise. Some people may not work hard if they think that too much of their income is being taken in tax. Some may not actively seek employment if state benefits are relatively generous. High taxes may also discourage some people from setting up new businesses and may also encourage some workers and firms to move to countries with lower tax rates.

Structured questions

1. a. Economic development involves an improvement in the welfare of the population. This may be the result not only of being able to enjoy more goods and services, but also living longer and having more freedom and choices.

   b. Developing economies may differ from developed economies in a number of ways. A key difference is lower real GDP per head. This difference can lead to a number of other differences. These include low life expectancy, low savings, poor education, poor health care, low standard housing and poor infrastructure. They may also have a relatively high proportion of workers employed in the primary sector and export a narrow range of products.

   c. All economies are seeking to become more developed as it will improve the lives of their people. The crucial aims of government macroeconomic policies relate to improving people's material living standards by raising output, lowering unemployment, keeping inflation low and ensuring that people have the opportunity to buy a range of products, including some from other countries. Government policies on education and health care can raise life expectancy, employment opportunities and the quality of people's lives.

   Governments are aware that increased economic development can lead to future economic development by creating a virtuous circle. For instance, a more educated labour force can increase output and the higher income earned by households, firms and the government can result in more money being spent on a range of areas that will improve economic welfare.

    d. Rapid economic growth may increase economic development but it is uncertain whether it will always do so. Economic growth involves an increase in the output of goods and services. Such an increase can improve people's material living standards. Employment may also increase and the extra tax revenue gained may lead a government to spend more on education, health care and measures to reduce poverty.

There is, however, no guarantee that rapid economic growth will result in more economic development. The higher output may have been caused by switching resources from making consumer to capital goods. In the short term this will reduce people's material living standards although it should increase them in the longer term. The extra output might also consist of weapons. During a period of threatened military conflict, output may rise but the quality of people's lives may fall.

Rapid economic growth may also have been achieved as a result of people working longer hours and at the expense of greater pollution and congestion. Greater stress may also be placed on workers as rapid economic growth is likely to involve the need for them to adapt to new jobs and new technology. In such circumstances, economic development might decline despite economic growth.

The benefits of economic growth may not be evenly spread and if income is very unevenly distributed, the quality of only a few people's lives will increase. Official economic growth figures may also give a misleading impression of what is happening to output. The country's output may be unchanged but if the informal economy declines with more economic activity being declared, economic growth will be recorded.

When a high proportion of a country's inhabitants are experiencing absolute poverty, rapid economic growth is likely to result in economic development. When, however, a country's inhabitants have achieved high incomes they may become more concerned about the quality of the environment and may seek increased leisure time.

2.   a. An uneven distribution of income means that households do not receive the same amount of income – some will receive a large share of the total and some a small share. For instance, the richest 10% may receive 60% of total income whilst the poorest 10% may only receive 0.5%.

    b. Rwanda is likely to, and does, experience more absolute poverty than the USA. Only a small proportion of the US population struggle to afford adequate housing, sufficient food and other basic necessities. As income is very unevenly distributed in the USA than Rwanda, however, the gap between the rich and the poor is greater in the USA. This makes relative poverty more of an issue in the USA than in Rwanda.

c. One cause of poverty is unemployment. When people are out of work, they usually experience a fall in income. The longer they are out of work, the greater their chance of falling into poverty. They will experience relative poverty and depending on whether state benefits are available or not and what their level is, they may experience absolute poverty.

Even those in employment may experience poverty if they receive very low wages. Unskilled and unorganised workers employed by firms that possess stronger bargaining power may be lowly paid.

Another cause of poverty is old age. The elderly may be poor if there are no or low state pensions, they have no or inadequate private pensions and no or inadequate savings.

d. A government can influence the distribution of income in a number of ways. The provision of state benefits to the sick, disabled, unemployed and the elderly will be likely to make income more evenly distributed. This is because it will raise the income of what are usually low income groups.

A progressive tax system, which takes a higher proportion of the income of the rich, will reduce income inequality. The higher the top direct tax rates are, the more the disposable income of the rich will be reduced. In contrast, a regressive tax system which may rely more on indirect taxes is likely to increase income inequality.

A national minimum wage, set above the equilibrium wage that is paid to low paid workers, will make income more evenly distributed, provided it does not lead to higher unemployment.

Government spending on education and health care can also make income more evenly distributed if it is targeted at the poor. Improving the education of the poor should increase their chances not only of gaining a job but also of gaining a reasonably well paid job. Improving the health care of the poor should mean that they will lose fewer working days and be less likely to lose their jobs through sickness.

A range of other government policies can influence the distribution of income. For instance, privatisation tends to increase income inequality. This is because the pay of top executives in private sector is often much higher than the heads of nationalised industries.

3. a. There may be a natural increase in the size of a country's population. This would occur if the country's birth rate exceeded its death rate. If the rate at which children are being born exceeds the rate at which people are dying, there will be more people in the population.

The other possible cause of an increase in the size of a country's population is net immigration. This involves more people coming to live in the country than are leaving the country to live elsewhere. Of course, the increase in population size could be the result of a combination of a natural increase and net immigration. There might also be a natural decrease which is more than offset by net immigration or a natural increase which adds more people to the population than are lost through net emigration.

b. A government could influence the size of the population of its country in a number of ways. These include removing restrictions on immigration, raising the school leaving age and providing greater accessibility to family planning.

Removing restrictions on immigration would be likely to increase a country's population size if the economy is doing well or it provides greater freedoms than other countries. Such a policy approach might be implemented to increase a country's labour force. This is because most migrants are of working age and are often attracted by better job opportunities and better pay.

Raising the school leaving age is likely to reduce the birth rate for a number of reasons. One is that it is likely to delay the age at which people marry. A third reason is that some women who have received more education tend to pursue a career and to do so, restrict their family size.

Greater accessibility to family planning by, for instance, providing state family planning clinics will enable those families which want to limit their family size to do so more effectively. Of course, such an approach may conflict with the religious views of come countries.

c. Whether an increase in the size of a country's population is beneficial for an economy or not will depend on the current size of the population and the cause of the increase.

If a country's population is above the optimum size, an increase in population may reduce output per head. It may also put pressure on facilities such as housing, health care and education. A rise in the birth rate will reduce the labour force in the short term as mothers take time off to have children. If more children are being born or people are living longer, there will be more people dependent on the working population. Taxes may have to be raised to finance more health care facilities, primary school education and pensions and residential care.

In some cases a rise in population size may lead to overcrowding, destruction of the natural environment and may put pressure on limited food supplies.

There are, however, a number of benefits that can come from an increase in the size of the population. This is particularly true if a country is underpopulated. For instance, Australia has encouraged immigration of people of working age in order to increase the country's labour force and make greater use of its natural resources. Immigrants can bring in new skills and are often geographically and occupationally mobile. If this is the case, the quality and flexibility of the country's labour force will increase. More workers will reduce a country's dependency ratio. In recent years the increased burden placed on the UK's labour force by a rise in the number of pensioners has, in part, been offset by net immigration of people of working age.

An increase in the birth rate now will raise the size of the labour force in the future. A growing population, whatever its cause, will result in larger markets. If it is combined with a rise in demand, firms may be able to exploit economies of scale to a greater extent and expanding markets may encourage firms to invest in new technology.

4. a. Despite fears about an approaching recession, job opportunities might have been better in the UK than in the countries that the immigrants come from. Wage rates and working conditions may also have been better in the UK than in the immigrants' countries of origin.

    b. One advantage that the UK could gain from net immigration of workers is that it would reduce the burden of an ageing population by lowering the dependency ratio. There would be more workers to support the number of retired people.

        Net immigration of workers can also enable skill shortages to be filled. In recent years the UK economy has had problems filling vacancies for both low and high skilled jobs. As a result, foreign fruit pickers and doctors, for instance, have been recruited.

    c. A government would want to see a reduction in poverty as this would mean that the living standards of the poorest people in the country would be rising. Increasing the living standards of the population is one of the key objectives of governments.

        A reduction in poverty, resulting from higher employment may also mean that a government does not have to pay out as much in benefits. This may enable it to spend more on other areas such as improving infrastructure.

        In addition, a fall in poverty caused by more people being in work would raise government tax revenue. This, again, would enable a government to spend more or reduce a budget deficit.

    d. A recession may increase absolute poverty as it is likely to be accompanied by both a rise in unemployment and a fall in government tax revenue.

        A recession is a fall in real GDP over a period of six months or more. Lower national output is likely to lead to cyclical unemployment as firms will cut back on the number of workers employed. Unemployment is one of the prime causes of poverty.

        During a recession both direct and indirect tax revenue is likely to fall. This is because income and expenditure will be lower. With less tax revenue, a government may cut back on the benefits it pays. Such a reduction would hit the poor.

During a recession, low skilled, low paid workers tend to be more likely to lose their jobs than higher skilled and higher paid workers. This, combined with a likely cut in state benefits, will probably increase the gap between the rich and poor.

Homework assignments

1. a. The sources are remittances, financial investment, foreign direct investment and foreign aid.
    b. Someone from the Philippines may go to work abroad because she or he cannot find work at home. The person may also be tempted to work abroad by the prospect of higher wages. A key reason why people seek to work in other countries is to improve their living standards and the living standards of their families. Working as a nurse in the USA, for instance, pays considerably more than working as a nurse in the Philippines. There are also more job opportunities for nurses in the USA.
    c. A merit good is one which people fail to appreciate the true value to themselves of consuming and one which has beneficial effects on third parties. The evidence in the passage on training concentrates on the second aspect. It mentions that much of the benefit of training that the governments of Jamaica and Grenada provide to people studying to be doctors is reaped by other countries.
    d. Two factors that may attract foreign direct investment to a country are a low corporation tax rate and a large supply of skilled labour. If the corporation tax is low, foreign firms would know that they will be able to keep a high proportion of any profit earned. A large supply of skilled labour should mean that the firm will be able to produce products of a high quality and keep its unit labour costs low.
    e. The emigration of workers from developing countries may promote their countries' development in some circumstances whilst harming it in other circumstances. The effects will depend on the scale of the emigration, the types of workers who leave and whether they settle abroad permanently.

    Workers usually send back money to their home country. As the passage notes, in many developing countries these remittances account for a significant proportion of foreign currency. This inflow of money can help boost demand in the developing countries and pay for improved education and health care. The workers may also send back ideas to their home countries including information on new technology and new management techniques. Some workers may return home to work after a few years having received extra training and picking up more skills abroad. Those who settle permanently abroad and set up businesses there often trade with their country of birth, and so increase that country's exports. The emigration of unemployed, unskilled workers may reduce pressure on employment opportunities. With less competition for jobs, the wage rates of those who remain behind may rise.

There are, however, a number of disadvantages of people going to work abroad. These disadvantages are likely to be greater if the workers are skilled, stay abroad for some time and leave in large numbers. Skilled workers have usually received training and education, often paid for by the government and the benefits of that expenditure may be reaped more by other countries. The loss in potential output from the departure of these workers may be greater than any money they send home. Indeed, the passage mentions that skilled workers do not tend to send much money back to their country as they often take their families with them.

The loss of skilled workers may also discourage foreign direct investment. Multinational companies may be deterred from setting up in a country if they think labour productivity is low. In addition, some domestic firms may move abroad if the lack of skilled workers pushes up their costs and prevents them taking advantage of advances in technology.

The emigration of skilled workers may set in place a downward spiral in skills. A lack of trained and qualified teachers and doctors will reduce the quantity and quality of education and health care available in a country. This, in turn, will reduce the productivity of the next generation.

Some workers who emigrate may leave dependents behind, including elderly parents, and may not send money back to them. In this case, there will be a greater burden placed on the remaining labour force.

2. a. Two effects of an ageing population are an increase in the cost of state pensions and a greater demand for health care. With people living longer, the state has to pay out more in pensions. The elderly require the most medical attention and their demand for health care increases significantly with age.

   b. Two causes of a decline in population are a fall in the birth rate and net emigration.

   c. The replacement rate in this case refers to the number of children born per woman needed to replenish the population, that is keep it at the same size.

   d. Japan's dependency ratio is increasing. There are more non-workers becoming dependant on fewer workers. The passage mentions that there will be fewer workers to every retired person.

   e. The effects of a declining population will depend on its cause, its extent and whether the population is currently at, above or below the optimum population size.

   If the cause of a declining population is an increase in the death rate, this will obvious reduce economic welfare. A natural disaster or a war may reduce a country's population quite significantly. Such an event is clearly undesirable. Net emigration is another possible cause of a decline in population. The problem here is that it usually consists of people of working age, a number of whom are likely to be skilled workers. If the workers do not take their dependants with them, there will be a rise in the dependency ratio. The workers may send home money but a fall in the size of the labour force will reduce productive potential. If the country's population is below the optimum size, the emigration of workers will reduce output per head.

A fall in a very high birth rate in an overpopulated country, however, may be beneficial. Having fewer children in the population can reduce pressure on schools, hospitals, housing and food. Moving the country closer to the optimum population size will enable better use of available resources.

3. a. The world's population is approximately 6.5bn, 2.5bn lack basic sanitation, so the proportion is 2.5bn/6.5bn × 100 = 38.46%.

   b. Water is not evenly distributed. The passage mentions that whilst the average US citizen uses 500 litres per day, in Gambia people only consume 4.5 litres a day.

   c. Demand for water in the future is likely to increase. This is because the world population is growing and income and output are increasing. It takes a considerable volume of water to produce products and as people get richer they demand more products and use more water themselves. For instance, a rich family in the US may have three bathrooms in their home, may wash their car regularly and may even have a swimming pool.

   d. Lack of water hinders development in a number of ways. It affects the ability of people to drink clear water, flush away human waste and to wash, and causes diseases and deaths. Health care resources which could have been used for other purposes have to be used treating people with illnesses resulting from a lack of water. The illnesses also increase the number of days' sickness that workers experience and reduce their productivity.

   A large amount of water is used by agriculture and manufacturing and so a lack of water can limit output. Such a limit would restrict material living standards, employment and economic growth. Tax revenue will also be limited and this will restrict the amount the government can spend on reducing poverty and improving education and health care.

   A lack of water can even result in wars which clearly reduce the welfare of people.

   e. There is an opportunity cost involved in developed countries providing grants to developing countries to improve their supply of water. The tax revenue used could have been put to another purpose, for instance, improving the health care of the citizens in the developed countries.

There is also a risk that the grants may not be used very efficiently and, in some cases, there may be corruption with the grants not being used for their stated purpose.

The benefits, however, could outweigh the costs. If the grants do help improve the supply of water, the health of the people in the developing countries should improve and the output of these countries should increase. Enabling developing countries to grow at a more rapid rate should increase demand for the exports of developed countries. Higher exports will, in turn increase aggregate demand and the output of developed countries.

Improvements in the economic growth and economic development of developing countries should also reduce the need for aid from developed countries in the future. In addition, the risk of diseases and wars spreading from developing to developed economies should reduce.

SECTION-8

Definitions

1. q	2. j	3. r	4. s	5. p
6. o	7. a	8. t	9. g	10. e
11. f	12. d	13. i	14. c	15. b
16. h	17. l	18. n	19. m	20. k

Missing words

1. current, goods, services
2. credit, financial
3. scale, exchange
4. falls/decreases, rises/increases
5. structural
6. exchange
7. specialising/trading
8. international, absolute, comparative
9. terms, trade, goods
10. exchange, export, import
11. interest rate, currency
12. rise/increase, direct
13. interest rate, increase
14. deficit, imports

15. reducing/decreasing/falling, falling/decreasing/declining
16. tariffs, domestically
17. control, quality
18. unemployment, replaced
19. competitive, low
20. choice/efficiency/quality, prices

 ## Calculations

1. a. Utopia has the absolute advantage in producing wheat as it can produce more per worker.
   b. In Erewhon the opportunity cost of producing one tractor is 5 wheat (25/5). In Utopia it is 7.5 wheat (75/10).
   c. Erewhon has the comparative advantage in producing tractors as the opportunity cost of producing a tractor is lower in Erewhon.
2. The value of the Kenyan shilling has fallen relative to the US dollar. More Kenyan shillings have to be exchanged to gain one dollar. This makes Kenyan exports cheaper, in terms of dollars, and imports more expensive in terms of Kenyan shillings. The US price of the 210Ksh Kenyan will change from US $ 3 to US $ 2.1 dollars. The Kenyan price of a US $ 20 US import will rise from 1,400 shillings to 2,000 shillings.
3. The terms of trade is: index of export prices/index of import prices x 100 = US $ 5/ US $ 4 × 100 = 125.

 ## Interpreting diagrams

a. The value of the pound sterling has risen because of a decrease in the supply of pounds on the foreign exchange market. Two possible causes of this could be a decrease in the UK's demand for imports and a decrease in UK firms investing abroad.
b. The rise in the value of the pound sterling is likely to increase the UK's trade deficit. This is because it will raise the price of UK exports whilst lowering the price of UK imports.

 ## Drawing diagrams

a. A rise in the value of Pakistani exports would mean that the buyers would purchase more rupees in order to pay for the exports. The rise in demand will push up the value of the Pakistani rupee.

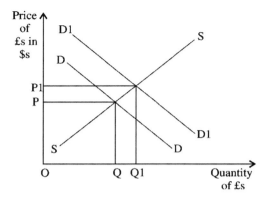

Fig. 1

b. Speculation that the value of the Pakistani rupee will result in some holders of rupees selling them and demand falling. Both effects will push down the value of the rupee.

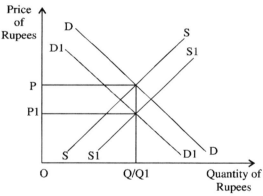

Fig. 2

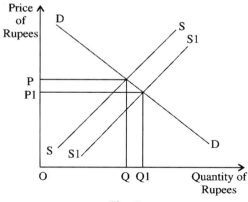

Fig. 3

c. If Pakistani firms buy out firms in India, they will sell Pakistani rupees for Indian rupees. The increase in the supply of Pakistani rupees on the foreign market will push down the value of the Pakistani currency.

Multiple-choice questions

1. A

   If production costs vary to a greater extent between countries, there will be more exchange of products as firms seek to buy at a lower price. C and D discourage international trade as they increase the cost of purchasing products from abroad. B would mean that firms may have to adapt products for the export market and this would again push up their price.

2. D

   Royalty payments appear in trade in services as an invisible item. Authors and owners of patents are paid for their ideas. A, B and C are visible trade items.

3. A

   The balance of trade in goods and services covers visible and invisible exports and imports. A debit item involves money going out of the country. Imported raw materials are a visible item and an increase in their purchase will involve more money going out of the country. The sale of insurance would appear in the balance of trade in goods and services but as a credit item as it will result in money coming into the country. C and D would appear in the financial account.

4. C

   Income, that is investment income, is one of the four sub-sections of the current account.

5. C

   A country's current account deficit will decline if either export revenue rises and/or import expenditure falls. A rise in incomes abroad is likely to increase the amount of exports sold. B would be likely to increase spending on imports and A and D would be likely to reduce export revenue.

6. C

   Most international trade is based on comparative advantage with countries concentrating on making products that they have a comparative advantage in.

7. C

   A country has a comparative advantage in producing a product if it gives up the opportunity to produce less of another product or products to make it than other countries.

8. D

   This is an unusual case as whilst Y has absolute advantage in producing both products, there is no comparative advantage. Both Country X and Country Y have to give up three TV programmes to make one car. Country X and Country Y will not know which products to concentrate on.

9. C

A government may be concerned that specialising in one or two products may make it vulnerable to changes in supply conditions or a fall in demand.

10. A

A fall in the exchange rate reduces export prices. If demand for exports is elastic, the fall in price will cause a greater percentage rise in demand and so a rise in export revenue.

11. C

A freely floating exchange rate is determined by the market forces of demand and supply whereas a fixed exchange rate may be maintained by a government buying and selling currencies.

12. A

Raising US interest rates is likely to encourage foreigners to buy US dollars to place in US financial institutions. An increase in the demand for dollars would raise the value of the currency. B and C would cause the supply of dollars to rise, and so push down its value. D would cause the supply of dollars to rise as US citizens will sell dollars to buy imports. It would also cause demand for US dollars to fall as demand for UK exports would decline. Both effects would push down the value of the US dollar.

13. A

When the value of the UK pound falls against the US dollar, it means that more pounds have to be exchanged for each dollar. It will also mean that UK exports will fall in price whilst UK imports will become more expensive. Note that US imports from the UK are the same as UK exports to the US.

14. C

A deterioration in the terms of trade means that export prices/import prices x 100 has fallen. This must mean that import prices have risen relative to export prices. D can be rejected as the terms of trade are only concerned with price and not volume. A rise in the exchange rate would mean an improvement and not a deterioration in the terms of trade. A deterioration in the terms of trade does not necessarily mean that a country has a deficit in its trade in goods. This is because a rise in the relative price of imports will be likely to reduce import expenditure relative to export revenue.

15. C

If the figure increases, it must mean that export prices have risen relative to import prices. A rise in inflation, and indeed just inflation, would mean that the price of the country's products will be rising. A would reduce a country's terms of trade as export prices will fall and import prices will rise. B would be likely to cause the number to decline as export prices would be expected to fall. D may cause demand for imports to rise which would cause import prices to rise and again the terms of trade figure to fall.

16. D

    Tariffs are taxes on imports. Tariffs placed on agricultural products will protect domestic farmers by raising the price of imported food. They will also raise tax revenue. A, B and C will protect domestic agriculture but will not raise revenue. Indeed, C will involve the government in some expenditure.

17. B

    A reduction in quota levels would mean that fewer imports could enter the country. This would reduce the competitive pressures on domestic firms. A does not directly influence the level of protection. C and D would reduce the level of protection.

18. D

    Tariffs will raise revenue for the government and will protect domestic companies that manufacture buses. In contrast, bus travel companies may have to pay more for their buses as the protection given to domestic producing companies may mean that they will charge more for buses. If the bus companies have to pay more for buses, they are likely to raise the fares which in turn will lower welfare of bus passengers.

19. C

    Dumping is an unfair practice and it is widely accepted that countries are justified in imposing restrictions on countries that engage in such a practice. If a country has a long standing current account deficit, it would need to tackle the cause of the problem. Protectionism reduces rather than increases the choice available for consumers. Countries may seek to protect employment at home but do not try to protect employment overseas.

20. B

    The payment of dividends to foreigners appears as income in the current account. A, C and D would appear in the financial account.

Similarities

1. Both are products traded between countries.
2. These are different names for intangible items traded between countries.
3. These are both components of the current account.
4. Both influence the price of a country's exports.
5. In both cases the price of the country's currency would be increasing.
6. Both are policies designed to reduce a current account deficit.
7. These both influence the value of a floating exchange rate.

8. Both may be used to protect domestic industries from foreign competition.
9. These are both types of industries which some governments believe need protection.
10. Each is a possible disadvantage of protectionism.

 Differences

1. The current account is concerned with short term movements of income and expenditure between countries. In contrast, the financial account covers the longer term movements of direct and portfolio investment between countries.
2. A trade in goods surplus means that the revenue from the sale of exports exceeds the expenditure on the import of goods. A trade in goods deficit, however, means that import expenditure is greater than export revenue.
3. Internal trade is trade within a country whereas international trade is trade between countries and so takes place across national borders.
4. A cyclical current account deficit is caused by a change in incomes at home or abroad whereas a structural deficit arises from a lack of international price or quality competitiveness.
5. A devaluation and a depreciation of the exchange rate both involve the price of the currency falling. A devaluation is caused by government intervention, moving the exchange rate from one fixed price to a lower fixed price. A depreciation in contrast, is caused by an increase in the supply of the currency and/or a fall in demand for the currency arising from market forces.
6. A fixed exchange rate is one which is set and maintained at a particular level by the government. It will change infrequently. A floating exchange rate, however, is determined by market forces and can change on a frequent basis.
7. Free trade means that there are no restrictions on what products can be exchanged between countries. Protection, on the other hand, involves placing restrictions on what can be bought from abroad and sometimes even on what can be sold abroad.
8. Sunrise industries are new, growing industries whereas sunset industries are old, declining industries.
9. Hot money flows are short term movements of money between countries in search of high interest rates and to take advantage of movements in exchange rates. Foreign direct investment involves longer term movements of finance, seeking to set up businesses abroad.
10. Credit items are those which bring money into the country whereas debit items are those which take money out of the country.

Data exercises

1. a. The percentage increase in net capital flows to India was 400% (US $ 36bn/ US $ 9bn).

    b. Less confidence in the dollar would mean that Indians would buy fewer dollars. The fall in demand for dollars would mean that Indians would have to sell fewer rupees to purchase dollars. The decrease in the supply of rupees would be expected to raise the value of the rupee. There may also be an increase in demand for rupees as some foreigners switch from buying dollars to buying Indian rupees.

    c. The sale of its currency by a central bank would increase the supply of that currency on foreign exchange markets. This would lower the value of the currency. Figure 4 shows that an increase in the supply of Indian rupees will shift the supply curve to the right and lower the price of Indian rupees.

    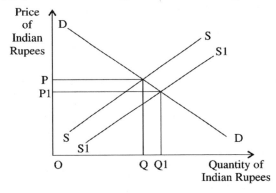

    Fig. 4

    d. Whether the Indian economy will benefit from a fall in the value of the rupee will depend on how foreign consumers react, the level of capacity in the economy and the impact that higher import prices have on inflation.

    A fall in the value of the rupee will make Indian exports cheaper in price. This will be likely to increase demand for Indian exports. If demand is elastic, export revenue may increase. For this to occur, however, Indian firms would have to meet the extra demand. If more exports could be produced, export revenue would rise and any current account deficit would be reduced. Imports will rise in price and import expenditure will fall if demand for imports is elastic.

    A rise in net exports increases aggregate demand. Higher aggregate demand will raise output if there is spare capacity in the economy. The higher output is likely to result in a fall in unemployment as firms take on more workers.

    If the economy is operating close to full capacity, an increase in aggregate demand resulting from a rise in net exports, may led to demand-pull inflation. Figure 5 shows an increase in aggregate demand pushing up the price level.

A fall in the value of the rupee will increase import prices. This rise may contribute to cost-push inflation, although it will depend on how much the country relies on imported raw materials.

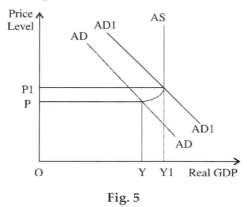

Fig. 5

e. One way a central bank could influence the value of its currency is by changing the rate of interest. If a central bank wants to reduce the value of its currency, it will reduce the rate of interest. A lower rate of interest may cause some people to move funds out of the country's financial institutions in search of a higher interest rate in foreign banks. Hot money flows leaving the country will increase the supply of the currency on the foreign exchange markets. The higher supply will drive down the price of the currency.

f. A decrease in exports may result in an increase in unemployment if it causes a fall in aggregate demand. Lower aggregate demand may cause firms to reduce their output and so reduce the number of workers they employ. If, however, an economy is initially operating at full capacity, a decrease in aggregate demand may reduce inflation but leave output and employment unchanged as shown in Figure 2.

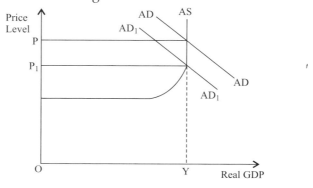

Fig. 6

A decrease in exports may also be offset by an increase in another component of aggregate demand such as consumption.

2. a Export revenue – import expenditure = trade balance. In the US case, this was US $ 140.1bn - ? = - US $ 56.5bn. So import expenditure = ? = US $ 140.1bn + £56.5bn = US $ 196.6bn.

   b. A trade in goods deficit means that expenditure on imported goods exceeds revenue earned on exported goods.

   c. A widening trade deficit will tend to reduce the growth in aggregate demand. For instance, a country's aggregate demand in 2009 might be US $ 600bn, consisting of C (US $ 450bn), I (US $ 100bn), G (US $ 120bn) and a trade deficit (X – M) of (US $ 80bn - US $ 150bn). In 2010, C + I + G might be US $ 700bn. If the trade deficit stayed at US $ 70bn, the economic growth rate would be US $ 30bn/US $ 600bn × 100 = 5%. If, however, the trade deficit increased to US $ 90bn, the growth rate would be reduced to US $ 10bn/US $ 600bn x 100 = 1.67%.

   d. The US may have exported more cars because of a rise in incomes abroad. If people in other countries become richer, they are likely to buy more cars, including from the USA. Other reasons why the US may have exported more cars are a rise in the quality of US cars, a fall in US inflation and the removal on tariffs on US cars.

   e. A fall in the exchange rate will make export prices, in terms of foreign currency, cheaper and will make imports, in terms of the domestic currency more expensive. If demand for exports and imports is elastic, it would be expected that a lower exchange rate will improve the trade in goods position.

   There are, however, circumstances where even if demand is elastic, the trade in goods position will not improve. If foreigners demand more exports, export revenue will not rise if it is not possible to produce more exports. Firms must be able to take on more workers and purchase more capital goods to produce more products.

   Foreigners may also want to buy more exports but if there are import restrictions, firms may have difficulties selling more products. Indeed, if import restrictions are raised, exports may fall.

   A fall in the exchange rate will also not improve the trade in goods position if the quality of domestic products falls relative to foreign products or if domestic products are marketed less efficiently.

   In addition, export prices are influenced not only by the exchange rate. There may be a fall in the exchange rate but this effect may soon be offset by inflation in the domestic economy.

   f. A country is likely to export products in which it has a comparative advantage. This, in turn, is influenced by the country's factor endowments. For instance, Hong Kong has workers with expertise and high skill levels in providing financial services. Kenya has the land and the climate for growing a range of crops including flowers and tea.

The level of demand is a significant factor. A country may be able to produce a product at a lower opportunity cost than other countries, but if there is no demand for the product, it will not be able to export it. The existence of trade restrictions may also prevent a country from exporting a product. These restrictions may even originate from the country's own government. If there is a shortage of a product, a government may decide that it should not be exported and so may impose an embargo on its export or may decide to discourage its export by imposing an export tariff.

g. A rise in imports may come at the expense of domestically produced products. This may mean that aggregate demand will fall leading to a reduction in output and employment, It may also mean that the current account will move into a deficit or into a larger deficit.

On the other hand, if exports are rising in line with imports, aggregate demand may be unaffected and the current account position may remain unchanged.

If the rise in imports is accounted for by a rise in the imports of raw materials and capital goods, these may contribute to an improvement in the country's economic growth and trade performance especially if some of the imported capital goods embody advanced technology.

Higher imports of finished goods may arise because the country is experiencing higher income. As income rises, households will buy more goods and services, some of which will be imported. In this case, higher imports will reflect higher living standards.

3. a. Two motives for imposing tariffs are to protect domestic industries and to prevent dumping.

b. Exports being artificially cheap means that they are being sold at less than cost price. Exporters may be able to do this if they are subsidised or receive, as mentioned in the passage 'favourable tax treatment' and 'low cost loans'. They may also be prepared, for a short period, to make a loss on their exports.

c. US consumers will benefit from Chinese firms dumping exports of paper in the short term. The benefit will be in the form of a lower price. In the longer term, US consumers may face a higher price and reduced choice if the Chinese exporters drive US sellers out of business.

d. One argument for the Chinese government providing help to its paper producers is to protect a declining industry. Such protection may prevent a rise in unemployment. This is because it may enable the industry to be gradually reduced in size. Workers who retire or move to other jobs would not be replaced, so that the number of workers employed could be slowly reduced.

e. I might recommend that the Chinese government should retaliate by imposing trade restrictions on US products if I think such a move would force the US government to remove its tariffs on imports of Chinese paper. This approach might succeed if the USA is selling a high volume of products to China and the tariffs are placed on the most popular products and those the USA might find difficult to sell elsewhere.

It is, however, a high risk strategy. It may provoke a trade war, with each country raising tariffs higher and higher, in retaliation. Such an outcome would restrict export sales, lower the purchase of imports and raise the price of imports. Those industries which sell a relatively high proportion of their products abroad are likely to produce less and make some of their workers redundant. The industries that are protected from foreign competition may keep their output and employment high in the short term but it is unlikely to be a good use of resources. This is because the country will not be able to specialise in what it is best at. This will reduce the country's total output and employment.

The higher price of imports may lead to cost-push inflation. Firms will have to pay more for imported raw materials which will raise their costs and prices. Those firms selling products which compete with imports may also feel under less pressure to keep their costs and prices low, if imports are more expensive.

f. A lower cost will usually enable firms to sell a product at a lower price and so give them a competitive advantage over their rivals and result in them having higher sales. This, however, may not always be the case. Tariffs may offset the cost advantage by pushing up prices above those of rival firms. Firms in rival countries may also be subsidised by their governments or may have lower transport costs which may enable them to sell their products at a lower price. In addition, people may not want to buy the country's products if they are of lower quality than their rivals.

g. A current account surplus has a number of advantages. Moving into a surplus or into a larger surplus will increase aggregate demand and so may increase economic growth. It will also increase the country's reserves of foreign currency and may strengthen the country's reputation as a strong economy.

Governments, however, usually aim for a balance on the current account in the long run. This is because such a balance will ensure that the country is neither living beyond its means nor forgoing the opportunity to consume more goods and services. It also creates greater economic stability. A current account surplus can contribute to inflationary pressure whilst a current account deficit is making a negative contribution to aggregate demand.

In addition, a current account balance is likely to mean less fluctuation in the exchange rate than would occur with a surplus or deficit.

Structured questions

1. a. Three components of the balance of payments are trade in goods, trade in services and income. Trade in goods or the visible balance covers the exports and imports of tangible goods such as clothes, computers and mobile phones that take place over a calendar year. A trade in goods surplus means that export revenue exceeds import expenditure.

    Trade in services or the invisible balance is a record of the export and import of services, such as education and financial services, again over a period of a year. A trade in services deficit would mean that the country is spending more on the imports of services than it is earning from selling exports.

    The main component of income is investment income. This covers profit, interest and dividends received from abroad minus profit, interest and dividends paid to people living outside the country.

    b. A current account deficit is likely to mean that the country is spending more on imports than it is earning from exports. In such a case, the economy is consuming more products than it is producing. If, however, the country's producers made more of the products the country is consuming, the country's output and employment would be higher.

    A current account deficit would also put downward pressure on the country's exchange rate. This is because there would be a greater supply of the currency than demand for it on foreign exchange markets. More of the currency would be sold to buy foreign products than would be purchased to buy domestically produced products.

    c. There are a number of factors that could explain the difference in the current account performance of the USA and China. One is differences in costs of production. China has recently been experiencing low costs of production which has helped its price competitiveness. It has started to produce a greater variety of products.

    Two other factors that affect price competitiveness and and so current account performance, are inflation and the exchange rate. China's inflation rate actually exceeded that of the USA in 2008 and so was not a relevant factor. China's exchange rate, however, has been low and this is thought to be a major reason why China has enjoyed a current account surplus in 2008. It resulted in China's export prices being low and its import prices being high. Indeed, the USA complained that China was deliberately keeping its exchange rate low in order to boost its trade position.

Other factors that could, in theory, explain the difference in trade performance are a difference in the quality of products produced, differences in how good their marketing was and what was happening to income levels in the countries producing these products. The USA does actually produce good quality products, is good at marketing and as with China, is trading with most countries in the world. This means that these factors are unlikely to have explained the difference in performance in 2008. The main reasons appear to have been China's low costs of production, its move into new markets and a low exchange rate.

2. **a.** Free international trade should enable countries to specialise on the basis of comparative advantage. With the ability to buy from and sell to any country in the world, a country's producers should be able to concentrate on making products that have the lowest opportunity cost. Producing products they are best at should mean output is high and costs are low.

   Another reason why free trade should keep costs down is the greater competition it provides. If consumers have the ability to buy products from anywhere in the world, producers will not only have to keep their costs and prices low but also to keep their quality high.

   Free trade also promotes the spread of new ideas and new technology which again should raise output, improve quality, keep costs down and promote competition.

   b. Three arguments for protectionism are to allow infant industries to develop, to prevent dumping and to improve the trade position.

   Infant, that is new, industries may need protection to grow because at first their costs of production may be higher than well established foreign industries. If they are given time to grow, they may be able to lower their costs as they take greater advantage of economies of scale. If a government can identify which new industries have the potential to gain a comparative advantage, this policy may improve the country's economic performance in the longer term. There is, however, a risk that a government may seek to protect an industry that will never be viable. Even if an industry does have the potential to be competitive it may become reliant on protectionism and not strive to reduce its costs and raise the quality of its products.

   To prevent dumping is a widely accepted argument for protectionism. This is because it is seen as an unfair trade practice. It involves selling products at less than cost price. There are two main motives for doing this. One is to get rid of surplus stocks and the other is to drive out domestic producers. Whilst consumers may gain a short term advantage in the form of low prices, they are likely to lose out in the longer term as the exporters will probably push up prices if they gain a larger share of the market. If dumping is not prevented, some efficient domestic producers may be eliminated by less efficient foreign producers.

To improve the trade position is a less viable argument than to prevent dumping. Whilst in the short term it may lower import expenditure, it may also lower export revenue in the longer term if other countries retaliate.

c. Two other government policy measures that could be used to correct a current account deficit are a rise in income tax and increased spending on training.

Increasing income tax in this case would be referred to as an expenditure reducing method. The aim would be to lower expenditure on imports and possibly to increase exports. Increasing income tax would reduce people's disposable income. This is likely to mean that they will spend less on both imports and on domestically produced products. The fall in domestic demand for their products may mean that domestic firms will put more effort into foreign markets.

There are, however, positive disadvantages in increasing income tax. If consumption falls by a greater amount than any rise in net exports, aggregate demand will fall. This reduction in aggregate demand may slow down the country's economic growth and may even lead to a recession. It may also result in unemployment and reduce the incentive to work. In addition, if the current account deficit is of a structural nature, the increase in income tax will not provide a long term solution.

Increased government spending on training may prove to be a more effective long term policy. If the training is of a good standard and is in the appropriate areas, productivity should rise. An increase in productivity should lower unit labour costs and increase the international price competitiveness of the country's firms.

This measure, however, may take one or two years to have an effect. It will also involve an opportunity cost, as the resources used to provide the training could have been put to another use such as improving education.

There is also no guarantee that the training will be in the right areas or will succeed in raising productivity.

3. a. A floating exchange rate is determined by market forces. As it does not involve any government intervention to influence the exchange rate, foreign currency does not have to be held for this purpose. In practice, even with a floating exchange rate a government is likely to keep some reserves of foreign currency in case the value of its currency was falling to low levels. However, less foreign currency is likely to be held and this reduces the opportunity cost.

A floating exchange rate also means that a government does not have to sacrifice other objectives in order to influence the exchange rate. For instance, if a country has a fixed exchange rate facing downward pressure, its central bank may raise the rate of interest. Such a move could have a harmful effect on employment and economic growth.

An additional benefit of a floating exchange rate is that it should move the current account towards balance. If imports exceed exports, for instance, the supply of the currency will be greater than the demand. This will lower the value of the currency and make exports cheaper and imports more expensive. These price changes may raise export revenue and lower import expenditure.

b. A country's exchange rate will rise in price if there is an increase in demand for the currency and/or a decrease in its supply. These changes may be brought about by government intervention, in the case of a fixed exchange rate, or by market forces, in the case of a floating exchange rate.

A rise in the rate of interest will attract hot money flows into the country as foreigners seek to take advantage of it by placing money into the country's financial institutions. This movement of short term financial investment will increase the exchange rate. Longer term, inward financial flows including direct investment and financial investment will also push up the exchange rate. Foreign direct investment and portfolio investment may be attracted into the country by, for instance, a good economic performance and high profits.

A surplus of exports over imports will also increase the demand for the currency relative to its supply and so push up its price. A central bank may buy or sell its currency to influence its value under a fixed exchange rate system or to add or reduce foreign exchange reserves under a fixed or a floating exchange rate system.

In addition, speculation may cause a rise in the exchange rate. Speculators may purchase a currency if they believe it will rise in value in the future. If they purchase enough of the currency, they can bring about what they are expecting to happen.

c. A rise in a country's exchange rate will affect a country's macroeconomic objectives. It will raise export prices and lower import prices. If demand for exports and imports is inelastic, a rise in the exchange rate will increase export revenue and reduce import expenditure. In this case, the country's current account deficit would be reduced. It is, however, more common for demand for exports and imports to be elastic. In this case, export revenue will fall and import expenditure will rise. These changes will increase any current account deficit and may turn a surplus into a deficit depending on the size of the changes.

A widening of the gap between export revenue and import expenditure will reduce a country's aggregate demand. The impact this has on a country's output and employment will depend on the initial level of economic activity and the size of the fall in aggregate demand. If an economy is operating at full employment with excess aggregate demand, a small fall in aggregate demand may not have much effect on output and employment. If, however, an economy has a considerable amount of spare capacity and the rise in the exchange rate results in a large fall in aggregate demand, output and employment may fall by a noticeable amount. Figure 6 shows a fall in aggregate demand form AD to AD1 causing a large fall in output from Y to Y1.

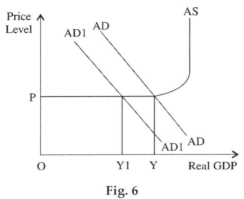

Fig. 6

A rise in the exchange rate is likely to reduce inflation. It will raise export prices but the country's inhabitants do not buy their country's exports and these are not included in consumer prices indexes. The fall in import prices it causes will, however, put downward pressure on the price level for several reasons. One is that the price of imported raw materials will fall, thereby lowering costs of production. The price of finished imports will decline and these products are included in the country's consumer price indexes. With lower import prices, domestic producers will feel more pressure to keep their prices and costs low and workers may be less inclined to press for pay rises.

A rise in export prices and a fall in import prices will also affect the distribution of income. Exporters will lose out if demand for their products is elastic. Firms which use imported raw materials, in contrast, will gain. Households who take holidays abroad will also gain as their currency will enable them to purchase more.

4. a. The current account deficit concerns a country's external trade position whilst the budget position involves the government's current financial position. A current account deficit arises when a country's import expenditure plus investment income and current transfers that have left the country is greater than the combined export revenue, investment income earned abroad and current transfers that have come into the country. In contrast, a budget deficit occurs when government spending exceeds tax revenue.

b. A fall in the value of the currency will result in a decrease in export prices and an increase in import prices. The price of exports is not taken into account in constructing a country's consumer prices index. This is because the country's inhabitants do not buy its exports.

The change in the price of imports, however, may have an effect on inflation. The price of imports is included in a consumer prices index as the country's inhabitants buy imports. If the prices of finished imported products rise, there will be a direct impact on inflation. A rise in the price of imported raw materials will increase firms' costs of production and so may contribute to cost-push inflation.

More expensive imports may also reduce pressure on domestic firms that are competing with the imports to keep their prices low.

c. A wide range of information could be examined to assess the performance of Pakistan's economy in 2008.

The country's inflation rate in 2008 and in a number of years before 2008 should be assessed. A low and stable rate of inflation would be regarded as price stability and this is what governments aim for. A comparison should also be made with other countries' inflation rates to judge what is happening to the country's international price competitiveness.

A variety of information about the country's labour market should be examined. The most obvious is perhaps the unemployment rate. Again governments aim for low unemployment. They also want any unemployment to be of a short duration. 2008's unemployment rate should be studied in comparison with previous years and other countries' unemployment rates. A government would also want the quality of the jobs available to its workers to be improving in terms of their working conditions, training and pay. In addition, the productivity of workers should be considered. Raising productivity levels will increase an economy's productive potential.

The economy's economic growth rate should be considered over a period of time and its actual economic growth rate should be compared to an estimate of its potential economic growth rate.

Information on changes in real GDP per head, distribution of income and pollution, for instance, would be useful in considering what has happened to living standards over time.

In terms of the current account and budget deficits and the exchange rate, it would be useful to consider what has been causing the changes. For example, a current account deficit may arise from a country's products becoming less internationally competitive or it may be the result of an economy importing more raw materials as it is increasing its output. The second cause may result in a current account surplus in the longer term but the first cause is more serious.

A growing budget deficit may arise because a government is committed to spending too much relative to its ability to raise taxes. It may, however, be the result of a government introducing reflationary fiscal policy. A falling exchange rate can contribute to inflation and may discourage foreign direct investment but it may also correct a current account deficit.

Changes in the proportion of output and employment accounted for by the different industrial sectors might also be considered. A growing tertiary sector might suggest an improved economic performance.

Homework assignments

1. a. Four reasons why demand for Indian chilli increased were failed harvests in other countries, an improvement in the quality of Indian chilli, concern about the possible use of pesticides in Chinese and Pakistani crops and a growing taste for spices in the West.
    b. The passage indicates that India does have the capacity to increase its exports of spices. It mentions that whilst India supplies 50% of global spice exports, these exports account for only 8% of its annual production. It could switch more of its products to the export market. The existence of unemployment in India, also means that more spices could be produced by bringing more resources into use.
    c. Sales of spices are an Indian export and are a credit item as they bring more money into the economy. An increase in their sales will improve India's trade in goods position and so its current account position.
    d. A good pepper harvest in Vietnam would reduce the price of Vietnamese pepper. This is likely to encourage some consumers to switch their purchase from Indian to Vietnamese pepper. The decrease in demand for Indian pepper will cause the price to fall from P to P1 and supply to contract from Q to Q1 as shown in Figure 7.

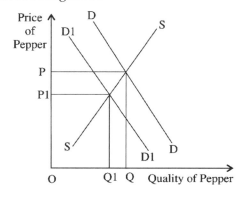

Fig. 7

Answer Key

e. In deciding whether to devote more resources to growing spices, Indian farmers should consider future demand, future costs of production, what rival producers will be doing and any possible government intervention in the market.

Indian farmers may be persuaded to grow more spices if they are convinced that world demand will continue to grow. They must also consider their costs. Rising revenue will only increase profits if costs do not rise in line with or by more than revenue.

The Indian farmers will also have to consider what competition they may face from farmers in other countries. If they think they do have a comparative advantage in producing spices they should increase their production in line with demand.

In addition, Indian farmers should take into account whether the Indian government is likely to subsidise spice production or, on the other hand, tax exports of spice. A subsidy would make them more likely to increase the resources they devote to growing spices whilst an export tax may discourage them from doing so. The prospect of foreign governments placing import restrictions on spices may also stop them from growing more spices.

2. a. Both members of a free trade area and of a customs union agree not to impose trade restrictions on each other's products. Members of a customs union, however, go a stage further. They also agree to impose the same external tariff on non-members.

b. One of the factors that will influence whether the Venezuelan economy will benefit from membership of Mercosur is the extent to which it trades with the other members in contrast with how much it trades with non-members. The more it trades with the members and the less it trades with non-members, the more it will benefit. This is because it will reap the advantages of having no trade restrictions with its main trading partners and will not suffer much from having to impose tariffs on imports from non-members. Obviously the size of the tariffs which have to be removed and the external tariff are influencing factors. Other influencing factors include how Venezuelan firms respond to the competitive conditions in a customs union and how Mercosur develops in the future.

c. It would be disadvantageous for a government to follow the same fiscal and monetary policies as other governments if it faces different economic conditions and problems. For instance, if the other countries have a high rate of inflation and low unemployment, they would benefit from an increase in the rate of interest and in the rate of income tax. In contrast, this country may face low inflation and high unemployment and so its economic performance may be improved by both a cut in income tax and in the rate of interest.

d. The existence of a customs union may harm non-members as their products will now have tariffs imposed on them in the customs union. This will raise the price of their exports in the customs union, making it more difficult for them to compete with the products of member countries.

Some customs unions, most noticeably the European Union, have also on occasion subsidised their agricultural products and sold them at below cost price in non-member countries. Such a practice makes it difficult for non-members not only to sell their products to people in the customs union but also to their own population.

Non-members, however, may gain from the existence of a customs union if membership of the trade bloc results in the faster economic growth of their members. Richer economies will buy more products.

If the non-members are concentrating on products not made by members, they may be able to sell more. The increased competition among members may also increase their efficiency and reduce the price of the products they sell to non-members.

If non-members see a customs union being very successful, they may decide to form their own customs unions.

3. a. Price competitiveness is the ability of a country's firms to sell their products at a lower price than other countries.
   b. (i) International competitiveness and growth are usually positively related. If an economy's international competitiveness increases, it should export more and import less. This will increase aggregate demand, which will increase actual economic growth, if there is spare capacity.

   Economic growth can also promote international competitiveness. An increase in productive potential can reduce inflation and so raise price competitiveness.

   (ii) Again productivity and international competitiveness are directly related. A rise in productivity should reduce costs of production and so raise international price competitiveness.

   (iii) A rise in international competitiveness would tend to push up the exchange rate. This is because demand for exports will rise whilst demand for imports will fall, thereby increasing demand for the currency and reducing its supply. In contrast, an increase in the exchange rate will reduce international competitiveness as it will raise export prices and lower import prices.

   c. As tourist minister I would seek to make the country's tourist industry more competitive by increasing the training of those working in the industry. If the training is successful, the price charged to tourists might fall and the quality of the service should improve.

I would seek to encourage the tourist firms to invest in, for instance, new hotels and attractions. Updating accommodation and attractions will be likely to encourage more people to visit the country as would better marketing. I might seek a government subsidy for the tourism industry, emphasising the importance of the industry and the need to improve its performance in a very competitive international market.

Greater coordination with complementary products, such as transport, should again raise the quality of tourism and may reduce its costs.

I might also put pressure on the government to keep the rate of inflation down and possibly to lower the exchange rate. If a country's inflation rate falls below that of rival countries, its price competitiveness will increase. A lower exchange rate, by reducing the price of holidays in the home country whilst raising the price of foreign holidays, should encourage both – more foreign and more native people to holiday in the country.

Useful Resources

Newspapers and Magazines

Quality newspapers and economics magazines can help you to keep abreast of the latest developments in your economy and in the global economy. They can provide you with examples to illustrate your answers, statistical information and with articles that deepen and widen your knowledge and understanding. Two economics magazines are published in the UK for students. These are aimed at AS/ A level students but you should find the articles accessible and useful. The addresses of the two magazines are:

- Economics Today: Economics Today Ltd, Stocksfield Hall, Stocksfield, Northumberland NE43 7TN England. Email: www.anforme.co.uk/
- Economic Review: (Subscriptions) Turpin Distribution, Pegasus Drive, Stratton Business Park, Biggleswade, Bedfordshire, SG18 8TQ, England.Email: custserv@turpin-distribution.com Go to www.philipallan.co.uk

Television and Radio Programmes

A number of television and radio programmes focus on economic issues. Check listing schedules on a regular basis.

People

Do not overlook people as a resource. They can be very useful. Your teacher plays a key role in developing your understanding and skills. Your family and other members of your community may also be able to tell you about their experiences as workers, members of trade unions, employers, savers and spenders. They may also share their views about economic events.

Books

The companion book to this book is 'Cambridge IGCSE Economics' which I have written. It is published by the Cambridge University Press India Pvt Ltd, 2013.

The Internet

The internet can be a useful source of information but you must exercise discrimination while using it, as it offers an indiscriminate exposure to a plethora of information. You

Useful Resources

must also be aware that websites can change their addresses.
Two useful search engines are:
- www.google.com
- www.yahoo.com/

Among the websites that you might find useful are:

www.bbc.co.uk/schools/gcsebitesize/business - A useful revision site produced by the British Broadcasting Company (BBC).

www.bized.co.uk/- This site contains a range of economic information targeted atstudents. lt includes case studies, a diagram bank, a dictionary and glossary, a macroeconomic model, power point presentations and news items.

www.cia.gov/cia/publications/factbook/index.html- The website of the Central Intelligence Agency (CIA) of the USA. You can obtain information on most countries by going to 'country profiles' and pulling down the country you are interested in.

www.commonwealth.org.uk - a website that provides information about the economic performance of a large number of countries.

www.conference.board.org - The website of the US Conference Board, which focuses on global economic issues.

www.econ.cam.ac.uk - University of Cambridge's website, which contains some interesting articles.

www.economist.com/countries/ - A website run by The Economist magazine which provides briefings on individual countries.

www.economywatch.com/world - Another website that provides information on individual countries, this time provided by Moody's Analytics, a company that supplies economic analysis data and forecasts.

www.europa.eu - The official website of the European Union.

www.federalreserve.gov -The website of the US Central Bank. This provides information on monetary policy and the US economy.

www.gov.bw - An interesting website on the economy of Botswana, produced by its government.

www.greenpeace - Greenpeace's site which produces information on environmental issues.

www.hn-treasury.gov.uk - The UK's Treasury's website which provides information on the UK government's budget among other data.

www.ictsd.org - This is the website of the International Centre for Trade and Sustainable Development.

www.ifo.de - German Institute for Economic Research. This provides (in English) information on economic growth and the performance of firms.

www.ifs-org.uk- Institute of Fiscal Studies. This independent research organisation produces reports on, for instance, the budget, poverty and inequality.

www.imf.org - The website of the International Monetary Fund that gives information on countries and global economic performance.

www.mdgs.un.org/ - A United Nations website which contains a report on the progress made towards the millennium development goals.

www.news.bbc.co.uk/l/hi/business/economy - This website of the BBC is very good at providing news in a clear and concise way.

www.oecd.org - The website of the Organisation for Economic Cooperation and Development. This website provides information on industrial member countries.

www.quia.com - A collection of activities and quizzes produced by teachers from a range of countries.

www.twnside.org.sg - Third World Network's website which includes a wide range of useful information on, for example, climate, development and free trade agreements.

www.tuc.org - The website of the Trade Union Congress which represents the major trade unions in the UK.

www.tutor2u.net - This website provides a range of information and activities for students. Check out, particularly, 'Select Revision Notes' which will take you to 'GCSE Economics'.

www.undp.org - The United Nations Development Programme. First click on 'Human Development Reports' and then go to 'Countries' to find useful comparisons between several countries.

www.unctad.org - The United Nations Conference on Trade and Development. This website provides country fact sheets.

www.wto.org/ - World Trade Organisations website. This concentrates on international trade and provides a map of disputes between member countries.